D0056685

Be Your Own
Personal
Trainer

Also by James G. Garrick, M.D., and Peter Radetsky, Ph.D.

PEAK CONDITION: WINNING STRATEGIES TO PREVENT,
TREAT, AND REHABILITATE SPORTS INJURIES

Also by Peter Radetsky, Ph.D.

PACE WALKING: THE BALANCED WAY TO AEROBIC HEALTH
(with Steven Jonas, M.D.)

Be Your Own Personal Trainer

Design your own program for
peak physical fitness and
sports performance

James G. Garrick, M.D.,
and
Peter Radetsky, Ph.D.

Illustrations by
Marianna Amicarella

Crown Publishers, Inc., New York

Publisher's Note: This book contains exercise instructions to be followed within the context of an overall health program. However, not all exercises and instructions are designed for all individuals. Before starting this or any other exercise program a physician should be consulted. The instructions in this book are not intended as a substitute for professional medical advice.

Copyright © 1989 by James G. Garrick and Peter Radetsky

All rights reserved. No part of this book may be reproduced or transmitted in any form or by any means, electronic or mechanical, including photocopying, recording, or by any information storage and retrieval system, without permission in writing from the publisher.

Published by Crown Publishers, Inc., 225 Park Avenue South, New York, New York 10003.

CROWN is a trademark of Crown Publishers, Inc.

Manufactured in the United States of America

Library of Congress Cataloging-in-Publication Data

Garrick, James G.
  Be your own personal trainer.
  Includes index.
  1. Physical education and training. 2. Physical fitness. I. Radetsky, Peter. II. Title.
GV711.5.G38   1989   613.7′1   88-7018

ISBN 0-517-57023-8
10 9 8 7 6 5 4 3 2 1
First Edition

Contents

For Becky, Amy, J. C., and Nancy,
and for Sam, Jessica, and Sascha

Special thanks to Marianna Amicarella, Corinne Pistone,
and J. C. Garrick

Be Your Own
Personal
Trainer

Introduction:
Be Your Own Personal Fitness Trainer—You Can Do It

I really missed exercising," Dave Simpson says. "You can get into a rut, working all the time, trying to make it. I just woke up one morning and decided it was time to take stock of things."

"Uh-huh," agrees Dr. James Garrick, director of the Center for Sports Medicine in San Francisco.

"So I started running again."

The only problem is, "again" refers to fifteen years ago, when Dave played basketball in college. He has done next to nothing since. But once a jock, always a jock. Thirty-six years old or not, Dave took off as though he'd never been out of training.

He goes on with his story as the two men move toward the entrance of the fitness club. Garrick has just finished a presentation on personal fitness training, the kind of talk he often gives in fitness facilities around the Bay area. Even before the applause was done, Dave had rushed—that is, to be more precise, limped—from his seat to join the circle of people around Garrick. With typical tenacity he has outlasted them all.

"I tell you, Doc, I did four miles the first day and sprinted the last four hundred yards." Carol, Dave's wife, joins them at the reception desk. She nods sadly. "It was great. I got a little tired, sure, but I felt terrific. The next day I couldn't get out of bed."

Garrick laughs. "Do you think you might've overdone it just a teense?"

"That's not all," Carol says.

"Then I took up tennis. I'd always wanted to try tennis, but between one thing and another I never had time."

"Did you start playing tennis before or after you were unable to get out of bed?" Garrick asks.

Dave laughs. Carol shakes her head. "I'm not that bad," Dave says. "First I got back to running to build up my endurance. Then I started tennis. Now I do both."

Sounds great, but now he has a sore and swollen Achilles tendon. He won't stop running because he doesn't want to fall out of shape for tennis, and despite the fact that his weekend matches make his ankle so sore he can't run for a couple of days afterward, he won't stop playing tennis because it's his love.

Sound familiar? Dave's is a common problem: an excess of enthusiasm and a shortage of judgment. It's one thing to get back to exercise after fifteen years—that's terrific. It's another thing to throw yourself into it with such gusto that you trash your body and injure yourself. And it's still another to subsequently take up not one but two sports activities, each of which makes your injury worse, and neither of which you're prepared to put aside, or even take it easy with, until you're once again healthy.

But Dave shouldn't feel bad—he's not alone. It seems to be the nature of exercising that it's awfully hard to find the right approach and pace. And it seems to be human nature that we tend to think of ourselves as we're not. It can be tough to admit that you're no longer twenty-one and an athlete when that's how you've thought of yourself all these years. Dave will have to find a more realistic way to approach his exercise. If he doesn't, in time he may come to remember his struggles with Achilles tendinitis as the good old days.

And Carol? A petite thirty-three-year-old, Carol is a nonathlete. Ask her and she'll tell you so, no two ways about it. She didn't do sports in college, hasn't done sports since, and has never missed it one bit. In fact, she wouldn't be doing sports now if Dave hadn't decided that it was important for the two of them to do this thing together. Besides, Carol was getting to be a little heavier than she'd like. She agreed—it was time to do something.

The question for her was, do what? She ran with Dave a few times and hated it—too lonely, too boring, and it *hurt*. Besides, Dave simply ran away from her. "You're holding me back," he would say, or words to that effect. "I can walk faster than you can run." And pretty soon all she would see of him would be his back, and from a great distance at that. So running definitely was not going to be her thing.

Next, she tried tennis. She had last played during high-school PE—at least she knew how to hold a racket. Dave had fallen in love with tennis. Maybe this was the sport they could do together.

So Carol took a few lessons and, gritting her teeth, joined a C team in a local tennis league. There were just three problems. The first was that she hated the sight of herself in a tennis outfit. She *had* put on weight, more than she thought. The second was that Dave didn't want to play tennis with her. She couldn't blame him —it did get awfully irritating having to retrieve balls she hit over the chain link fence. The third was this little pain on the outside of her elbow that was next to nothing when she started but little by little had begun to grow worse, until now it hurt every time she even gripped a racket.

Garrick patiently listens to Carol's sad story. He's used to people peppering him with questions after one of these talks, but there's something about the Simpsons that sparks his interest. A particular sincerity? A particular desperation? In any case, he leads Carol to the snack bar, sits her down, and gently pokes the outside of her elbow with a finger. "Is this the spot?"

"Yes," Carol says, flinching ever so slightly.

"Does it hurt when you straighten your arm and pull your wrist under?"

Carol tries it. "Yes."

"You've got a textbook case of tennis elbow," Garrick announces. Then he catches himself. "Sorry, you didn't ask for my opinion. You can take the doctor out of the office but you can't take the office out of the doctor—or something like that."

Carol laughs. "No, please go on. I'm tired of hurting all the time."

"Well," Garrick says, "if I were you I'd back off the tennis for a while and do other things to keep in shape."

"That's why we joined here," Dave says.

"It was the worst mistake we ever made," adds Carol.

Garrick sighs and sinks into his chair. "I'm all ears," he says.

They joined the health club to be able to work out with weight machines. Dave, a strapping dark-haired fellow who looks like the athlete he thinks he is, had done weights while at college, and although the machines these days are much more sophisticated and varied than the relatively primitive equipment he had used fifteen years ago, one look at them made him feel as though he had never stopped lifting. In fact, when the instructor attempted to start them out with a relatively light, beginning program, Dave pointed at Carol and announced, "You work with her—I already know how to do this stuff."

He then proceeded to head straight to the leg press machine, figuring that he had to build up his calf muscles to get rid of the persistent pain in the back of his ankle. As it turns out, he was right—you *do* want to strengthen your calf muscles to deal with Achilles tendinitis, but you *don't* want to do it while you're still hurting, and definitely not by using a leg press machine with too much weight. He stacked up a healthy pile of ten-pound plates and attempted to work his calf muscles by raising and lowering the weights with his toes, with the result that the pain in his Achilles tendon became so bad that he couldn't run, play tennis, or even work out at the club for two weeks.

"Stupidest thing I've ever done," he says. "Sometimes I wonder when I'll ever learn."

"Don't be too hard on yourself, honey." Carol gives him a tender pat on the shoulder. "You just didn't know any better."

"That's right," Garrick says. "It's a lot easier to decide to start working out than it is to know how to go about it. However"—he raises his eyebrows and drops his voice to a conspiratorial stage whisper—"you might have listened to the instructor."

"Then my elbow started to get worse," Carol says.

"Uh-oh." Garrick sighs. "Didn't you listen to the instructor either?"

"I did listen," Carol says. "That's the trouble. He put me on that machine where you pull the bar down over your head. Know which one I mean?"

"Yep," Garrick says. "The lat pull-down bar."

"That's it. But it was too big for me, and I must have put too much weight on it or something, because when I tried to pull down I felt something in my elbow and it started to hurt worse than ever."

Carol has hardly been back on the court since and has developed a healthy distaste for fitness clubs and weight machines and tennis and running—and just about everything associated with the word *exercise*. She has concluded that her many years of inactivity constituted a wise course indeed. A person has to be crazy to go through this stuff.

"We're just a real mess." Carol shrugs. "But in four months—God help us—we're going to spend two weeks at a fitness resort."

"We have to go," Dave says. "It's on the house. The investment company I work for has put some money into the place. Besides, *I* want to go."

Carol and Dave fall silent. They stare at Garrick—hopefully, trustingly.

"This isn't fair," Carol says suddenly. "This is how Jim makes his living. We can't take advantage of him like this."

Garrick laughs. "Don't worry about it. You've gotten me interested. I feel strongly that people *can* do something about their physical condition but that lots of times they don't have the foggiest idea of how to go about it."

"Boy, that's us, all right," Carol says.

"It's just not as easy as it seems," Garrick says. Carol nods her head vigorously. "You just can't charge out and start doing things you've never done before—you can get hurt that way."

"Tell me about it," says Dave.

"By the same token, you don't want to be too cautious, either. You've got to set reasonable goals based on who you are and what kind of shape you're in, and you've got to know how to arrive at those goals. Then you're in business. That's when working out can be a real joy."

"Sounds good to me," Dave says.

"Okay," says Garrick, "if you don't mind I'll give you a few suggestions. But you have to promise me something."

"Mind?" Dave says. *"Mind?* Are you kidding? I'll promise anything."

"I've heard that before," says Carol.

"No, I mean it. I'm sick and tired of hurting and not being able to do the things I want."

Garrick fixes them with his best stern-doctor stare. "You have to promise me that you'll do what I ask you. Because if you continue to overdo it, we won't be talking casually here at the club about getting you in shape—instead you'll be paying me a visit at the office, and we'll be trying to figure out how to deal with a couple of chronic injuries that might keep you from doing any of the exercises you like to do, ever."

"We'll be good." Carol looks at her husband. "I'll see to it."

Dave and Carol represent the two extremes of people who exercise, the gung-ho enthusiast and the reluctant nonathlete. But they have one thing very much in common with each other and many of the millions of people who work out: they just don't know how to go about it. Well, so what? That's life, right? There's so much going on that we can't be experts in everything. Sometimes life can seem like a three-ring circus in the midst of which you're constantly searching for your seat.

Doing exercise is one of the ways in which many people attempt to bring order, health, and accomplishment into their lives. It's ironic that finding your stride in exercising can be so difficult, especially when often the upshot of this confusion is not only dissatisfaction with actually doing the exercise and lack of benefits in the long run, but injury as well. It's bad enough not to get much out of your attempt to improve your level of physical fitness—but it's much worse to get injured along the way.

Yet it needn't be like this. "You just didn't know any better," Carol said to console Dave, and she was right. Once you do know better, once you know how to go about exercising, everything changes. What was once a forbidding, frustrating experience quickly becomes rewarding and enjoyable. It all has to do with recognizing your strengths and shortcomings and acting accordingly.

Let's take another look at Dave and Carol in this light. First of all, Dave's determination to start doing something about their state of physical fitness is admirable. There are no two ways about it— exercise, done intelligently and appropriately, can be one of the healthiest and most enjoyable activities possible. It helps us feel better and reduces our risk of several major diseases and unhealthy conditions, among them heart disease. It increases the heart's ability to pump life-sustaining blood and helps the body burn off unnecessary fat. It increases stamina and strengthens muscles and bones. And the social benefits are often similarly attractive. It helps us look better, feel better, live more confidently. Dave has the right idea, no doubt about it.

But he went about it in precisely the wrong way. You just can't expect a thirty-six-year-old body to act as though it's twenty-one. You just can't expect suddenly to throw yourself into any strenuous activity without inviting frustration. And you can't expect to hurt yourself and then ignore the injury without eventually facing the inability to do anything at all.

As for Carol, if Dave was bullheaded and unrealistic, Carol was just plain lost. Exercise was a brand-new world for her. She had no idea where to go or how to proceed. She felt hesitant and a bit frightened from the beginning. She badly needed someone to help her along slowly and supportively, and Dave certainly wasn't that person. Dave needed to recognize that he hadn't done anything for fifteen years and start back as a baby learns to walk, little by little, while Carol was faced with an even tougher proposition. She somehow had to experience the fun and benefits of exercise for herself. Dave was already hooked—albeit hooked on his memories of times past. Carol had no such terms of reference. For her, it was all new.

But all that's over and done with. They botched it once. Now it falls to Garrick to give them another shot at it.

The first thing he must do is help them get rid of their pain. And that means that Dave and Carol must back down to a level of exercise that doesn't hurt (in their case, next to nothing) and then gently and purposefully restretch and restrengthen their injured parts. Pain is *not* gain, not when it comes to injuries. Before they do anything else, they must get their injuries under control.

The next step for Carol and Dave is to begin exercising in a manner appropriate to who they are and what they want to do. In other words, they must figure out their exercise goals. Well, that's easy, at least in the short run: their goal is to get in shape so they won't collapse during their two-week vacation.

So Garrick suggests that they continue to work out at the fitness club—but *not* together. For the sake of eventually being able to keep each other company, they had better do this early part separately. For Carol he suggests a low-impact aerobic dance class, with the goal of moving on to a regular aerobics class in four or five weeks—but not doing the entire aerobics section. The idea is that Carol take it slowly, find her stride little by little, and build up her body *and* interest before devoting herself more fully to the whole business.

A few weeks into her low-impact aerobics class, Garrick will start Carol on a gentle strengthening program. The first order of business will be to bring her forearms up to snuff, for tennis elbow, which hurts on the outside of the elbow, really is a problem of weak muscles in the forearm (and lack of proper tennis technique). At first Garrick will suggest exercises that Carol can do at home; later he'll coax her back into the exercise room to try the weight machines again. But this time she'll do exercises appropriate for her, at weights that are not too heavy, with specific goals in mind.

The overall strategy for Carol, then, is a general weight training program, emphasizing exercises to treat tennis elbow as well as to complement the general needs of tennis, and an aerobic dance program for general endurance and fitness.

Dave, on the other hand, is champing at the bit. As always, he's *ready*. Garrick has to help him stay active, find him an alternative to running and tennis until he can get rid of his Achilles tendinitis. So Garrick suggests a cycling program and shows Dave how to place the pedal directly under his heel so as to keep his ankle movement to a minimum. That'll provide aerobic conditioning. And he leads Dave back to weight machines, suggesting that he work on his upper body until his leg comes around—but this time *gradually* working up to the kind of weight he considers appropriate to his status as a returning athlete.

"I love it," Garrick comments along the way. "It's what makes life so interesting. Everybody's different. Carol has to be coaxed every step of the way. She's kind of like a timid fawn. But Dave's a bull elephant. The thing you have to watch with him is that he doesn't charge into a tree so big it'll knock him out."

Well, Dave is ecstatic. He may not be crazy about the cycling, which he considers boring, but he knows it'll get him back to tennis and running. So he tolerates it. But the weight work has him all charged up. He had anticipated that until his leg healed he wouldn't be able to do any lifting at all, forgetting that often one of the compensations of being injured is that you can exercise one part of the body while nursing the other. Working on his upper body is fine with Dave. He limps through the weight room, grunting and groaning to his heart's content, with visions of massive pecs and biceps dancing in his head, confident that he's getting himself into shape to go back to tennis and running sooner than anyone, Garrick included, realizes.

For his part, Garrick is happy to let Dave bluster along. "Just be sure not to go too fast," he reminds him. "If you do, you know which of my lists you're on. Agreed?"

''Agreed. You're the boss, Doc.''

Eventually Dave will be able to ease back into tennis and running, this time starting with a body that has been toned and strengthened for just that purpose, and with an awareness of the dangers of going too hard and too fast. At least, that's the plan. With someone like Dave, you never can be sure. But so far so good.

And, lo and behold, Carol finds she actually enjoys aerobic dance. She meets people just like her in the class, people who have no interest in putting on running shoes or a tennis outfit but like the idea of moving to music and appreciate the benefits that aerobic exercise affords. In time, Carol even comes to like the way she looks in a leotard—so does Dave—and she announces that she has no intention of stepping onto the tennis court during their upcoming vacation. Dave will have to do that on his own. With her newly acquired confidence, she's going to spend her time in the aerobic dance studio.

In effect, Garrick acted as Dave and Carol's personal trainer. He assessed their physical condition, provided them a program to bring themselves up to a generally balanced state of fitness, and then suggested ways to further prepare themselves for the specific exercise goals they had in mind. In Dave's case, the goals have remained the same from beginning to end. For Carol, the means have become the end—she found that aerobic dance was the kind of exercise she had been looking for from the start.

Unfortunately, they ran into all sorts of detours before finding their way. But it didn't have to be that way for them, and it doesn't have to be that way for you. The trick is to know how to go about it *before* you start. Here's how.

First, you figure out what kind of shape you're in. That means being aware of your physical condition. Both Dave and Carol had obvious injury problems that simply wouldn't allow them to do what they wanted to do. For many others, figuring out what kind of shape you're in is more subtle. For example, many of us have learned to cope so well with the residuals of old injuries that we're hardly aware we may have a problem that will rear its ugly head once we start to exercise. You simply must know at the beginning what kind of shape you're in, or you run the risk of finding out later on in ways that you'd rather not have to experience.

Second, you bring yourself physically up to par. That's not to say to the level of fitness you'll need to fulfill your exercise goals —that comes later. But you want to be generally fit and balanced. For example, one arm or leg shouldn't be appreciably weaker than the other, or you're going to experience problems later on; one shoulder shouldn't be far less flexible than the other, or you'll run into some real difficulties later—on the running track, in the dance studio, on the courts, in the pool. You must bring yourself to a balanced state, a state of readiness, before beginning any kind of specialized exercise program. It's the old story: unless your body is ready to crawl, you won't be able to walk. When you can walk, then you can run. And you have to be able to run before you can sprint.

Third, you need to know what exercise opportunities are available. Specialized workouts require specialized techniques and equipment. These days there's a myriad of both—so much, in fact, that the world of fitness can be a confusing blur for the uninitiated and hardly less so for those who know their way around a bit. It's important to know what's out there before you jump in.

Fourth, you need to know what to do to reach your goals. If you want to work out to improve your tennis, as Dave did, you must know how. If you want to exercise to improve your swimming, golf, or skiing, or just for the sake of exercising itself, you have to know how to go about it. All exercises don't work for all activities. In fact, an exercise that's helpful for one activity may be detrimental to another. Blundering into it and learning as you go is just that: a blunder. You need to know how to go about it beforehand.

And last, you need to know how to do the exercises. Climbing onto a weight machine will do you little good if you don't know what to do next, or if you use too much weight, or if you don't fit into the machine. Just ask Carol. It's important to know proper technique, how quickly to progress, how to avoid being hurt, and what kind of regimen to follow. Working out is one area in which you *don't* want to learn by trial and error. You should have a plan in mind ahead of time and a sense of what to do and what not to do as well.

Sounds good, right? But as Jim Garrick says, "It's a lot easier to decide to start working out than it is to know how to go about it." The Simpsons needed Garrick to point them in the right direction —but what about the rest of us? How can we reach our fitness goals, whether they be to perform our favorite sports activity better or simply to become more fit and active, without resorting to sometimes inconvenient and often expensive professional help? The answer is this book. The chapters that follow include all of the information you'll need to become your own personal fitness trainer, and much, much more. There has never been a book quite like it. What Jim Garrick has done for athletes ranging from tennis pros to ballet dancers, from college and professional football players to figure skaters, from world-class runners to occasional exercisers like most of us—and for Carol and Dave Simpson—he'll do for you.

Be Your Own Personal Trainer contains the wisdom of over twenty-five years of taking care of active people. The book provides a high-quality, individualized, and *safe* workout guide that goes far beyond anything you'll find elsewhere. The information is here. What's necessary on your part is to apply it carefully and conscientiously. If you do, by the time you arrive at the end of the book you'll be much happier with your level of fitness and your ability to do your favorite sports activity. You'll enjoy yourself along the way. And you'll know more good and useful things about yourself and your body than you ever dreamed possible. *Personal Trainer* is just that: your own private, individualized personal fitness guide.

How to Get the Most from *Be Your Own Personal Trainer*

First, it's important to realize that all parts of the book work together—that is, one chapter leads into the next. Remember, you have to learn how to crawl before you can walk and walk before you can run. In the same way, each chapter gives you information that you'll need before going on to the next. As with anything that involves exercise, you have to start right and proceed gradually and consistently if you're to achieve your goals. You can't take shortcuts, and you can't skip steps—that way lies frustration at the least and injury at the worst. We suggest that you start at the beginning of the book and work your way through.

But let's say you already know how to run. Can't you just skip to the section that tells you how to run better? The answer is no, not really. It's simply not a good idea. First things first. Any personal trainer worth his salt first assesses your condition, then brings you up to a balanced state of fitness before devising a workout to make you even better at your favorite activity. This book is no exception. And you'd be amazed at how many people are reasonably proficient at their favorite sport while harboring the nagging results of an old injury or deficiency. Stick with what you're doing and you may get away with it—start doing something new, or more strenuous, and you're heading for trouble.

So we recommend that you start at the beginning of the book and apply the suggestions as they are appropriate to you. Here's what you'll find.

Chapter 1, Assessing Your Condition, will show you simple, accessible ways to find out exactly what kind of shape you're in.

In Chapter 2, Getting Balanced, you'll learn how to recover from injuries that have kept you away from your favorite activity and how to gain a balanced state of fitness throughout your entire body.

Chapter 3, Matching Your Goals to a Fitness Program That's Just Right for You, provides insight into what kind of fitness training possibilities are available and which will be just the one for you.

Chapter 4, How to Train for Your Favorite Sports Activity, suggests how to supplement that activity with other kinds of exercise so as to perform better and enjoy it more. It also suggests how to stay as strong and fit as possible if you're injured and can't do your favorite activity.

Chapter 5, Working Out for Strength, Endurance, and Flexibility, offers a thorough exercise guide that you can apply to whatever your fitness goals might be (as well as to whatever ails you).

All together, the chapters comprise a complete course in personal fitness training. Whatever your exercise goals and needs, you'll find out how to go about them here. It's an extended personal consultation with Jim Garrick, your guide to better condition and to a level of enjoyment in exercise that you may not have thought possible.

How to Use *Be Your Own Personal Trainer*—A Blueprint

Let's go back to Carol and Dave Simpson. They relied on Jim Garrick in the flesh, not on the printed page, but let's imagine that they turned to this book before they started to work out on their own. How might they have gone about it? How might the book have saved them time and misery? In what direction might it have taken them? Following the Simpsons' imaginary journey through the book will provide an example of how you can use it.

First, Dave. Being Dave, he jumps in with both feet. He assesses his condition by doing the formal aerobic conditioning tests in Chapter 1. But no matter how he scores on these tests—in the midrange, most likely—the informal tip-offs on page 25 mean the most to him: he easily becomes winded rushing the length of an airport concourse to catch a plane. He's tired of dropping into his seat panting, in a pool of his own perspiration. It's clear to him that he needs aerobic conditioning.

Next, Dave turns to Chapter 2 to bring himself up to a balanced state of fitness. He gives himself the suggested self-examinations and on page 60 discovers that he is indeed prey to Achilles tendinitis. And right then, before rushing out to run too far and too long and injuring himself as a result, he does the strengthening and stretching exercises suggested on page 187. Those exercises condition his calf muscles to the point at which they're ready for the hard work his running and tennis will impose on them. All of this, mind you, *before* he starts to hurt. Now he's balanced and ready to reach his goal of being generally fit.

Dave then turns to Chapter 3 to look over his exercise possibilities and discovers on page 75 that running is one of the best aerobic conditioners there is but that it also carries a relatively high risk of injury and is particularly tough on old injuries as well. If he's going to run, he'll have to pay constant attention to his tendency toward Achilles tendinitis. He also turns to the section beginning on page 94 and learns the differences between the various kinds of fitness facilities. He realizes that since he likes company and certain amenities such as a comfortable locker room, sauna, steam room, and Jacuzzi, he's probably better off joining a general fitness club.

Chapter 4 advises Dave on how to approach his running (he should begin at a reasonable pace and distance and *gradually* progress) and suggests a variety of aerobic exercises he can do to supplement his running. Following the advice beginning on page 79, Dave begins to cycle on those rainy, blustery days when running is out of the question. And the Muscle Work section beginning on page 175 convinces Dave that it's a good idea to stretch and strengthen his thigh muscles and to continue the calf muscle work he has been doing to stay away from Achilles tendinitis.

Chapter 5 shows Dave just how to do these stretching and strengthening exercises. The section beginning on page 200 starts him working on the quadriceps muscle in the thigh (he uses the leg extension machine at the fitness facility), and beginning on page 186 Dave learns more about how to keep his Achilles tendinitis at bay (he starts to use the leg press device—with an appropriate amount of weight).

And so rather than charging ahead, hurting himself, and ending up in Jim Garrick's examining room, Dave takes advantage of his own private, extended, ongoing consultation with Garrick through *Be Your Own Personal Trainer* and begins to exercise in a productive and *safe* manner. As he continues to work out, even if he changes his mind about his goals and needs, Garrick will still be available at the turn of a page.

As for Carol, her journey through the book begins in quite a different way. First, the formal exercise tests in Chapter 1 don't interest her at all. It's the informal tip-offs beginning on page 25 that say something to her. Yes, she *does* have some trouble carrying sacks of groceries from the car to the house. Yes, climbing a long flight of stairs or walking around San Francisco *does* cause her to become winded. And yes, she *does* depend on Dave to do the simplest tasks, such as moving the trash cans to the street or carrying boxes of books. She never thought much about these things before but upon reflection is not surprised to discover that they are tip-offs for the need to be in better condition.

Chapter 2 uncovers no previous injuries for Carol but reinforces what Chapter 1 made her suspect: she's generally weak all over. She doesn't so much need to balance her condition as to improve it overall.

On page 84 of Chapter 3, Carol finds the perfect way to do so: aerobic dance. And, more specifically, aerobic dance videotapes. Like many people, she knew they were available but never felt the inclination to give them a try. But suddenly the idea of being able to exercise by herself, in the privacy and safety of her own home, is very appealing to Carol. If nothing else, no one will see her in a leotard.

But which tape should she buy? That's no problem, for she has the book to advise her what to look for in an aerobic dance video and how to use it once she has made her purchase. Carol heads for the video store.

Chapter 4 gives Carol specific information about aerobic dance (as well as a brief portrait of a woman who has been successful at it—the section begins on page 158) and suggests exercises she can do to supplement her aerobic dance if she wants to. After trying out a videotape and discovering that she likes this kind of exercise very much, Carol eventually musters the courage to try a class in person. She thumbs back to Chapter 3 for some suggestions on how to find the right class for her.

Later on, after she has become comfortable in aerobics dance class, Carol turns back to the book again. Her instructor has gently suggested that although she's doing very well and has lost weight and gained conditioning, it wouldn't hurt if she were a bit stronger. In Chapter 4, page 165, she discovers what exercises she can do to strengthen herself for aerobic dance. Chapter 5 shows her how to do them.

Finally Carol finds herself showing up at Dave's fitness club from time to time to work out on the very same machines that Dave uses with such enthusiasm. They didn't plan it to happen in quite this fashion, but in their own way and their own time, Dave and Carol have found some common ground in exercise after all.

This is what might have happened had *Be Your Own Personal Trainer* been available to the Simpsons before they started to exercise. It wasn't, but it *is* available to you. What remains now is for you to use the book to reach your own exercise goals in your own time and your own way.

Remember, you *can* do it. And you can do it in a way that's just right for you. Be like the Simpsons—take advantage of Jim Garrick. Let him be your personal trainer.

PART ONE
Getting Started

1 Assessing Your Condition

Daria is a spirited forty-one-year-old woman with blond hair, a hearty laugh, and infectious vitality. She's trim, strong, and fit. Meeting her for the first time, you'd never suspect that no more than nine months ago she was thirty pounds overweight.

"She really had a weight problem," Garrick says. "She tended to use food to satisfy other things. When she was feeling stress she'd eat, not because she enjoyed food but because she was nervous."

Daria nods agreement. She can admit it now that she has turned things around. Now she carries only 110 pounds on her 5'4" frame. Now she laughs and freely discusses her former weight problem. And now she can recognize some of its telltale symptoms.

Daria and her husband have their own accounting firm, but her real love is growing things. She has a small garden plot in the backyard and a mind-boggling collection of planters and window boxes inside. After a day behind the desk, she makes sure to spend an hour or so tending her ferns and flowers and experimental varieties. "I used to find myself really pushing to keep going," she says. "It wouldn't take much to get me out of breath and really, really tired."

Then Daria became so ill that she was pretty much confined to bed for months. "That was the big change," she says. "I'd always taken my body for granted, but when I got really sick I didn't want to do that. I wanted to take better care of myself."

So, once she was back on her feet, Daria decided to do just that. She tried running and swimming, but things didn't really start happening for her until Garrick suggested that she enroll in an aerobic dance program at a nearby swim and racket club.

"I just needed a physical release," she says. "I can do aerobics for an hour easier than I can run for an hour or swim for an hour."

And besides that, she was lucky. The instructor Garrick suggested turned out to be particularly sensitive to her needs and abilities. "He was great. He related to me one hundred percent where I was at. I'd been in other classes before where if you're not perfectly fit and wearing a beautiful leotard, you're ignored. Not here. He would feel good if you could only do three sit-ups. That was fantastic. Now if I don't do two minutes' worth, he's annoyed with me."

Daria stuck with it. At first she was so self-conscious that she refused to wear a leotard, preferring the biggest, baggiest sweats she could find. When she walked into the studio and saw mirrors along the walls, she almost walked right out. The prospect of having to look at herself while she worked out was too much. Still, she stuck it out. And the weight started to come off.

At the same time, she started to watch what she ate. "I always tended to enjoy foods that were healthful—I never was a big meat or fat eater—but at certain points sweets would satisfy some kind of longing in me. Now I don't want a candy bar. Now I treat myself to good things. I'll go out and buy a basket of blueberries, even though it's a dollar ninety, rather than a candy bar. Because I enjoy the workouts so much, I hate to get all logy with sugar."

And now Daria is much, much happier with herself. "There's no comparison. Even in aerobics the difference between just a couple of months ago and now is amazing. I used to drag my butt through class. It's really neat. It's really exciting to see muscles grow. Today I even wore a leotard. It was the first time ever."

And her newfound strength has spilled over into her everyday life. "I'm doing better work at the office and a lot more at home. It's really nice to use my body. I can go longer, I'm stronger, I'm more alert. Now instead of worrying about how I'm feeling, I'm concentrating on how the flowers grow. Know what I mean?"

"Yep," Garrick says. "Glad it worked out for you."

"*You're* glad," she says. "Not nearly as much as I am. How can I thank you?"

"Keep it up," Garrick says. "Grow good flowers."

Daria's experience mirrors that of many people who successfully carry out an exercise program. In Daria's case, it wasn't much of a program, at least at the beginning, but she stuck with it. Despite her embarrassment at having to go into a class overweight and out of shape, despite the agony of pushing her body to do things she hadn't ever done before, she stuck with it. She wanted to change her life so badly she was willing to do whatever it took to get there. You have to *want* to exercise and become fit— want to badly. Later on come the rewards of being in good condition and enjoying the process.

Daria was inspired to exercise because of dissatisfaction with her everyday life. There are lots of formal tests that are aimed at gauging your level of physical fitness, but what really counts is how well, or not so well, you're able to do the ordinary things in your life. Daria's extra weight aside, she simply couldn't do what she liked best—grow things.

It's the everyday things that count. For example, if you're not able to carry your bags of groceries to the car or the apartment without inordinate huffing and puffing, it's time to do something about your physical condition. If you have trouble hurrying the length of an airport concourse to catch a flight, it's time to get in better shape.

And what's interesting is that your ability to handle everyday activities transfers into your sporting activities. It may be obvious that becoming excessively winded while rushing along an airport concourse reflects your inability to run that extra lap. It may be somewhat less obvious that huffing and puffing while carrying your groceries mirrors the feeling of swimming through molasses by the time you hit your tenth lap or the certitude that your body is falling apart while you're trudging up to the ninth hole of the golf course. But it may not be obvious at all that if a half hour with the hedge clippers makes your shoulders ache, a strengthening program will probably help your tennis game as much as your yard work. Everyday tasks can be a tip-off as to what kind of condition you're in for your favorite sporting activities. People involved in sports can tell much about themselves and their general condition by how well they're able to accomplish everyday tasks, just as performance in exercise activities can say much about your ability to get through the rest of your day. We're only allotted one body, after all.

What follows in this chapter are suggestions on how to assess what kind of physical condition you're in—you and nobody else. The next chapters will discuss what you can do about it. We'll talk about three distinct areas of fitness: *aerobic condition, strength,* and *flexibility.* None of these capabilities exists separately in your body, of course—there everything works together—but taken individually they pretty well define what you can and can't do in the realm of physical activity.

Aerobic condition has to do with how efficiently your body converts breathed-in oxygen to usable energy. It's aerobic fitness primarily that enables you to run an extra lap or make the last minute mad dash to catch your flight without arriving at your seat sweating and shaking.

The need for strength and flexibility is obvious. If you're not strong enough, you'll have as much of a problem maintaining a skier's crouch as you will carrying the groceries home. And if you're not flexible enough, you may not be able to rear back on your serve or reach around to scratch your back.

Finally, we'll talk a little about *fat* and how to determine if you're overweight. Interestingly, and not surprisingly, problems in any of the fitness areas above are often accompanied by an overabundance of fat. It's a fact that Daria knows all too well.

The tests range from everyday activities that you can use to assess your condition anytime you like, with little or no preparation, to formal activities that may require a particular environment, a stopwatch or tape measure, and counting repetitions. One approach is not necessarily better than another. The formal approach will allow you to compare yourself with others who take the same tests and thereby give you a sense of where you fit in a larger context. The informal approach will have more meaning in the context of your own daily life.

Whichever way you go about it, the important thing is to become aware of yourself and how satisfied you are with your physical well-being. Had Daria not eventually realized how much she missed not being able to garden, she might never have done anything about her condition, despite her weight. And being aware of your physical condition helps you define your fitness goals. No sense working only for endurance if it's strength you need. By the same token, you can be fairly strong and still have real trouble jogging around the block.

If you have no specific goals in mind, this chapter is a first step in defining them. If you already have a goal, this chapter will help you find out if it's realistic. For what follow are the beginning steps of your own personal path to fitness. We can suggest *how* you can go about it, but no one but you can tell you *why* you're embarking on this journey. So as you try out the tests and tip-offs to follow, start thinking about what you want at the end of the process. Start clarifying your own individual reasons for improving your condition. Your goals and our means—a potent combination. Read on.

What's Your Aerobic Fitness Level?

"What I need is a program to help me lose weight."

"I need something to improve my wind. I'm tired of not being able to go up a flight of stairs without panting."

"I want better endurance. As it is, I poop out after one set."

"My problem is cholesterol. I need something to reduce my blood cholesterol level."

If any of these reactions describes your situation, you've come to the right place. Being aerobically fit helps solve all these problems. Aerobic conditioning has to do with how efficiently your body converts oxygen to energy. The process requires a healthy cardiovascular system to circulate blood, which carries energy, throughout your body. Aerobic exercise strengthens your heart, allowing it to work less hard and still meet your body's need for blood energy. When you're aerobically fit, your heart pumps more slowly at rest as well as during exercise. As with any pump, the less your heart has to work, the more efficient it is and the longer it may last.

Aerobic exercise reduces the risk of disease. For example, one to three hours per week of aerobic exercise significantly lowers the risk of heart attack. Aerobic exercise lowers levels of harmful cholesterol, too much of which can lead to arterial disease, and helps reduce blood pressure. Aerobic exercise helps you deal with stress. And over time aerobic exercise actually changes your metabolism so that you tend to use accumulated fat for energy and you lose weight.

So exercising for aerobic reasons can have wide and long-lasting effects. Combine those with the increase in wind and stamina enjoyed by people in good aerobic condition, and it's clear that working for aerobic fitness is a good idea for anyone—whether you're involved in sports activities or not. Here are some ways to determine what kind of aerobic shape you're in and whether it might be a good idea for you to do something to make things better.

FORMAL AEROBIC TESTING

Here are three simple tests that don't require access to sophisticated equipment or esoteric environments. If you can find a high-school track and get hold of a stopwatch, you can do the first two of these tests. All you'll need for the last is a low bench or table. They're aimed at reasonably healthy adults.

A caution: if you experience dizziness, lightheadedness, nausea, or severe shortness of breath from any of these tests, or if you simply want to stop, don't go on. That's indication enough that you're in poor aerobic condition. See a doctor.

One-Mile Timed Walk

This is a particularly good test for the nonexerciser, as walking is probably the most accessible and easy of all aerobic activities. It's also a good test for people who do exercise activities that don't involve running per se—swimming, for example, or aerobic dance.

Walking is an activity that just about anyone can do.

This test is specifically designed for healthy adults between thirty and sixty-nine years old. If you're younger or older than that, the fitness categories may not be quite so accurate for you. Still, they'll give you an indication of what kind of aerobic shape you're in.

Most high-school running tracks are one quarter mile in circumference, so the following test requires four trips around a typical outdoor high-school track. If you're using an indoor track, be aware that it's probably shorter. In that case, determine your number of revolutions accordingly.

If you fall into the good to excellent categories, bravo! You most likely need little aerobic conditioning work. If you're either high or low average, it's a tip-off that although you're not in bad aerobic shape, it wouldn't hurt to get a little bit better. And if you fall into the fair or poor categories, better get to work. Nonexercisers will probably find themselves at this end of the chart.

One-Mile Timed Walk

Time (in min. and sec.)		Aerobic Condition
Women	Men	
11:40 and under	10:12 and under	Excellent
11:41–13:08	10:43–11:42	Good
13:09–14:36	11:43–13:13	High Average
14:37–16:04	13:14–14:44	Low Average
16:05–17:31	14:45–16:23	Fair
17:32 and above	16:24 and above	Poor

Adapted from Rippe J., Ross J., McCarron R., et al., "One-Mile Walk Time Norms For Healthy Adults." *Medicine and Science in Sports and Exercise,* **18:S21, 1986.**

One-and-a-Half-Mile Timed Run

This is an especially good test for runners, as it involves the activity they're most familiar with. It's important to realize that if you can't run a mile and a half in a time that suggests good aerobic condition, it doesn't necessarily mean you're in bad shape. Running simply may not be for you. You might be a strong aerobic walker or swimmer, for example, but just not used to running. In that case, the problem may be one of strength, not aerobic condition. That's why we offer more than one kind of test.

One-and-a-Half-Mile Timed Run

Age Groups

Fitness Category		13–19	20–29	30–39	40–49	50–59
I. Very Poor	(men)	>15:31*	>16:01	>16:31	>17:31	>19:01
	(women)	>18:31	>19:01	>19:31	>20:01	>20:31
II. Poor	(men)	12:11–15:30	14:01–16:00	14:44–16:30	15:36–17:30	17:01–19:00
	(women)	16:55–18:30	18:31–19:00	19:01–19:30	19:31–20:00	20:01–20:30
III. Fair	(men)	10:49–12:10	12:01–14:00	12:31–14:45	13:01–15:35	14:31–17:00
	(women)	14:31–16:54	15:55–18:30	16:31–19:00	17:31–19:30	19:01–20:00
IV. Good	(men)	9:41–10:48	10:46–12:00	11:01–12:30	11:31–13:00	12:31–14:30
	(women)	12:30–14:30	13:31–15:54	14:31–16:30	15:56–17:30	16:31–19:00
V. Excellent	(men)	8:37– 9:40	9:45–10:45	10:00–11:00	10:30–11:30	11:00–12:30
	(women)	11:50–12:29	12:30–13:30	13:00–14:30	13:45–15:55	14:30–16:30
VI. Superior	(men)	<8:37*	<9:45	<10:00	<10:30	<11:00
	(women)	<11:50	<12:30	<13:00	<13:45	<14:30

* > means "more than"; < means "less than."

From Cooper, K. H., *The Aerobics Program for Total Well-Being* (New York: Bantam Books, 1982). Reprinted with permission.

Step-Up Test

Finally, here's a simple test anyone can do, and in your own home at that. No tracks, no running, no walking, no leaving the house. All you need is a bench or footstool or low table about twelve inches high (a sturdy coffee table is about right), a stopwatch, and something to help you pace yourself—a metronome, say, or a quick, rhythmic piece of music. Here's how it works.

Step onto and down from the bench for three minutes at a rate of about twenty-four step cycles per minute. Each step includes an entire cycle—step up with your right foot, step up with your left foot, step down with your right foot, step down with your left foot.

Once you're done with your three minutes, sit down and immediately begin to monitor your heart rate for one full minute. The idea is to determine your cardiovascular system's ability to recover from the exercise. An easy way to measure your heart rate is by feeling the pulse in your neck, just below the jaw line. You can then compare your recovery heart rate against the norms established for people between the ages of twenty and forty-six. For example, if you're a woman and your heart rate after your three minutes of step-ups is 118 beats per minute, you're in average aerobic condition.

Step-Up Test

Beats per Minute

	Men (age 20–46)	Women (age 20–46)
Excellent	81–90	79–84
Good	99–102	90–97
Above Average	103–112	106–109
Average	120–121	118–119
Below Average	123–125	122–124
Fair	127–130	129–134
Poor	136–138	137–145

Adapted from YMCA, *Y's Way to Fitness* (Chicago: The YMCA of USA, 1982). Reprinted with permission of the YMCA of the USA.

EVERYDAY AEROBIC TESTS

The above tests can help you assess your aerobic condition in terms of the rest of the population and certain physiological norms. For many people, however, such criteria don't mean all that much. It's what's going on in your life that counts.

The following tests involve everyday occurrences. The trick here is to become *aware* of what's going on in your life and not take your current level of condition for granted. For example, it simply isn't necessary to huff and puff while hurrying along an airport ramp to make a flight. It isn't necessary to feel as though your heart might pound clear through your skin. And it isn't necessary to arrive at the terminal especially early just so you won't have to move more quickly than your usual lazy amble. Lack of wind and stamina aren't simply facts of life—they are probably no more than a result of your lack of fitness.

So don't assume that what is, is—assume that what is can be changed for the better if you do something about it.

Here are some easy, everyday tests you can give yourself to assess your aerobic condition. If you put your mind to it, you can think of other ones, even better ones for your particular situation. Again, it demands only awareness and the point of view that the way you are now needn't necessarily be the way you'll remain forever.

• Can you walk the length of an airport concourse without becoming overly winded?

• Can you climb subway stairs or the flights of stairs to your home without feeling as though you're going to collapse?

• Can you climb the hill to the office? Can you climb the stairs to the office if the elevator is out?

• Can you carry sacks of groceries from the store to the car or apartment?

• Do you always have to ask the bagger to load the groceries in the car for you?

• Can you carry your own luggage from the baggage claim to the car or bus?

• Do you always check your bag at the curb for the sake of convenience or simply because you can't carry it inside?

• Have you bought comparatively expensive luggage just because it has wheels?

• Can you take a brisk walk at high altitude? (Altitude makes you particularly sensitive to problems of fitness.)

• Can you climb the stairs to your vacation rental cabin?

• Can you carry the tent from your car to the campsite? Even if the campsite is up a hill?

• Can you walk in San Francisco (or any hilly city) for an evening without suffering later on?

SPORTING ACTIVITY TESTS

• Can you walk rapidly around the block? For fifteen minutes?

• Can you carry your own golf bag around the course? Can you carry it from the cart to your car?

• Can you shoot baskets with a friend or your child without feeling as though you're going to collapse?
• Can you ski a six-minute run nonstop?
• Can you swim five laps without stopping? Ten? Twenty?
• Can you bodysurf for ten minutes straight?
• Can you play more than one set of tennis singles?

Again, the important considerations as far as aerobic condition are concerned are wind, endurance, heart rate level, and just plain energy.

How Strong Are You?

It's hard enough to objectively assess your aerobic condition, but at least there are some standards available. When it comes to strength, the task becomes even more difficult. As individual a matter as aerobic condition is, strength is even more so.

For example, if you sit at a desk all day, you don't need to be very strong. It's probably a good idea to be in reasonable aerobic condition, for reasons of general health if nothing else, but how strong do you need to be to push a pencil or use a computer? How strong should you be to punch out numbers on the telephone or type on a word processor? However, if you sit at a desk by day and are a cyclist or hiker or swimmer in the evening or on weekends, then it's a different story. Then you need strong legs and strong shoulders and arms. Then not only is aerobic conditioning important, but strength is important as well. Strength helps determine whether you enjoy your activity and are successful at it.

So strength is an individual thing. (As long as it's fairly symmetrical strength, that is. Most of us are stronger on one side than the other, of course, but if that discrepancy is too pronounced it may mean that you have an injury to contend with. More on that in the next chapter, Getting Balanced.) What you do determines how strong you need to be. Applying a general standard to strength may not be to the point at all.

Still, there are general standards. The President's Council on Fitness requires schoolkids to do a certain number of pull-ups and sit-ups in a certain amount of time. Attain that level and you're strong enough—fail and you need to be stronger. Other organizations have their own requirements. For years one of the most popular fitness guides has been the *Royal Canadian Air Force Fitness Plan*. It ranks your level of fitness by age, in terms of your ability to accomplish an exercise routine that includes such strength activities as sit-ups, back V-ups, and push-ups. The U.S. Marine Corps has a similar test to rank fitness, requiring men and women to perform a variety of activities and assigning their performance a point value. Score a certain number of points and you're in good enough shape. Fail to hit the minimum number and you have work to do.

But where strength really counts is in everyday living. Are you strong enough to do the everyday things you need to do? And are you strong enough to do the special things—sporting activities, for example—that you want to do?

The following questions are the kinds you might ask yourself. Again, the trick is to become aware of what's going on in your life day to day and not take your current level of activity for granted. One of the joys of exercise is the implicit promise that for most of us, it's possible to do more and better than we've done so far.

With all these tests, notice not only how you feel while performing them but how you feel the next day as well. If what you do is beyond your capabilities, you'll feel it the next day for sure.

EVERYDAY STRENGTH TESTS

• Can you climb three flights of stairs rapidly? Do your thighs burn? Do your knees hurt?
• Can you carry a twenty-five-pound sack of charcoal or dog food or kitty litter? With one arm?
• Do you have trouble lifting luggage into and out of the trunk?
• Do you have trouble lifting luggage off the airport baggage carousel?
• Do you have trouble lifting the spare tire into and out of the trunk?
• Can you lift an automobile battery into and out of the car?
• Can you carry your trash can to the street every week for pickup?
• Can you pull the cord to start a balky power mower?
• Can you rock your car back and forth to free it from ice in winter?
• Can you push your car to start it?
• Can you lift a box of books?
• Can you move furniture in your home?
• Can you use a hedge clipper for any length of time?
• Can you paint the ceiling?
• Can you change a bulb in a ceiling light?
• Do your legs hurt after walking downhill?
• Is it hard to get up after squatting in the garden?
• Can you carry your five-year-old child? Ten-year-old? Fifteen-year-old?

SPORTING ACTIVITY TESTS

• Do you have to stop skiing because of jelly muscles or burning thighs? After how long?

• Are you never able to ski more than a couple of hours the first day? Do you hurt like crazy the next day?

• Do your arms feel like spaghetti after five laps in the pool? Ten laps? Twenty?

• Do your thighs burn after kicking with swim fins? Do your legs cramp?

• Can you bend at the knees for low shots on the tennis court, or must you lean over at the waist?

• Do your shoulder and arm ache after a set of tennis?

• Do your shoulder, arm, and back ache after bowling a few games?

• Can you ride your bike uphill without burning, aching thighs?

• Do you have to walk your bike up hills?

Everyday Tip-offs

If a half hour with hedge clippers makes your shoulders tired and sore, it's an indication that you need to be stronger. A strengthening program will most likely improve your tennis game as well as your yard work.

If you sleep on a soft bed and wake up stiff and sore, it's an indication that your back and stomach muscles aren't strong or flexible enough. The better shape you're in, the better you tolerate soft beds. A strengthening program will not only help you sleep better, it'll improve your performance in just about any sport you can think of.

If your knees ache when you sit in a theater, it's an indication that your thigh muscles could use strengthening. A good quadriceps strengthening program will increase your comfort during the movie and help with biking, running, tennis, basketball, and other sports as well.

If walking hills like those in San Francisco makes your calves sore and causes shin splints, it's an indication that the muscles in your lower legs need strengthening. Doing so will improve your jumping and running ability as well as your ability to walk home from work.

How Flexible Are You?

Like strength, flexibility is an individual matter. And determining how flexible you are may be the least important of all these tests. You need only be flexible enough to do what you want to do. (As long as you're symmetrically flexible, that is. If you're far more flexible on one side than the other, you most likely have a problem—the residue of an old injury, for example, or a current injury. More on that in the next chapter.) It simply isn't necessary to be able to bend yourself into a pretzel unless you're involved in an activity that demands pretzel shapes. Gymnasts, dancers, and a few others are; most of us aren't.

In fact, striving for flexibility for its own sake can be more harmful than good. For example, at the Center for Sports Medicine we see lots of problems arising from stretching classes. People go into these programs determined to become as flexible as the instructor—an unreasonable goal in most cases—and the result is often injury. Too much stretching can do more than stretch muscles and tendons: it can weaken ligaments and injure joints. You simply have to decide how flexible is flexible enough and then stay at that level. For better or for worse, some of us just aren't destined to be very flexible. Somehow or other we survive.

EVERYDAY FLEXIBILITY TESTS

- Can you fasten a back-closing bra?
- Can you brush the hair on the back of your head?
- Can you pull the back of your collar down over your necktie?
- Can you tuck in your shirt in back?
- Can you wash your hair in the shower?
- Can you reach to the back seat of the car without turning your body completely around?
- Can you scratch your back? Even that hard-to-reach place that always itches?
- Can you tie your shoes without having to sit down?
- Can you sit Indian-style, with legs crossed?
- Can you sit on your heels?
- Do your legs hurt when you walk uphill? If so, your calves may not be flexible enough.

SPORTING ACTIVITY TESTS

- Can you pull all the way back on your golfing backswing?
- Can you rear back to hit a tennis serve? Can you toss the ball directly over your head, or do you have to toss it a bit in front of you?
- Can you raise your arms high during freestyle swimming, or do you just barely skim the water?
- Can you bend for low net shots in tennis?

Everyday Tip-offs

If you can't reach into the back seat of the car, becoming more flexible might help your golf and tennis.

If you can't tie your shoes without sitting down, becoming more flexible will help you get those low net shots.

Finding Your Appropriate Weight

Daria has lost about thirty pounds. Now she's well within the acceptable weight range for her height. But how do you know what's an acceptable weight? If you're not obviously overweight, how do you know if you're too fat? How do you know if your health is suffering?

It's not an easy question to answer. For years the Metropolitan Life Insurance Company, among others, has published weight tables by sex and height. We've included Metropolitan's below. It's a sensible, if not foolproof, guide to an appropriate weight for your

Weight Table by Height and Sex

Height	Weight	
	Men	Women
58		100-131
59		101-134
60		103-137
61	123-145	105-140
62	125-148	108-144
63	127-151	111-148
64	129-155	114-152
65	131-159	117-156
66	133-163	120-160
67	135-167	123-164
68	137-171	123-167
69	139-175	129-170
70	141-179	132-173
71	144-183	135-176
72	147-187	

From the 1983 Metropolitan weight tables. Courtesy of the Metropolitan Life Insurance Company.

height. For example, the acceptable weight for a woman who is 5′8″ is between 123 and 167 pounds. For a man of the same height, it's between 137 and 171 pounds. A person of slight build should be at the lower end of the scale, medium build somewhere in the middle, large frame toward the high end. According to most medical experts, if you're more than 20 percent heavier than the midpoint of your recommended weight, you're obese. And with obesity comes an increased risk of such problems as high blood pressure, diabetes, and possibly heart disease.

WEIGHT TABLE BY HEIGHT AND SEX

But these tables aren't perfect. For one thing, they're based on a sampling—primarily whites and middle-class blacks—that may not reflect acceptable weight for the entire population. And what about special cases—for example an athlete, a football linebacker, say, who's 6 feet tall and weighs 225 pounds? That's well above 20 percent more than his acceptable range. Is he obese? Probably not, for that extra weight is most likely in the form of muscle rather than fat.

So a more accurate test of obesity is probably the percent of fat in your body rather than weight alone. It's generally considered that in men up to 18 percent body fat is allowable. In women the figure is 26 percent. Unfortunately, it's harder to determine body fat percentage than it is to find out how much you weigh. You can't just step on a scale to discover your percent of body fat. There are methods involving such esoteric procedures as ultrasound, X-rays, caliper measurements, and underwater weighing, but these are relatively costly and inaccessible tests. There are simpler tests based on measurements of girth, but these too are more involved and complicated than many people are willing to put up with.

Suffice it to say that the most practical test of all may be your everyday perception of yourself. A visit to the scale or glance in the mirror can tell you a lot about your condition, as long as you don't base your judgment on misleading standards. For example, those super-slim models on TV are not overweight, certainly, but you don't have to be that skinny to be fit and healthy. If you don't measure up—or down, that is—to your favorite fashion model or film star, it doesn't necessarily mean you're overweight. Better that you should compare yourself to yourself, to the way you used to be when you felt best about yourself. That is a more realistic and more nearly attainable standard.

The lesson is especially relevant as we age. Love handles and saddlebags seem to be one of the almost unavoidable consequences of getting older. They're not necessarily attractive or healthy, but they're not the end of the world either, especially if you keep them under control. And the best way to do that is through exercise. As with everything we suggest in this book, the idea is to become aware of what's going on with your body and do something about it intelligently and realistically.

Starting with the next chapter, we'll suggest what that something might be.

2 *Getting Balanced*

Russ is twenty-seven years old, a high-school teacher, and a born-again exerciser. After not having done any formal working out since he was in ninth grade (we'll discuss why in a moment—it's a sad story), he regularly lifts weights and swims. He has it down pat. He swims every other morning, lifts every other afternoon, and takes Sundays off. At least, that's the plan. But since he started working out more than a year ago, he has kept to his schedule no more than a handful of times. His problem has to do with why it's important to make sure your body is balanced before you embark on an exercise program.

"When I was a freshman in high school," Russ says, "I played football. I can still remember it vividly. We were doing tackling practice—it didn't even happen in a game. I was running with the ball, and the kid who was supposed to tackle me came toward me on my right side. He slammed into my knee, I heard something snap, and the next thing I knew I was on the ground clutching my leg."

"Then what happened?" Garrick asks.

"I'd just as soon forget it," Russ says.

He was carried off the field, rushed to the emergency room in an ambulance, and spent the next two weeks in bed. He hobbled around with a cane for a month after that and never played football again. In fact, when he showed up at a practice toward the end of the season, no longer leaning on his cane but still unable to straighten or bend his knee all the way, the coach accused him of dogging it so he wouldn't have to be tackled again.

"Does your knee still bother you?" Garrick asks.

"Well, it stiffens up when it's cold and wet. And it goes out on me once in a while—always at the worst times, of course."

"Of course," Garrick says. "That's the way these things work. What do you mean, 'goes out'?"

"All of a sudden it bends the wrong way, as though it's going to break apart. And it hurts like hell."

"Hmm. What was the diagnosis when you first injured it?"

"That's the trouble, I don't know. The doctor never said."

"Well, let's find out," Garrick says. He gently works Russ's knee from side to side. "Now just relax your knee. I won't hurt you. C'mon, more than that."

"I can't," Russ says.

"That's okay," Garrick says. "You've blown out your medial collateral ligament. You've been able to live with it all these years by substituting sheer muscle. You can't relax your guard even when you want to."

"That's why I began an exercise program," Russ says. "I've gotten along pretty darn well. Sometimes I even forget about it. I decided it was high time to forget about it all the time."

He knew that swimming is easy on the legs, so he decided to give that a try. And he had read somewhere that the best thing to do for a bad knee was to strengthen the thigh muscles, so he started to work out with weight training machines. The instructor agreed with him and started him out doing knee extensions and squats.

Within a week his knee was so sore he could hardly walk. He continued to work with upper body weights, but soon he did something to his shoulder on the lat pull-down machine. And from that time on it has been a balancing act of swimming when his shoulder felt good enough, working out with weights when the rest of his body felt good enough, and frequently being able to do neither.

"It's been terribly frustrating," he says. "I feel worse than I did when I started. All because I thought it was time to do something about my physical condition."

"Don't be too hard on yourself," Garrick says. "You had the right idea. But most people don't realize that before you can dive into a workout program your body has to be ready for it. And that means rehabilitating old injuries first."

"You mean I have to strengthen my knee before I can start strengthening my knee?"

Garrick laughs. "Just about. You have to bring your bad knee up to the level of your other knee before going on from there. If you don't . . . well, you know what happens if you don't."

Russ knows all too well. His motives were good—he just went about it in the wrong way. He simply wasn't ready to start weight training. He needed to bring his body to the point where it was ready to go ahead.

That's where this book comes in. This chapter will show you how to get your body ready to go about exercising for your particular needs and goals. And that involves dealing with old injuries.

As the previous chapter suggested, you may not be strong enough or flexible enough for your particular needs, or your cardiovascular condition may not be at a level suitable to achieve your goals. In that case, the remedy may seem simple: set up a program designed to rectify the problem and go at it. Right?

Wrong. Wouldn't it be wonderful if life were that straightforward? But it's not. The reason is that we bring to this endeavor a less than perfect instrument called the body. No two bodies are exactly alike—everyone knows that. But what's easy to forget is that every body comes with its own history. And when it comes to sports and exercise, that history almost invariably includes injuries.

Were we robots, a race of C3POs able to replace worn or damaged parts with brand-new ones, a history of injuries wouldn't mean much. You've had a knee injury? No problem. Just hop on down to the parts bin and snap in a new one. Hurt your ankle? Time for a replacement. But robots we aren't, and the sad truth of the matter is that once we sustain an injury, especially if it's a serious injury, there's every likelihood that that particular part will never be quite the same again. Your knee may have more or less recovered from your past injury, for example, but at the least it's probably behaving a little differently than it used to. Just ask Russ.

Most of us compensate pretty well for these changes. In fact, it sometimes may seem that after a certain point in our lives staying active involves an endless procession of compensations. We constantly make adjustments to counteract our bodies' idiosyncrasies, often without even noticing it. Who cares if your old knee injury prevents you from starting and stopping on a dime the way you used to when approaching the net or that your shoulder injury keeps you from rearing back on your serve as before? So what that your back problem has reduced your distance off the tee or that your old ankle sprain makes running on uneven terrain a touchy proposition? Life goes on. You refine other aspects of your game, start driving for accuracy instead of distance, make sure to run on the high-school track rather than through the park.

All well and good. But when it comes to setting up a personal fitness program, old injuries rear their ugly heads and stay there. Compensate for them or ignore them at your peril—especially those injuries that cause one part of your body to be weaker than the corresponding part.

For example, consider Russ. He had been getting along with his old knee injury all these years, but once he began an exercise program that included knee extensions and squats, the imbalance in his leg strength on one side compared to the other caused him some real difficulties. In the same way, if your shoulder strength is imbalanced one side to the other, better think twice about beginning push-ups or pull-ups. And so it goes. The rest of this chapter will go into such concerns in detail. The point is that you must bring your body up to a balanced, generally stable level of fitness before beginning any program designed to improve your condition further. If you don't, you may find that, rather than becoming more fit, you're becoming more hurt. If you do, your chances of beginning a healthy, effective workout program are good indeed.

So the purpose of this chapter is to help you do three things:

• Identify old injuries that you haven't yet completely recovered from.

• Know how to rehabilitate those injuries so that you can go on to your own personalized general fitness program.

• Know when you should stop doing things on your own and see a doctor.

For the goal of working out is certainly not to reopen old wounds —it's to heal them and improve from there on. This chapter will help make sure that you don't get hurt when you embark on your fitness program and that you're primed and ready to gain the greatest benefits from your efforts.

General Suggestions

Before you even begin, you should ask yourself some questions. And don't fool yourself. Answer them honestly. As much as it hurts to admit to injuries, it hurts far more to suffer them.

Do you have any pain or swelling in joints or muscles during daily activity? It doesn't have to be much. Ideally, your joints shouldn't hurt or swell at all. You may experience muscle soreness, especially if you overdo—that's only natural and not necessarily worrisome—but it shouldn't linger. And joints should remain pain-free. You should hardly notice them, almost as though they're not there at all.

Have you ever had any surgery involving joints or your back or stomach? And remember, arthroscopic surgery counts. That little probe and those miniature instruments entering your body may not have seemed like much at the time, but when you rehabilitated the joint you certainly knew that you had undergone surgery. Anytime your body is incised and invaded, that's surgery.

Do you feel as though any joints are loose or unstable? They don't have to feel loose by much. This is one of those subtle concerns, often difficult to measure and pin down. In the extreme, yes, a doctor can push and pull and demonstrate the instability of your joint. But often it's just not that obvious, especially because we tend to compensate for joint instability by tightening muscles in the area. A doctor can tug as much as he wants, but you may be holding things tightly in place by muscle power, and so little or no looseness may show up. And besides, one person's looseness is another's stability. You just have to trust your feelings in this regard. A joint that just sort of *feels* loose probably *is* loose.

Do you regularly avoid certain sports or activities because of pain, swelling, weakness, or fear of reinjury? Again, your hesitancy may be subtle, and it may be based on incidents that happened quite some time ago. Never mind. You probably have good reason to be cautious. There's no one who knows your body nearly as well as you.

If you answered *yes* to any of these questions, you should pay particular attention to the rest of this chapter. We'll explore various troublesome parts of the body and suggest how to go about recognizing problems and dealing with them so as to get your body up to snuff. Again, it's very important to go into any workout program in a balanced state of fitness, even if it isn't a particularly high level. At least then you can work on your body without fear of neglecting one area while overdoing another. Otherwise, you only invite trouble.

If we don't cover your particular problem here, or don't cover it in enough depth, *don't hesitate to consult with your doctor before beginning the workout programs in this book or any other.* Remember the old saying—an ounce of prevention is worth a pound of cure. When it comes to the body and working out, it's certainly true.

The Knee

The knee is the most common source of sports and fitness injuries. Indeed, instead of asking, "How are you doing?" one athlete might as well ask another, "How's your knee?" Knee injuries are that common.

Over 25 percent of all sports injuries involve the knee, and when it comes to surgery the figure is over 75 percent. In runners, knee injuries are by far the most common complaint. For aerobic dancers they rank either first or a close second. And, believe it or not, even swimmers suffer knee injuries—breaststrokers, that is. The motion of the frog kick can be hard on the joint.

PAST KNEE INJURIES

In general, knee injuries have two sources. One involves previous knee injuries. It's simply a fact that ligaments, cartilage, and tendons, the targets of most knee injuries, are not particularly forgiving. Once hurt, they may never quite get back to their former condition. So unless you pay particular attention to rehabilitating a knee injury by strengthening the muscles in the area so that they can help out the injured parts—and many people don't—your knee may always be a shade weaker or looser than before. A knee once injured is often more easily reinjured.

If your previous injury has necessitated surgery or immobilization in a cast, another potential problem may be involved: premature wear of the joint—in other words, arthritis. Over half of all knee injuries involving cartilage or ligament damage can cause your knee to wear out earlier than it might have otherwise. The tip-offs are aching or swelling when you use the knee, locking or giving way, loss of flexibility. While these problems may not be bad enough to keep you away from a sports or fitness activity, don't ignore them when deciding which activity to pursue. For example, cycling is easier on the knees than running. If your knee bothers you because it's worn or damaged, better think of at least alternating cycling with running, if not trading in your running shoes for a bike.

Again, if you suspect that you experience any of these residuals of prior injuries, you should consult your doctor before embarking on a fitness program.

CURRENT KNEE INJURIES

The most common source of knee injuries is overusing the knee. People who like to exercise aren't always smart about their activity. It can be awfully hard to stop when you should or curtail your activity when you should. The result is often an overuse injury.

Overuse injuries are usually caused by attempting an activity that's too strenuous for your current level of strength or endurance. In fact, not having a strong enough quadriceps muscle—the large muscle in the front of the thigh—is the single most common cause of sports-related knee complaints. It's the quadriceps muscle —especially the small portion called the vastus medialis, just above and to the inside of the kneecap—that has the responsibility of keeping your kneecap tracking properly. If the muscle isn't strong enough, and if you overwork the knee, the kneecap can subtly veer off course, causing a host of knee problems.

At first you may notice that your knee aches after activity. Then, as the injury becomes more severe, your knee may hurt and grow stiff when you sit with your leg bent for long periods of time. (The symptom is called "positive theater sign," as it afflicts people jammed into crowded theaters. That fellow whose outstretched legs you tripped over during the movie probably has a knee problem.) Then you may notice pain when you climb or descend hills or stairs. The pain is usually in the front of the knee, behind or surrounding the kneecap. And finally your knee may swell and feel tight, or it may even collapse when you least expect it.

At the very least, these symptoms indicate a need for a stronger quadriceps muscle. And that's something you can take care of yourself. Here's how to go about determining what kind of work your knee may need.

KNEE EXAMINATION

First, do what any good doctor does—ask yourself these questions:
- Have you ever been advised to wear a knee brace?
- Does your knee feel loose?
- Does your knee give way or lock?
- Does your knee swell with activity?
- Is your knee swollen now?

If your answer to any *of these questions is* yes, *see a doctor.* You most likely have a knee problem serious enough to need professional treatment.

If *all* your answers are *no,* then ask yourself the following questions:
- Does your knee hurt when you climb up or down hills or stairs?
- Does your knee hurt or ache when you sit for long periods of time with your leg bent, as in a theater?
- Does your knee feel weak, as though it's going to give way?

If your answer to *any* of these questions is *yes,* then before beginning a fitness exercise program you should make sure that the strength of your "bad" leg is equal to the strength of the other leg. We'll suggest how to do that in a moment.

If *all* your answers are *no,* go on to the next part of the examination. You may be in fine shape, but often these discrepancies are subtle and don't show up in such obvious ways until the problem is well along. The thing to do now is to catch them early on. The way to do that is by self-examination.

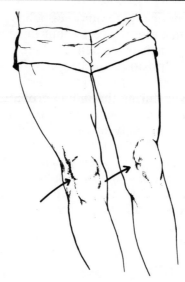

Sit on the floor with your legs extended straight in front of you, or sit in a chair and rest your heels on a footstool. Now look at the depressions or dimples on either side of your kneecap. Are they equally prominent on both knees?

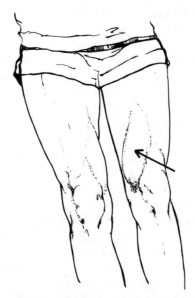

While still sitting with your legs extended, tighten the muscle in the front of your thigh—that's the quadriceps. The part just above your kneecap and to the inside is the vastus medialis. Observe how large the muscle is compared to the other side. Feel the tone of the muscle. Are both sides the same in size and hardness?

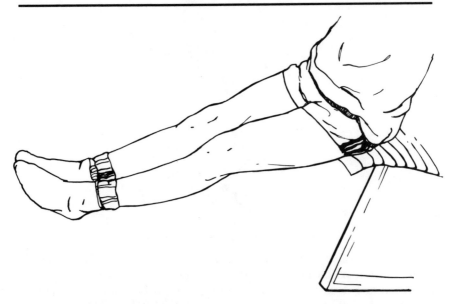

Sit in a chair and extend your legs in front of you. Do both knees straighten out to the same degree?

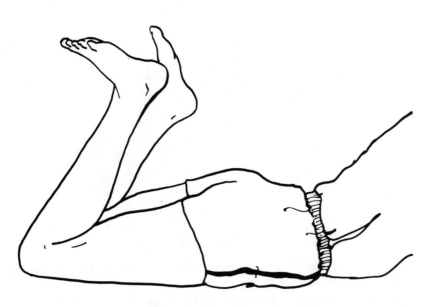

Lie on your stomach. Bend your knees as far as you can. Are both your heels an equal distance from your buttocks?

Are you able to do a one-legged squat? Try lowering yourself slowly down with one leg—it doesn't matter how far you can go—and then see if you can do the same on the other side. The farther you can go, the stronger you are, but the point of the test is to see if you can squat the same on both sides, painlessly.

How much weight can you lift with one leg? Can you do the same on the other side?

This test demands a knee extension machine—it's just not practical to do it at home. Try to lift at least 15 percent of your body weight. Any less than that suggests that you're weaker than you ought to be, even in your good leg. But, again, the point of the test is to see if you can lift the same amount on both sides.

Be sure to lift with one leg at a time. It doesn't work to lift one hundred pounds, say, using both legs at the same time and then conclude that you can lift fifty pounds with each leg. People often cheat without realizing it by using the good leg to do the brunt of the work.

If your legs test out pretty much the same in these exercises, it's an indication that both knees are similarly strong and flexible—in other words, that you're balanced from side to side. You're probably able to go on with a fitness program.

But if one side is consistently stronger or weaker than the other, it may mean trouble. Any difference that exists between one knee and the other suggests that a previous knee injury hasn't been completely rehabilitated or that there's a potential problem just waiting to occur. So if your examination turns up a discrepancy from side to side, better strengthen the weak side before beginning any fitness program that will involve the use of your knees. Here's how.

KNEE STRENGTHENING PROGRAM

Quadriceps Tightening Exercises

These are the easiest and most accessible knee strengthening exercises you can do. They're also among the most effective.

Sit with your legs straight out in front of you. Contract your quadriceps. Imagine that you're trying to pull your kneecap toward your waist. Now feel the vastus medialis with your fingertips. It should be hard to the touch. If it's not, the contraction isn't working.

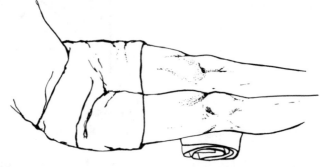

Try the same exercise with a rolled-up towel beneath your knee. Try to flatten the towel beneath your knee. Now feel the vastus medialis with your fingers. It should be hard.

Hold the contraction for six seconds, then relax for two to three seconds and contract again. Do three to four repetitions of this exercise fifteen to twenty times during the day.

And keep it up indefinitely. This is one exercise that's good to do no matter what kind of shape you're in. Do it on your good side as well. A strong vastus medialis muscle is your best insurance against knee problems.

Knee Extensions

If you have access to a knee extension machine, here's an exercise that can supplement your quad tightening efforts.

First, determine how much weight you can lift and hold with your good leg. Lift the weight slowly and hold it steadily, with your knee straightened all the way, for three seconds.

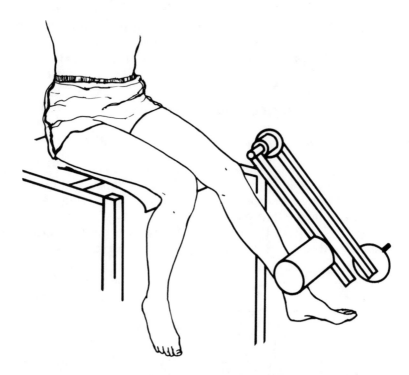

Now take one quarter of that weight (25 percent) and try a lift with your weaker leg. Again, lift slowly and hold the weight for three seconds.

If you can lift 25 percent of the weight you handled on your good side, then increase to 50 percent. If you can lift 50 percent, try 75 percent, and so on. When you get to the point at which you can't lift the weight, you've found your current capability.

Now it's time to begin strengthening the bad leg. Begin by doing ten repetitions at half the amount of weight you've determined you can lift with your bad leg. For example, if you can lift forty pounds with your bad leg, do ten reps at twenty pounds. Again, lift up slowly, hold for about three seconds, and let down slowly. Then do ten reps at three-quarters of your maximum weight—in this case that would be thirty pounds. Then do up to ten reps at your maximum weight, forty pounds. You may not be able to do that many—simply do as many as you can. Finally, to cool down, do twenty quick reps at one-quarter weight—ten pounds in this case.

Again, that's ten reps at half weight, ten reps at three-quarter weight, up to ten reps at full weight, and twenty quick reps at one-quarter weight to cool down. That's a good workout for one day.

Gradually increase your weight over the following days, sticking at any one level until it becomes comfortable, then moving on until finally you can lift 90 percent or more of the weight on your good side. At that point, your leg strength is approximately equal side to side. Depending on how weak you are to start with, it may take a couple of weeks to equalize your leg strength side to side, but you'll probably begin to notice a difference in a week. Don't think that you have to progress too quickly. A five-pound weight increase is plenty—enough to increase difficulty but not enough to cause injury. You want to build up your bad knee, not tear it down. How fast you can build up isn't the point—it's how well and how lastingly.

These exercises may cause some aching and sore muscles, but they should not cause pain in the knee. If your knee itself hurts, see a doctor.

These exercises will help rehabilitate previous knee injuries and prevent future ones. They'll help balance your knee strength from side to side. Once you've done so, that's the time to begin a fitness program. But until then, be wary of starting any fitness program that involves the knees. In particular, these are the activities that you should approach with caution or simply avoid until your knee strength is balanced.

Exercises to Avoid

- Knee extensions with excessive weight
- Leg presses
- Running or treadmill exercise
- Stair climbing or step-ups
- Squats or lunges
- Rowing with knees bent beyond 90 degrees
- Cycling with the seat too low

OTHER COMMON PROBLEMS

Shin Splints

If the front of your lower leg hurts when you run or jump, you may be suffering from shin splints. No one really knows just what causes shin splints, but they may be the painful result of muscles ripping away from the shin during activities that involve pounding and pressure along the shinbone.

The best way to guard against shin splints is to stretch and strengthen the muscles in the lower leg.

To stretch the muscles in the back of the calf, do the same exercises we recommend for Achilles tendinitis (page 60). To strengthen the muscles, do toe raises (see page 187).

To strengthen the muscles in the front of the lower leg, try the exercises we recommend for ankle weakness (page 197). In particular, pull up your foot against resistance—a piece of surgical tubing (see page 198) or an inner tube nailed to the sides of a piece of wood will provide homemade resistance.

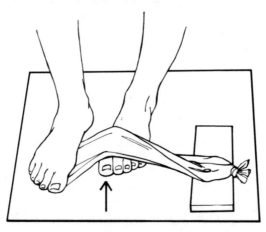

Do these exercises slowly in sets of ten, three times a day. You can accomplish much the same kind of strengthening during normal daily activities by taking a few seconds to walk on your heels. The exercise forces you to flex your ankle and thus contract the muscles in the front of your lower leg.

Muscle Pulls or Strains in the Thigh

A pulled muscle in the thigh, whether it be the quadriceps muscle in front of the thigh or the hamstring muscle in the back, is one of the most common injuries in sports. They're not usually terribly serious injuries and can be effectively rehabilitated. But if you don't rehabilitate the injury and restrengthen the injured muscle to the point where it's again equal in strength to the other side, thigh pulls or strains can easily occur again.

If the amount of weight you can lift with one leg is markedly larger or smaller than that of the other—more than 20 percent difference from side to side, say—you should strengthen the weak side for sure.

To strengthen a weak quadriceps muscle, practice leg extension exercises (see page 209).

To strengthen weak hamstrings, try hamstring curls. You can do these exercises at home by using surgical tubing. Simply sit in a chair with your knees bent, slip your leg through a loop of tubing, and pull your heel toward your buttocks. As you become stronger, increase the resistance by stretching the tubing to a greater extent, so that it's less elastic.

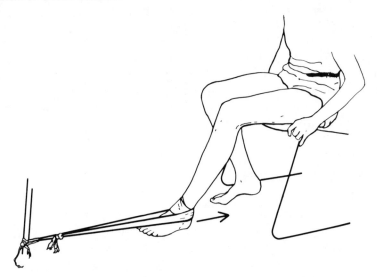

The easiest way to do the exercises, however, is with a hamstring curl machine. It's also the most precise approach, as you can measure the amount of weight you're lifting. Simply follow the approach for strengthening on page 183.

The Back

Nearly everyone has experienced at least some low back pain, so a sore back shouldn't necessarily keep you away from sports or fitness activities. In fact, doctors often prescribe fitness-enhancing exercises to treat or relieve back pain. You may be doing your back a favor by working your body into shape.

The problem with back injuries is that when they hit, they really hit. There's no other injury that's so debilitating. Though you can get along relatively well with a sore arm or leg or shoulder, even continue exercising by doing activities that bypass the injured part, when it comes to a back injury you're in trouble. It's simply hard to do anything at all with a back that's out of commission. So it's a good idea to do everything you can to keep your back sound.

Of course, besides being debilitating, some back injuries are dangerous, because the backbone protects the spinal cord, the brain's connection to the rest of the body. An injury affecting the spinal cord can affect the body's nervous system. At the worst, spinal column injuries can lead to paralysis and loss of bodily function.

The tip-offs to such serious injuries are *pain, numbness or tingling along the arms or legs, obvious weakness in the arms or legs, or sharp pain with coughing or sneezing.* If you have any of these symptoms, see a doctor before embarking on any new exercise or fitness program.

More often, though, back problems are not serious. Most consist of aching and stiffness following some unaccustomed activity —carrying boxes, working in the garden, trying to load a heavy suitcase into the trunk of the car. The way to treat and prevent these problems is to increase the strength and flexibility of the muscles surrounding your back.

BACK EXAMINATION

First, take your own medical history.
• Do you have pain radiating down your leg or legs?
• Do you have back pain or radiating pain when you cough, sneeze, or strain, as when moving your bowels?
• Do you have weakness in your legs, such as the inability to stand on your toes?
• Do you have any numbness or tingling in your legs or feet?
• Have you ever been diagnosed as having disk disease or a ruptured disk?
• Have you ever been told your back X-rays are abnormal?
• Have you had more than one episode of significant back pain or other back problems within the last twelve months?

If the answer to *any* of these questions is *yes,* you should consult a doctor right away. Any of them could be the tip-off to serious back problems.

If the answer to *all* of these questions is *no,* then ask yourself the following questions.
• Is your back stiff when you get up in the morning?

• Does your back ache after you've been sitting or standing for more than thirty minutes?

• Does your back ache the day after any unaccustomed activity —skiing or tennis, for example?

If the answer to *all* of these questions is *no,* then most likely your back is in pretty good shape. To be sure, go on to the next part of this examination.

If the answer to *any* of these questions is *yes,* then you should begin a back exercise program before going on to a general fitness program.

Sit on the floor with your legs extended in front of you. Now lean forward with your arms outstretched. Can you comfortably reach your fingertips beyond your kneecaps?

Lie on your stomach. Are you able to arch your chest and legs upward painlessly?

Are you able to move your back in all six directions—bend forward, bend backward, bend to the left, bend to the right, twist to the left, twist to the right? Can you do so comfortably?

Are you able to do five curl-ups? (See page 248 for a description of how to do curl-ups.)

If you answered *yes* to *all* of these questions, you're probably ready to go ahead with your fitness program.

If you answered *no* to *any* of these questions, you should proceed with the back strengthening program suggested below before starting any new fitness activity.

BACK STRENGTHENING PROGRAM

Back Stretches

Lying on your back, grasp the back of one thigh and gently pull your leg to your chest. Hold the stretch for fifteen seconds, then straighten out that leg and pull the other one to your chest. Hold for fifteen seconds, and then pull both legs to your chest. Hold for fifteen seconds. Relax and go on to curl-ups. Repeat the stretching exercises afterward.

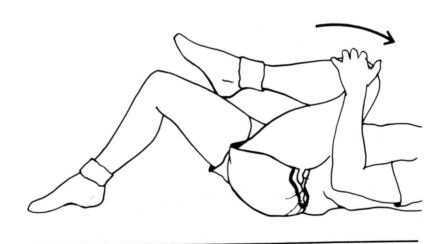

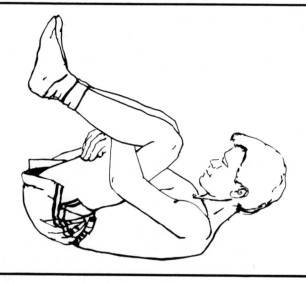

Curl-Ups

No, not sit-ups: curl-ups. There's a difference. If strengthening your stomach muscles is your aim, there's nothing more effective than curl-ups, and nothing safer.

Stomach muscles? Isn't this section about the back?

Well, so it is. But your stomach muscles help support your back. They're the back's front stabilizers. If you want to strengthen your back, you must strengthen your stomach muscles. Here's how.

Lie on your back on the floor with your knees bent and your hands resting together over your chest. Then press the small of your back into the floor and slowly curl your head and shoulders up, to the point where your shoulder blades have cleared the floor. Hold the position for a moment and then slowly curl back down. You should feel the contraction in your stomach.

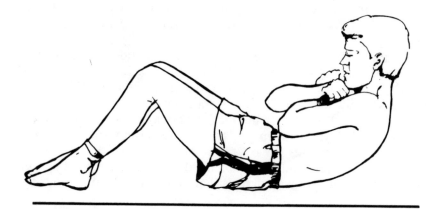

It's particularly important to do curl-ups slowly. Count slowly to six as you curl up, hold for a count of six, then count slowly to six again as you curl down. Don't hold your breath—keep breathing throughout the exercise—and make sure that your back is pressed into the floor. As soon as you tire and your back begins to arch, stop. And surely stop if this exercise causes any back pain.

Work up to five curl-ups three times a day. Don't be discouraged if it takes a while. Curl-ups are tough, but they may be the best thing you can do for your back.

Remember, do the back stretching exercises before you do curl-ups, then do the stretching exercises again afterward.

These exercises will help rehabilitate old back injuries and prevent new ones from getting started. If you can do them effectively, you're ready to start on your fitness program. Until then, however, avoid the following activities or approach them with caution. They can be hard on your back.

Exercises to Avoid

- Touching your toes
- Vigorous hamstring stretching
- Using excessive weights with any kind of lifting
- Sit-ups with your feet hooked

The Ankle

Nearly everyone has sprained an ankle at some time or other. It's the single most common sports injury of all. And the cause doesn't have to be sports-related. Puttering in the garden can do it; so can a leisurely stroll after dinner; so can nothing more than stepping in a hole or tripping over a child's toy. Anything that causes your foot to turn underneath you can cause a sprained ankle.

That's the bad news. The good news is that most people survive ankle sprains without any long-term problems. As a rule, the more quickly you get back to normal activities after your ankle sprain, the less likely that you'll have continued difficulties. The sprain that causes you to limp or hobble for only a day or two is unlikely to result in future problems. It's the more serious sprain, the one that requires crutches for over a week, or a cast, or any kind of surgery, that often leads to problems down the line. These sprains can result in persistent weakness that, unless dealt with, can cause an unstable ankle, recurrent twists or sprains, and pain and swelling.

Some aerobic fitness activities aren't particularly hard on the ankle. You can begin cycling and rowing programs while you're strengthening your ankle. In fact, such programs actually help rehabilitate the joint. But be careful of activities that demand jumping and quick starts and stops. Aerobic dance may be one, running another. And games such as tennis, softball, basketball, racketball, and volleyball are especially likely to reinjure already weak ankles and produce brand-new ankle injuries. If you have any history of recurrent ankle problems, you should approach these activities cautiously. It can be a good idea to wear an ankle wrap or brace until you've completed an ankle restrengthening program.

ANKLE EXAMINATION

First, take your own medical history.
- Do you have sharp, severe ankle pain for no apparent reason?
- Does your ankle lock or catch, requiring that you move, twist, or jiggle it in order to unlock it?
- Does your ankle give way or collapse and subsequently become swollen?
- Is your ankle constantly swollen? Is it swollen now?

If your answer to *any* of these questions is *yes,* better see a doctor. You may have an ankle problem too serious to deal with on your own.

If your answer to *all* these questions is *no,* go on to the next part of the examination.
- Do you twist or sprain your ankle more often than once a year?
- Does your ankle feel stiff the morning following unaccustomed exercise?
- Have you had a significant ankle sprain anytime in the past?
- Does your ankle feel untrustworthy, especially when walking over uneven ground?

If your answer to *any* of these questions is *yes,* then it's likely that you need to rehabilitate your ankle. We'll suggest how in a moment.

If your answer to *all* of these questions is *no,* then it may be that your ankles are in pretty good shape. To be absolutely sure, give yourself an examination.

Sit on a chair in front of a mirror with your feet flat on the floor and take a good look at your ankles. Are they both the same size and configuration? Or does one appear swollen, lumpy, larger than the other? (See illustration on page 54.)

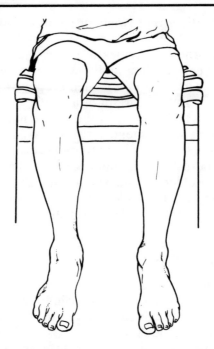

Stand on your toes with your back to a full-length mirror. Now look over your shoulder. Are the upper portions of your calves the same size and configuration? Or does one calf appear larger or more defined than the other?

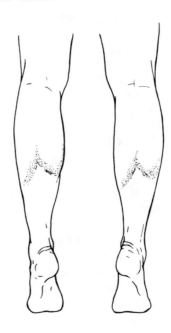

Sit with both legs extended in front of you. Now point your toes. Can you point the toes on both feet the same amount?

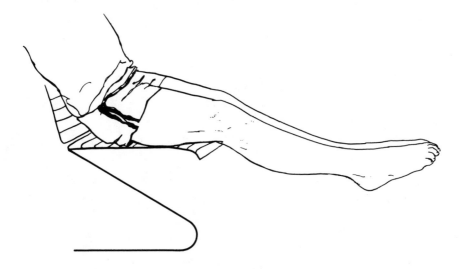

Stand approximately two feet from a wall. Face the wall and, keeping your knees straight, lean forward over your ankles. Can you lean as far on both ankles? Does it hurt your ankle to lean forward?

Stand with your feet parallel and squat down. Are you able to squat as deeply on both ankles?

Balance on the toes of one foot. How many seconds can you balance without support? At least twenty? Then balance on the other side. Is your balance time within five seconds of the first-side time?

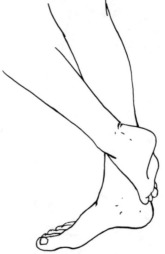

Can you hop up and down at least ten times on each foot without allowing your heel to touch the floor?

If you answered *yes* to *all* these questions, then your ankles are in pretty good shape. You can probably begin a fitness program without an increased chance of injury.

If you answered *no* to *any* of these questions, or if you otherwise note a marked difference between ankles, then you may be suffering the aftereffects of an old ankle injury. Before embarking on any fitness program with a high risk of ankle injuries, you should strengthen your weak ankle. Here's how.

ANKLE STRENGTHENING PROGRAM

Ankle Contractions

One way to strengthen your ankle is to contract it against resistance. Your ankle moves in four directions: up, down, and from side to side (and, of course, all the variations in between). Using a piece of surgical tubing, inner tube, or Thera-Band®, move your ankle in these directions against the resistance provided by the tubing. Do ten slow contractions in each direction at least twice a day.

You can buy surgical tubing—which is the strong, elastic tubing doctors sometimes use in surgery for suctioning out fluids—at many drugstores, medical supply stores, or hospitals. Inner tubes, of course, are available at automobile or bicycle supply shops. Thera-Band is a bit harder to find but well worth the effort. If a nearby medical supply store, physical therapy clinic, or hospital doesn't carry it, you can order it directly from the manufacturer: The Hygenic Corporation, 1245 Home Avenue, Akron, Ohio 44310; 1 (800) 321-2135, in Ohio (216) 633-8460.

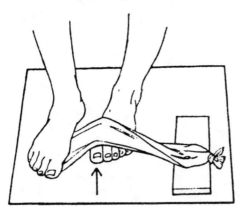

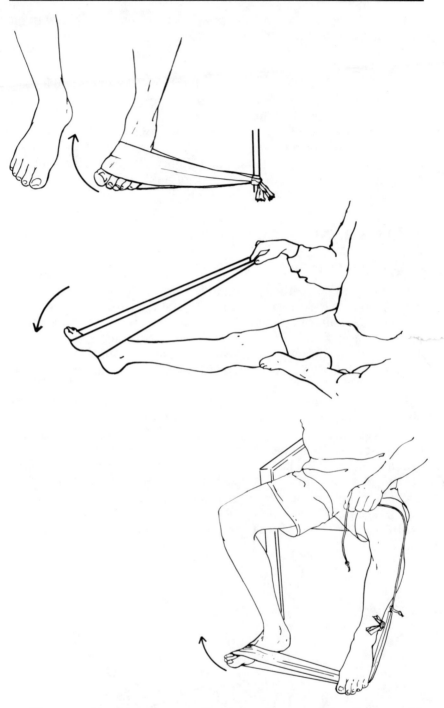

The muscles that are most important in preventing future ankle sprains are the peroneal muscles, the ones on the outside of your lower leg. These are the muscles that allow you to pull your ankle up and out. So it can be a good idea to make a special effort to exercise your ankle in that direction.

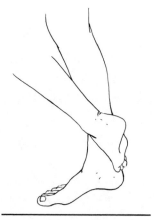

Ankle Balancing

Without hanging on to anything for support, balance for as long as possible on the toes of your bad foot. Do this exercise frequently during the day—while talking on the telephone, waiting for a bus, doing dishes, etc.

Toe Raises

Toe raises do a good job of strengthening many of the muscles that cross the ankle. If you do them with your knees straight, you strengthen the muscles in the upper calf.

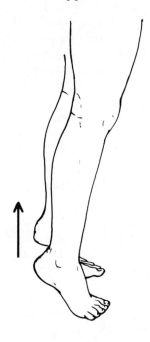

Do toe raises with your knees slightly bent and you strengthen the muscles in the lower calf.

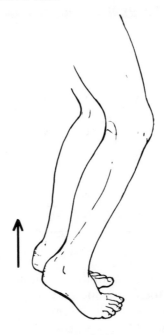

Do these exercises slowly each day in sets of at least twenty repetitions. Once you're as strong in one leg as the other, try toe raises one leg at a time.

These exercises will help rehabilitate previous ankle injuries and balance your ankle strength from side to side. Until then, be wary of any fitness programs involving a great deal of ankle movement. In particular, avoid the following activities or approach them with caution until your ankle strength is balanced from side to side.

Exercises to Avoid

- Agility running drills
- Jumping exercises

OTHER COMMON PROBLEMS

Achilles Tendinitis

If your upper calf muscles are unequal in size, you may be prey to Achilles tendinitis. If your Achilles tendon—the big, tough cord in the back of the ankle that connects your calf muscles to your heel—is swollen or tender to the touch, you're already suffering the injury.

Tendinitis is the inflammation of a tendon, and the Achilles tendon—the largest and most exposed tendon in the body—is particularly vulnerable to such inflammation. Achilles tendinitis is often the result of calf muscles that are too weak or tight. If you never fully rehabilitate these muscles after the injury, you can suffer Achilles tendinitis for a long time to come. Here's how to go about strengthening and stretching your calf muscles.

See page 187 for a description of how to do toe raises. Be sure to do some of them with your knee straight and some with your knee bent, to strengthen both the upper and lower muscles in the calf.

To stretch your calf, stand with your bad leg slightly behind the other, your feet pointing straight ahead. Keeping the heel of your back foot on the ground and your knee straight, slowly bend forward over your ankle. You'll feel the stretch in your calf and Achilles tendon. Don't bend so far that it hurts. Hold the stretch for a count of fifteen, then gently bend your back knee. That stretches the lower part of the calf muscle.

Stretch three or four times a day. Always do the stretches slowly and gently. Never bounce into the stretches or do them abruptly. That can lead to reinjury.

Foot Pain

If your foot hurts along the inside of the sole or at the front of the heel bone, you may be suffering the residuals of plantar fasciitis —that is, a stretched or torn plantar fascia. The plantar fascia is a ligamentlike rope of fibrous tissue that starts at the heel of your foot and runs along the inside of the sole, where it fans out and connects to the base of the toes. If you pull back on your toes, you can see the plantar fascia clearly. It helps to maintain the arch in your foot.

Muscles also help to support the arch, but if they're not strong enough it falls to the plantar fascia to do all the work. The result can be plantar fasciitis. It can make it difficult to do any exercise that involves putting weight on your feet, and that includes a wide range of fitness activities.

The thing to do about plantar fasciitis is strengthen the muscles in the area. Here's how.

Any of the strengthening exercises suggested for the ankle may help plantar fasciitis, as the same muscles are involved (see page 197).

Strengthening the small muscles in the foot may help as well. One way to do that is by picking up marbles with your toes. Another is to pull a towel beneath your foot by using your toes. Later on, as your foot becomes stronger, you can attach weights to the towel.

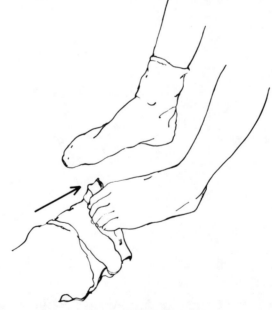

Exercise your foot muscles every day by doing at least three to five minutes of one or the other exercise.

The Shoulder

The shoulder is the most flexible joint in the body. It's also the least stable. Whereas the other joints in the body are held together firmly by ligaments, as in the ankle and knee, or by a deep ball-and-socket arrangement, as in the hip, the shoulder depends on strong, well-balanced muscles and tendons to keep it together. When your shoulder muscles are weak, or when the balance among them is somehow disrupted, a shoulder problem can easily result.

The difficulty is compounded by the fact that often the problem may not show up right away. When subjected to normal, daily, nonathletic activities, even a substantially weakened shoulder might seem to be in good condition, because you unconsciously avoid positions and motions that are uncomfortable. If it hurts to raise your shoulders, you begin to hunch your bad shoulder forward for protection. If it hurts to reach to the top shelf, you use your other shoulder without even thinking about it.

But when it comes to athletic activities, a shoulder problem can no longer slip by. You can't serve a tennis ball or swim the free-style without a full range of shoulder motion. You can't hit a golf ball or shoot baskets without a strong, flexible shoulder. And you can't use weight machines or do aerobic dance properly if your shoulder is weak or stiff.

So a healthy shoulder is absolutely necessary for many exercise activities. But if you've had a shoulder injury in the past, there's a strong likelihood that when you start a new fitness program or begin more strenuous activities you're going to have shoulder problems. As with ankle injuries, any previous problem that kept your shoulder disabled for more than a few days caused muscle weakness that will last forever—until, that is, you've rehabilitated the shoulder. Simply getting back to "normal" in a general way doesn't work. You've got to specifically restrengthen your shoulder muscles.

If you've had shoulder surgery, restrengthening is particularly important. In fact, shoulder surgery can often result in some permanent loss of motion.

If you've had such shoulder surgery, even if it was years ago, consult your doctor before you begin any new or strenuous fitness or sports activity.

SHOULDER EXAMINATION

The first thing to do in assessing your shoulder condition is take a quick medical history.

• Does your shoulder feel unstable, dislocate, or slip out of position?

• Does your shoulder catch or lock?

• Do you feel any numbness, tingling, or weakness in your arm or hand?

If your answer to *any* of these questions is *yes,* better see a doctor. These are symptoms of problems that may be too severe for you to handle yourself.

If *all* your answers are *no,* then ask yourself the following questions.

• Does your shoulder feel stiff or achy following unaccustomed or strenuous activities?

• Do you avoid using your shoulder for certain activities such as carrying suitcases?

If you answered *yes* to *either* of the questions, then you should strengthen your weak shoulder to the level of the other side. We'll show you how in a moment.

If your answer to *both* these questions is *no,* then your shoulder may be in pretty good shape. Go on to the self-examination to make sure.

Shoulder problems can be tricky. The symptoms are often subtle, so that you may not be aware of a problem until it is advanced enough to cause you real trouble. This self-examination offers a way to discover problems before they get to that point.

Stand facing a mirror with your arms hanging at your sides. Are your shoulders the same height? Do they appear about the same size?

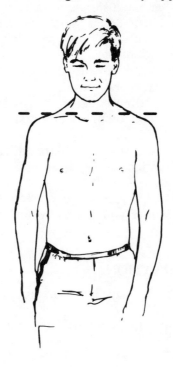

Looking in a mirror, raise your arms, with your thumbs pointing upward, to the front of your body until they are horizontal. Are the muscles in the front of the top of your shoulders, the anterior deltoids, the same size?

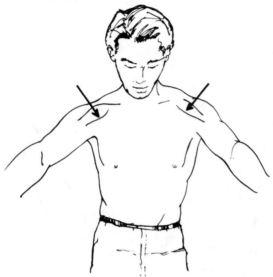

Looking in a mirror, raise your arms out from the sides of your body. Do the tops of your shoulders stay at an equal level as you raise your arms? Or does one shoulder elevate sooner than the other?

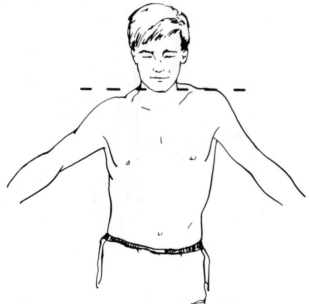

While standing, raise your arms from your sides and attempt to touch your hands above your head. Are you able to raise both arms above your head to the same degree?

Standing with your arms at your sides, bend your elbows and put your hands behind your back. Are you able to move both hands an equal distance up your back?

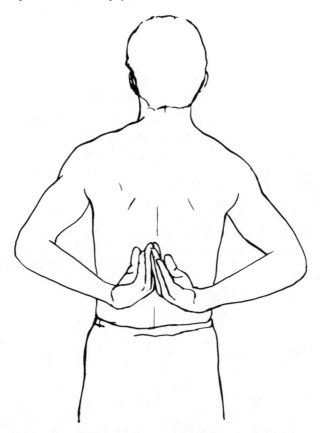

Lie on your back with your arms out from your sides and your elbows bent to a right angle. Now allow your hands to drop down to the floor. Do the backs of both hands touch the floor? If not, do both your hands come to within an equal distance of the floor?

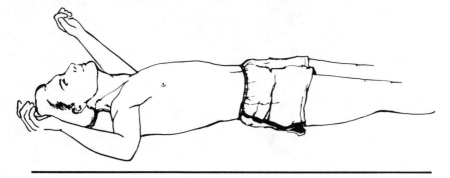

If you answered *yes* to *all* of these questions, it's likely that you have no particular weakness in either of your shoulders.

If you answered *no* to *any* of these questions, one of your shoulders is probably weaker and less flexible than the other. In that case, you should strengthen that bad shoulder before undertaking any general fitness or exercise program involving your shoulders. Here's how.

SHOULDER STRENGTHENING PROGRAM

These exercises move your shoulder through its entire range of motion and exercise virtually all of the muscles in the shoulder. You should do them without weights or resistance, simply utilizing the weight of your arm. They'll help restrengthen and rebalance your shoulder muscles and help you develop some endurance as well. They're awfully good exercises.

Do all these exercises only through a range of motion that's comfortable. If it hurts to do an exercise, cut down on the motion. Start by doing twenty repetitions of each exercise twice a day and eventually work up to fifty reps of each two or three times a day. Go slow; be easy on yourself. The trick is not to see how quickly you can progress, but how well.

Circles

Bend over at the waist and let the arm on your bad side hang in front of you. Then start swinging it in a clockwise direction. Use just enough muscle to kick the arm into motion and keep it swinging lazily. If it hurts to make a circle, make an egg shape or any other figure that feels comfortable. Do twenty circles in a clockwise direction, then twenty counterclockwise. The more you do, the more your range of motion will increase.

Sawing

Stand up straight, pretend that you're on one end of a double-handled saw, and start sawing. Saw back and forth with as much range of motion as you can muster. The more reps you do, the longer your sawing stroke will become. It's a good exercise because you're stretching at the same time as you're strengthening. And it puts your elbow through a complete range of motion as well.

Swings

Let your arms fall to your sides. Then raise them up to the side at right angles to your body and slowly lower them. Slowly raise and lower them, again and again, as though you're flapping an injured wing. These exercises are called abduction swings.

Raise your arms to a *comfortable level only*. As you continue to do the exercise, you'll become more flexible.

Shrugs

Now shrug your shoulders. That's all there is to it. The movement exercises the muscles in your shoulders and neck. If the exercise doesn't hurt, you may want to roll your shoulders up and forward then down, or up and back then down, making clockwise and counterclockwise circles.

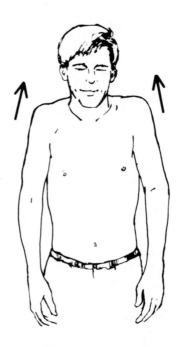

A week to ten days of these exercises will probably be enough. Along with the strengthening exercises to follow, they'll probably whip your shoulder into good enough shape so that you can begin a general fitness program. If not, you may want to see a doctor or physical therapist.

The exercises we've just suggested will go a long way to re-strengthen your shoulder. Here are a couple of others that employ resistance. You can use surgical tubing, Thera-Band, or wall pulleys for both of them.

First, bend over at the waist and with your arm pull back against the resistance without bending your elbows, almost as though you were starting a lawn mower by grabbing the pull cord with both arms at the same time. This exercise strengthens the rhomboids and middle trapezius, the muscles in your upper back that control the movement of your shoulder blades.

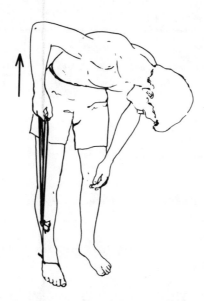

Do a couple of sets of ten every day. Increase the resistance as you grow stronger by stretching the tubing so that it's less elastic.

To strengthen the deltoid muscle on top of the shoulder, stand with your arms at your sides and with your bad arm pull up and out against resistance. Pull only as far as is comfortable. As you grow stronger, you'll be able to pull higher. Then increase the resistance. Do two sets of ten reps every day.

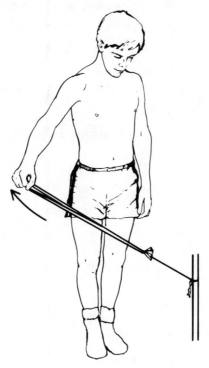

These exercises will help strengthen your bad shoulder and balance your shoulder strength and flexibility side to side. Until then, however, avoid the following activities or approach them with caution. They're particularly hard on the shoulder.

Exercises to Avoid

• Weight lifting utilizing the arms or shoulders—machines and free weights
  • Rowing machines
  • Nordic track or Nordic trainer
  • Push-ups
  • Pull-ups or chin-ups
• Games that particularly utilize the shoulder, such as tennis, softball, and golf

ANOTHER COMMON PROBLEM

Tennis Elbow

If you experience sharp pain on the outside of your elbow, you may be suffering from tennis elbow. It usually recurs because you never restrengthened the muscles in your lower arm adequately after your last bout with the injury.

One test to see if these muscles need strengthening involves picking up a chair by its back, much as you would lift a suitcase. If your elbow hurts when you lift the chair (and you'll know before you've lifted it an inch off the floor), then you should start a restrengthening program right away.

Rest your arm on a table or your knee with your palm down and grasp a light dumbbell or loop of surgical tubing. Curl your wrist back as far as possible. Try twenty slow repetitions twice daily. As you grow stronger, gradually increase the amount of weight and number of reps.

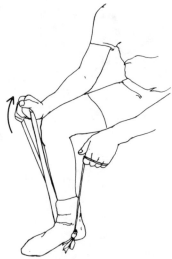

3 *Matching Your Goals to a Fitness Program*

So you've figured out which areas of your body need ﹀ and you've balanced your body so that now you can t﹍ a fitness program without running an especially high ri﹍ injury. Time to get started.

But how? Should you start running, swimming, walking? Sh﹍ you take up tennis or golf? Should you buy an exercise videot﹍ and work out at home or should you enroll in an aerobics cla﹍ Should you join a health club? If so, which one? To some﹍ venturing into the world of fitness for the first time, the variety choices can be overwhelming.

"I'm stuck. I don't know what to do. I don't know if I shoul﹍ run off to a health spa or an aerobic dance class or join a running club or a tennis league. I'm lost. It's a frightening feeling."

Millicent—Mil for short—is thirty-seven, a real estate broker, and one of those tightly wound balls of energy who simply can't sit still. Garrick has known her for years and is used to her fidgeting and blustering.

"C'mon, Doc," she says. "Give me a prescription. Tell me what to do. I've got to do something."

Garrick peers at her over the tops of his half-glasses, a look that says, *here we go again*. "Have you ever thought of doing something you like rather than exhausting every exercise possibility known to man?"

"And woman too," Mil says. "You know me—I've got to have a plan."

"I know," Garrick says. "I know. All I'm saying is that the way to make a plan is by figuring out which activities will do two things for you: help you reach your exercise goals and make you happy while you're doing it. If you don't like your workout program, or if it's inconvenient or too expensive, or hurts rather than helps you, it isn't worth the effort. Right?"

"I know that," Mil says. "But, my God, I could spend the rest of my life hunting for the right program. It's a jungle out there. I need a trusty guide." She bats her eyes at Garrick. "Know anyone?"

Good guides are hard to find. One reason is that often people knowledgeable in matters of fitness and conditioning have their own biases and enthusiasms, but what's right for them may not be right for you. Another reason is that people involved in physical conditioning are often employed by a fitness organization—a health club, say—that pushes a particular conditioning approach or type of equipment. These people make their living by selling you their wares. Rare is the fitness club staff member who will tell you, "I think you'd be better off at the club down the street." And yet another reason for the difficulty in finding good fitness advice involves the problem of injuries. Attendants at health clubs see a great many injuries, of course, and some may be able to offer good suggestions concerning how to get over them and avoid them the next time. But they see far fewer injuries than do sports medicine doctors or exercise physiologists, and may have neither the training nor the time to apply sound medical insights to your particular problem.

The upshot is that people beginning a fitness program may quickly find themselves on their own, adrift and not particularly pleased about it. Unless, that is, you're able to depend on someone who knows the world of fitness and can tell you the ins and outs of each approach as it affects your needs and goals.

That's where this chapter comes in. We'll take a look at the fitness choices available to you—an unbiased, thorough, and informed look. We'll suggest what each activity can do for your fitness needs and outline the advantages and disadvantages of each. Again, you're a partner with us in this business. You know your goals and needs better than anyone else. With this in mind, read through the activities to follow and pick the ones that seem most appropriate for you.

The important thing to realize is that no one activity is a cure-all, no one activity will do everything for everyone. Picking an approach depends entirely on who you are and what you want from your fitness training. Each activity offers its own gains and has its own problems. By deciding about each one in an informed way, you can tailor your workout to your own situation. You can match your goals to a fitness approach that will enable you to achieve them. That's what personal fitness training is all about.

Running

Advantages

If it's aerobic conditioning you're after, you can't do any better than running. A good run will readily push your heart rate into the aerobic range.

Running strengthens the lower body. It builds up muscle in your legs in particular. It will also do some good for your hips and back. But as running doesn't make you bear weight in your arms, it doesn't provide an especially good workout for the upper body.

You can measure your progress. As compared to many other activities, running provides measurable guideposts. If you ran a mile six months ago and can run ten miles today, that's progress. Or if it took you ten minutes to run your mile and you can do the same distance in six minutes today, that's progress. It can be comforting to have a precise measurement of your progress so you know exactly how much you're accomplishing.

There are well-established guidelines for runners. In fact, there may be no fitness activity about which more has been written than running. If in doubt about virtually any aspect concerning running, you can find an opinion. When you run, you join a wide and enthusiastic family.

You can run in a group. For those who abhor solitary exercise, running can provide company. Especially so because if you're huffing and puffing too much to be able to talk with your partner, you're running too hard for an aerobic workout. The idea is to work hard enough to raise your heart rate into the aerobic range but not so hard that you can't carry on a conversation with your neighbor. In that case, you're doing anaerobic exercise—relying on your body's stored energy rather than that provided by breathing in oxygen. That's fine, of course, but if cardiovascular benefits are what you're after, aerobic exercise is what you need.

Running requires a relatively low level of skill. Everyone knows how to run. All you need do to run for fitness is get out there and do it. Refining your technique may bring you dividends, but most people naturally run with the technique that's best for them.

Running is relatively inexpensive. It's not quite true to say that running requires no equipment—it does require shoes. But that's really the only expense.

It's important that you wear good shoes when running—that is, shoes designed for running rather than other activities. There are many brands and styles of running shoes on the market, too many for us to go into here. Suffice it to say that you shouldn't be in a hurry when picking a pair of running shoes. Try out the shoe in the shop (some shoe stores provide treadmills for this purpose), wear the kind of socks you'll be wearing when you run, and go in at the same time of day at which you usually run. If your feet swell at all during the day, at least they'll be the same size as when you begin your run.

The main thing to consider is comfort. A shoe that isn't comfortable in the shop won't become any more comfortable with use. As for durability, you can usually trust name-brand companies that have had particular models on the market for a couple of years. Most likely they've weeded out problems in their shoes. And shoe stores that specialize in running shoes often employ fellow runners. If you take into account the fact that they're pushing their own brands, these salespeople can share their experience and provide useful advice.

Running helps you learn more about your neighborhood. It's a terrific way to see the sights, get to know your town, explore the nooks and crannies.

Disadvantages

Running involves a relatively high risk of injury. These days it's almost a cliché to say that, but it's true. There are more running injuries than any other sports-related injuries. Runners who do more than twenty-five to twenty-nine miles a week are at particularly high risk, but approximately one in every four runners who put in just twenty-five miles a week will end up with an injury that's severe enough for a visit to a doctor. Those are not good odds. So if you run, be prepared to get hurt.

Running is particularly tough on old injuries. All that jarring and pounding doesn't do much good for old problems. If you've sustained knee, hip, or back injuries in the past, you might think twice about running.

Running is dependent on the weather. That's a statement that can be made about a lot of other activities, of course, but it's worth emphasizing here. Unless you have access to an indoor track, be prepared to give up running from time to time during the year. It can be a good idea to have a backup exercise activity—an *indoor* activity.

Swimming

Advantages

Swimming provides a good aerobic workout.

Swimming strengthens the upper body. In fact, swimming is a particularly good upper body conditioner. The arms, shoulders, back, and neck all receive a good workout.

It's interesting, however, that upper body cardiovascular conditioning is not the same as lower body cardiovascular conditioning. You'd think that any activity that forces the heart to beat in the aerobic range would provide as good a cardiovascular workout as any other. Not so. Only about 60 percent of upper body cardiovascular work carries over into the lower body, and vice versa. Strange but true.

Swimming is easy on the body. In fact, of all fitness activities, it may be easiest on the body. Water not only neutralizes gravity, and so removes the pounding of weight-bearing exercise activities, it cushions the body, providing a buffer between you and potential injury-producing hazards.

You can measure your progress. As in running, swimming allows for distance and time measurements. A hundred-yard free-style in 1.20 shows improvement compared to a 1.35. Likewise, you can measure how far you swim.

Disadvantages

It can be difficult to find a place to swim. It may be the fatal bugaboo for all but the most dedicated swimmers. Whereas you can run around the block or do aerobic dance in your living room, you must find a suitable body of water to swim in. For most people, that means a pool—and preferably a pool at least twenty-five yards long. In urban, crowded areas, it can be tough to find one. Anyone who has ever slugged his way through overcrowded lanes in an overcrowded pool, and has paid dearly for the privilege, knows the frustration involved in finding a good place to swim.

Swimming for fitness demands skill. That doesn't mean you have to be an Olympic-quality swimmer (and it doesn't even mean that you have to be able to do the classic strokes—sidestroke will do for an aerobic workout), but it does mean that you have to be able to do more than dogpaddle in the shallow end.

You must know how to swim. That may seem so obvious as not to need stating, but the fact is that many people simply don't know how. It's a skill you must learn, and parents who have watched while their children struggled to put their heads under water for the first time know that it isn't necessarily that easy to learn, either.

Swimming is a solitary activity. We could have put this statement in the Advantages list as well, for many people consider solitude one of the things that make swimming attractive. Conversely, it's certainly true that swimming can be a team sport and help people establish a bond that can last for years. But when it comes to actually doing the activity, there's no doubt that it's pretty tough to chat with your neighbor or even make satisfying visual contact when you've a mouthful of water and are half submerged in splashing and waves.

Fitness swimming is boring. Even dedicated swimmers say so. Back and forth, back and forth, lap after lap staring at the black line on the bottom of the pool—fitness swimming simply isn't for everyone. The most successful swimmers quickly learn to vary their workouts.

Walking

Advantages

Walking provides a good aerobic workout. It may seem surprising to nonwalkers, but you can accomplish as strong an aerobic workout by walking as you can with any other activity. The key is pushing your heart rate into the aerobic range.

Walking may provide a total body workout. If you do the exaggerated arm swing suggested in certain approaches to fitness walking or carry hand weights, you actually exercise your upper body as well as your lower body. It doesn't provide as strong an upper body workout as rowing, for example, but it's certainly better than running or regular walking.

Walking is easy to do and easy on the body. Everyone knows how to walk, so even though you may have to modify your usual walking style by swinging your arms vigorously, for example, walking for aerobic conditioning requires no difficult skills. And it's relatively easy on the body, with little of the jarring associated with running. For both these reasons, walking is a particularly good exercise for older people and pregnant women and a good beginning activity for nonexercisers.

You can measure your progress. Just as with running and swimming, walking offers time and distance measurements. You can compare your pace and endurance with previous efforts.

You can walk almost anywhere. Even running, as accessible as it is, demands a reasonably clear and open course. But you can walk just about anywhere. In fact, in cities many people walk to work, change their walking shoes for dress shoes, and then change back for the walk home.

You can vary routes and learn more about your neighborhood. As with running, there's no better way to get to know your surroundings than by walking through them. It's a good strategy to keep walking interesting.

Walking is relatively inexpensive. As with running, all you need are good shoes.

Walking is a terrific social exercise. It's hard to think of an

exercise more conducive to visiting with your fellow exerciser—
especially since the nature of aerobic exercise is such that you
shouldn't be too out of breath to carry on a conversation. The
increasing number of walking clubs attests to the social benefits of
the exercise.

Disadvantages

Walking is dependent on the weather. As with running, unless
you use an indoor walking course, there are days when you'll have
to give up your favorite activity. Better have an indoor backup.

Walking is boring. For some people it's an activity that simply
isn't physically challenging enough to sustain interest. Successful
fitness walkers learn to vary their workouts and walking courses.

*Walking requires concentration in order to keep your heart rate
in the aerobic range.* As you become better conditioned, especially, you must pay particular attention to heart rate. It's one of
the ironies of aerobic exercise—the better-conditioned you are,
the harder it is to raise your heart rate.

Now we'll take a brief look at commonly available conditioning
equipment. If you go through the list and wonder why we don't
mention weight training machines, remember that we're talking
about aerobic workouts here. Later on we'll look at weight training
equipment.

Bicycles, whether stationary or otherwise, are by far the most
accessible and most popular of all exercising machines. You can
find the rest of the equipment at fitness clubs or you can buy it—
although you're not likely to come upon some of these machines
in private homes. All of them offer a good aerobic workout.

Cycling

Cycling is unusual among fitness activities in that it can be done
outdoors or indoors. We're speaking here, of course, of street
bikes and stationary bikes (as well as devices that allow you to
convert your regular bike into an exercise bike). Cycling is also
unusual because the Johnny-come-lately of the activity, indoor
exercise cycling, which is undoubtedly the less exciting and interesting of the two kinds of cycling, provides a more consistent
cardiovascular workout.

Not that biking outdoors can't afford you a splendid aerobic
workout. It can—but not necessarily. The reason has to do with
the nature of aerobic conditioning, which demands a sustained
effort. You must sustain your heart rate in the aerobic range for at
least twenty minutes at a time to receive lasting cardiovascular

benefits. On a stationary bike it's simple—set the tension, turn on the timer, pedal at a predetermined rate, and you're set. But ride outdoors and you're confronted with upgrades and downgrades, periods when you pump like crazy and periods when you coast—all of which may be great fun but doesn't offer the kind of sustained workout cardiovascular conditioning requires.

We'll talk about both kinds of cycling here, but be aware that the benefits are more than likely different from one another. As to which one is right for you, it all depends on what you want from your exercise.

Advantages

Cycling offers a good aerobic workout. It's particularly easy to raise your heart rate into the aerobic range by cycling, especially if you ride against the resistance provided by stationary bikes (or bike uphill for a good stretch).

Cycling builds strength in the lower body. Cycling offers a terrific workout for your legs. In fact, it's often recommended by doctors and exercise physiologists as an especially good rehabilitation technique for lower leg injuries. It builds muscle quickly and lastingly.

You can measure your progress. Cycling is another of the activities that offer the possibility of time and distance measurements. In fact, you don't even have to go anywhere to cover lots of ground on a bicycle. Stationary bikes will measure how far you've ridden for you. Some people make the equivalent of cross-country trips on their stationary bikes.

Cycling is not wholly dependent on the weather. If it's snowing or raining outside, just jump on the exercise bike.

You can do other things while cycling. That is, on a stationary bike—we don't recommend that you try any diversions while negotiating traffic. Many people watch the evening news, read, listen to music, even conduct business while doing a good workout on their exercise bike.

Bicycles are relatively inexpensive, durable, and portable. You can buy a serviceable exercise bike for under $200. They do not require much space or maintenance. Comparable outdoor bikes cost more, perhaps twice as much. But considering the quality of the workout they afford and the length of time they last, it's pretty good value for the money.

Disadvantages

Cycling takes skill. True, it may not take much ability to jump on a stationary bike and pedal away, but if you're going to venture outdoors, you need to know how to balance on a bike. Not everyone does, and it's a skill that becomes more difficult to learn with age.

It also takes some skill, and experience, to set up the bike properly. Figuring out the proper seat height, handlebar position, and foot position in the pedals can take some time.

Cycling is boring. Not outdoors, perhaps, but the bane of exercise bike riders is the monotonous nature of the activity. That's why people do other things while cycling.

Cycling can be hard on old knee problems. It's an irony of the activity: just as cycling can help people recover from knee injuries by building up muscle in the area, it can aggravate old injuries by subjecting them to stress and strain. If you have knee problems, be careful of cycling.

In the majority of instances, however, you can set up your program to alleviate these knee problems. Just be sure to approach the exercise, and your position on the bike, carefully.

Cycling can be the most dangerous of aerobic activities. We're speaking here of outdoor cycling, of course. Thousands of cyclists each year are killed by automobiles. You *must* wear a helmet while cycling outdoors.

Exercise Bikes

A bike shouldn't easily tip over. Check to be sure that your bike's base is wide enough to be stable.

Look for a bike that you can readily mount and dismount. With some stationary bikes, the mere act of getting on or off can demand more flexibility and persistence than you're willing to devote. That can be a particular problem when you're injured.

A bike should have a comfortable seat. Remember, you may be logging lots of time on this machine, so you want it to be comfortable. Some bikes allow you to change seats—that can be a real advantage. These days there are replacement seats available that contour themselves to the shape of your body.

A bike should have adjustable handlebars. The configuration of the bike may not match your configuration. And if it does, it may not match the configuration of other people who may use the machine as well as yourself. Adjustability is a real plus.

A bike should have adjustable tension. Virtually all exercise bikes offer this feature, but they don't necessarily allow you to adjust the tension, or completely turn it off, while you're riding the bike. Both are features you should look for.

Other fancy features like programmable workouts and automatic heart rate measurements and the rest of the computer-assisted options can be handy and fun but are certainly not necessary for a good workout. They also drive up the cost. So again it all depends on what you want from your workout.

Rowing

Like cycling, rowing is an outdoor/indoor exercise activity. Here, however, we'll only talk about indoor rowing machines. Doing the real thing outdoors can be exhilarating and exhausting, but as it requires a suitable body of water, relatively few people are able to do it. Indoor rowing machines are accessible to virtually everyone.

Advantages

Rowing offers a good aerobic workout for the upper and lower body. In fact, rowing is one of the best all-around fitness activities you can do. Legs, back, shoulders, arms—it conditions them all.

Rowing is relatively easy on the body—if done correctly, that is. Proper technique is important.

You can measure your progress. Rowing is yet another of the activities that offer the possibility of time and distance measurements. Some machines measure how far you've rowed and compare your performance with that of an electronic pacer. You can carry on rowing races without ever leaving your fitness facility.

Disadvantages

Rowing requires good technique and instruction. Surprising as it may seem, you can't just climb into the machine and start working out—at least, you shouldn't. Just charging ahead with little thought to proper tension, length of stroke, or position of the seat can bring about injuries. It's a good idea to have an attendant at your fitness club show you the proper way to use the machine, as it's more complicated than meets the eye.

Rowing machines are expensive (some of the fancier ones run $300 to $600) and can be cumbersome. If you're thinking of buying one for your home, be sure you have plenty of room and are willing to shoulder the expense. (Some rowing machines, however, fold up neatly against the wall to a width of only about six inches.)

Rowing Machines

A rowing machine should be comfortable—always the number one requirement when considering exercise machines. If you don't like to sit in the machine, or the oar handle position is uncomfortable, you'll probably never use it.

A rowing machine should not be difficult to get into and out of. It may be comfortable once you're settled in, but getting there can be a bear. And if you're injured, this relatively minor problem can become insurmountable. Make sure you can easily get into and out of your rowing machine.

A rowing machine should not easily tip over—for obvious reasons.

You should be able to adjust the handles and tension and change your foot position in the foot supports—again for obvious reasons. Not all people are the same size or have the same strength, although some designers of these exercise machines seem to assume so.

Cross-country Skiing Machines

Advantages

Cross-country skiing machines are one of the best overall conditioners. They're not as well known as other fitness machines, but they offer as good a workout as any, if not better. These machines condition the entire body. It's as though you're doing an extended cross-country ski—and anyone who does that demanding sport knows the degree of conditioning it affords. In fact, cross-country skiing is such a good exercise that competitive cross-country skiers find it virtually impossible to maintain their condition by any other means.

Cross-country skiing is easy on the body. No pounding or special stress on joints—just smooth slipping and sliding.

You can measure your progress. These machines, too, offer the possibility of measuring time, distance, pace, and resistance.

Disadvantages

Cross-country skiing demands skill and requires instruction. It's not one of those machines that you can simply get into and start using immediately. Among other things, it demands a relatively high degree of coordination. Make sure you know how to use the machine before beginning your workout program.

It's expensive and cumbersome. If you plan to buy a cross-country skiing machine, better be sure you have plenty of room and are willing to invest at least $625.

Cross-country Skiing Machines

You should be able to adjust the upper (arm) and lower (leg) tension independently. If not, the machine may do you more harm than good. Make sure the tensions are completely—and easily—adjustable.

Treadmill

Advantages

It's a good cardiovascular conditioner. A treadmill offers the advantages of walking and running, which are considerable, with none of the disadvantages of having to find a course and deal with the weather. It can raise your heart rate into the aerobic range, and the activity is as good a cardiovascular conditioner as virtually any other. It's primarily a lower body conditioning exercise, but if you hold dumbbells while exercising, it can help condition the upper body as well.

Treadmills are relatively easy on the body. They keep to a minimum the wear and tear of weight-bearing exercise. If you choose to run on the treadmill, it may not be as hard on the body as running on an unyielding surface.

Disadvantages

Treadmills are not easy to use. It may seem like a snap—just hop on and walk or run away—but it's not. It's relatively easy to get thrown off treadmills, and they're tough to run on. Be sure to get some instruction before using the machine.

Treadmills are expensive and cumbersome. Like most of the equipment we've been talking about, treadmills demand lots of room and cost lots (and lots) of money. Be prepared to pay $2,500 and up for top-quality models.

Aerobic Dance

Aerobic dance deserves a category of its own. It's the most popular organized fitness activity in the country, and one of the best. We won't devote all that much space to it here, as reams have been written about aerobic dance—we'll simply highlight some pertinent info.

Advantages

Aerobic dance is a good aerobic conditioner for the entire body. For once the hype is true. Done intelligently, aerobic dance offers a thorough and healthy workout.

The quality of instruction is high. Aerobic dance seems to be one of those activities that attract effective and dedicated people. In most cases you can depend on the intentions of the instructors and the quality of instruction you'll receive.

You can begin at any level. Even if you find yourself in an

advanced class by mistake, you can simply go at your own pace—
no one will think less of you.

It's good for both sexes and any age. But males should be careful not to mimic the instructor, usually a female, too closely.
Women are simply more flexible than men. If men try too hard to
bend and twist as thoroughly as a female instructor, they may find
themselves hurting rather than thriving.

It's a good social activity. That (and the excuse of shopping for
a wardrobe of fashionable exercise outfits) may be what draws
people as much as the prospect of good aerobic conditioning. In
fact, the pace of aerobic exercise is based on the dictum that if
you're too out of breath to chat with your neighbor, you're doing
too much too hard.

The injury rate is low. Aerobic dance may be one of the safest
of all aerobic activities.

It's accessible and widespread. Aerobic dance is a particularly
good city fitness exercise, as it's offered all over the place. For
example, in San Francisco it's probably true that no one in the city
lives more than fifteen minutes away from a fitness club—and
aerobic dance is not confined only to fitness clubs. If you want to
try aerobic dance, it's easy to find a place to do it.

*Aerobic classes provide an instructor to answer questions and
offer advice.* It can be a pleasure to have someone knowledgeable
to depend on, especially for beginning exercisers.

It's relatively inexpensive. Although people spend lots of money
on all sorts of aerobic dance accoutrements, the only expense
that's really necessary is for a pair of good shoes—plus, of course,
the instructor's fee.

You can do aerobic dance on your own with videotapes. As the
phenomenal success of Jane Fonda's workout tapes have illus-
trated, people are interested in working out at home on their own.
There are some good tapes and some not-so-good tapes on the
market. We'll suggest what to look for in a moment.

Disadvantages

*For the most part, you have to go somewhere to do aerobic
dance.* Although people buy aerobic dance videotapes so they can
work out at home, many people prefer a more formal, social situation. And although aerobic dance classes are widespread and accessible, they still demand that you get up and go. For some
people, having to exercise at a prescribed time and place simply
isn't appealing—especially when you may have to buck inclement
weather or traffic or other hindrances in order to get to class.

It's easy to do too much too soon. It's the nature of aerobic
dance that people tend to become swept away by the activity. That

kind of enthusiasm is great, of course, but it often induces people to work much too hard much too quickly. Some aerobic dance injuries are simply the result of overenthusiasm.

Exercise Videotapes

There are lots and lots of tapes out there. Jane Fonda popularized the whole business, of course, and now it seems as though it's de rigueur for all celebrities worth their salt to come out with a video showing just how they keep themselves as watchable as they like to think they are. The problem for people interested in buying the tapes is how to know beforehand which are worth your thirty or forty bucks and which aren't. A famous name and attractive body on the box doesn't necessarily guarantee that what's inside delivers as advertised. And it certainly doesn't guarantee that what's inside is medically sound. If nothing else, you want these tapes to offer a safe workout.

So here are some suggestions for what to look for in exercise videotapes. You may not find all of these criteria met in any one tape, but the best ones incorporate most of them. And which ones are the best? It's hard to say, because it all depends on what you're looking for. (We know that Jane Fonda's tapes are medically sound, because we've been involved in making a number of them.) But, happily for the consumer, many of these tapes are available to rent before you decide to buy. It can be worthwhile to take a few home and give them a critical going-over before you plunk down your hard-earned cash.

The Box

First, take a look at the box itself. Pay particular attention to the back of the box—that's probably where you'll find specific information about the tape, if any. If a video box doesn't present specific, detailed information about what's inside, you might think twice about buying it. It doesn't have to be much info—there's only so much room on the box for that sort of thing—but it should address certain criteria. For example:

The tape should be approved by a recognized authority or scientific organization. And that person or organization should be presented by name. If not a doctor, then an exercise physiologist. If not either, then an organization such as the American College of Sports Medicine. And be careful of a simple "So and So, M.D." or "Ph.D." An M.D. or Ph.D. may know a lot about a particular field but not necessarily much about fitness and exercise and the injuries involved. Be sure that any M.D. or Ph.D. is identified by affiliation—with a sports medicine clinic, say, or a sports team or league.

The box should suggest the purpose of the tape. Is it an aerobic exercise tape? A weight training tape? A weight loss tape? After reading the box, you should have no doubt as to what the tape is for.

The box should suggest for whom the tape is intended. Is it a tape for beginners? Advanced exercisers? Pregnant women? Is it for older people or kids? The box should tell you.

The box should suggest who should be careful with the tape. Perhaps it's not intended for obese people, or people over forty, or people with prior medical problems. It may not be intended for senior citizens or preteens. Again, the box should make all that clear.

The box should suggest what's in the tape. And the more specifically the better. What kind of exercises, how many, lasting how long? You should not have to buy or try a tape to get an idea of what you're in for.

The tape should not promise the unrealistic. For example, it may be your dream to get rid of fat from certain parts of your body by doing specific exercises. Don't be misled. No matter what any tape promises, you're not going to rid yourself of saddlebags by doing side leg raises. Neither are you going to make significant cardiovascular or weight control gains by doing any less than twenty minutes of aerobic exercise three times a week. These are absolute minimal requirements, no matter what any tape promises.

The Enclosed Pamphlet

First, there should *be* an enclosed pamphlet. If your tape doesn't provide one, you might have second thoughts about buying that particular video. (Most tapes don't state on the box whether there's a pamphlet or not. You may have to ask the salesperson to open a box before you decide to buy.)

Second, if there is a pamphlet, read it. Many people don't bother to. They simply rip off the plastic, pull out the tape, stick it in the VCR, and get to exercising. But even if you don't read it right away, read it sometime—preferably before you're too far along in your exercise program. The pamphlet may supply information that supplements and amplifies what's in the tape—at least, it should.

And for prospective buyers, the pamphlet is the best preview possible of what's in the tape. If the pamphlet isn't clear, specific, understandable, and informative, the tape may not be either.

The pamphlet should describe in more detail what's in the tape. If the box gave you a pretty good idea, that pamphlet should leave no doubts at all. It should be the next best thing to actually viewing the tape. And it should provide necessary or supplemental information about the exercises in the tape.

The pamphlet should describe in more detail for whom the tape is—and is not—intended. If you had any lingering doubts as to whether this tape is intended for you, the pamphlet should dispel them.

The pamphlet should suggest who should be cautious about using the tape. Here's where any previous medical problems that might prevent you from doing exercises in the tape should be discussed.

The pamphlet should provide alternatives to the exercises described. It should suggest what you might do if, for example, you're not flexible enough to perform certain exercises or lack the endurance to complete certain sets.

The pamphlet should give directions as to how quickly or slowly to progress with the tape. It's particularly important that beginners be told how to ease into any exercise program. One of the surest ways to injure yourself is to charge into a new activity too quickly.

The pamphlet should describe proper attire, footwear, and equipment. You don't want to be surprised when you start watching the tape and learn that you need a certain piece of equipment or should wear a certain kind of shoe or clothing. By the time you've read the pamphlet you should know exactly what's in store.

The pamphlet should suggest how frequently to do the exercises. And when you should rest and how often. And provide other guidelines as to how to go about doing the exercise program.

The pamphlet should show you how to take your pulse and how to determine your aerobic heart rate. It's easy to do—all you need is to be shown how.

The Tape

The box and pamphlet can give you a pretty good idea as to what's going on, but it all comes down to the video itself. We'll talk here about aerobic exercise tapes, as they're by far the most common.

The tape should contain three phases. First, warm-up and stretch. Before beginning just about any exercise it's a good idea to warm up and stretch to help reduce injuries. *Next, an aerobic segment.* This portion should be at least twenty minutes long. Twenty minutes at least three times a week is the minimum workout time necessary to realize lasting aerobic benefits. *Finally, cooldown and stretch.* Tired muscles tend to tighten up. Stretching after your workout will help reduce aches and pains and keep your muscles relaxed and loose for next time.

The tape should include a running narrative. It should suggest

what the individual exercises are supposed to accomplish—specifically. For example: "This exercise is designed to strengthen the abdominal muscles, which will help hold your stomach in, improve your posture, and protect your back."

The narrative should suggest alternatives for specific exercises: "If it hurts to raise your arm out to the side, try the exercise with your elbow bent, like a chicken wing."

During the aerobic portion of the tape, the narrative should frequently remind you to take your pulse.

The tape should avoid activities and positions that can easily lead to injuries. Among those are arching your lower back, doing deep knee squats, and turning out your feet excessively. (Aerobics instructors often have had at least some ballet training and so by habit turn out their feet. But the position can cause injury in someone not used to it. The tape should make special mention of the danger of too much turnout.)

The tape should clearly show the position or posture in which the exercise should be done. If necessary, there should be two camera angles—one from the front and one from the side. Doing an exercise in the wrong position can be useless at best and dangerous at worst.

Watch and listen all the way through before using it. Once you start exercising, you may not pay much attention to the instructions. It's important that you hear them through at least once.

Begin exercising gradually. The tape or pamphlet may tell you how to begin exercising—but it may not. If in doubt, begin by doing the warm-up/stretching segment, then do five minutes of the aerobic portion, then fast-forward to the cool-down/stretch section and do that. Then increase the aerobic portion by two minutes each session—or every two sessions—until you're doing the whole thing.

Exercise consistently and regularly. This is very important if you're to realize any lasting benefits from your workout and if you're to keep the risk of injury to a minimum. Begin by using the tape at least three times a week, preferably every other day. When you work up to using the tape daily, it's a good idea to rest completely at least one day a week—even better, two.

If any exercise is painful or results in discomfort afterward, try the alternative exercise presented in the narrative; try the alternative given in the pamphlet; or avoid the exercise or decrease the range of motion required. *If the pain or discomfort persists, see a doctor.*

During the aerobic portion you should be able to carry on a conversation. It's a quick and easy way of determining that your heart rate is in the aerobic range—that is, between 60 and 85 percent of your maximum. If you're too out of breath to talk, you're

probably doing too much too hard. And, what's more to the point, you're probably not getting the fat-burning benefits of aerobic exercise.

The suggestions above cover aerobic exercise tapes, but there are other kinds out there as well. The question is, which kind should you buy? It all depends on what you want from your fitness program, of course. To help you decide, here are some pros and cons concerning each type.

NON- OR LOW-IMPACT VIDEOTAPES

Advantages

Non- or low-impact aerobic exercise places less stress on your legs and back. Because there's less bouncing and pounding, it's relatively easy on the body. These may be good programs for people with shin splints, knee problems, low back pain, and other aches and pains.

It's a good beginning program for nonexercisers. The lack of quick, jarring exercise makes these programs a good way to ease into the world of aerobic exercise.

It provides a healthy break from regular aerobic programs. Variety in your exercise can be a real boon, both physically and psychologically. It can be a good idea to do regular aerobic exercise one day and non- or low-impact aerobics the next.

It provides a good way to return to regular aerobics if you've been off for more than a week. It's an unhappy fact of life that an enforced layoff tears you down at least twice as fast as you built up. So if you've been off for a week or more, starting back where you left off invites injury. Beginning back with a non- or low-impact aerobics program can be an ideal way to build up to your former condition.

Disadvantages

It may not provide an aerobic workout. The workout may be so non- or low-impact that it has no impact at all. The way to tell if you're gaining any aerobic benefits is to take your pulse often during the aerobic segment of the tape. If your heart rate doesn't stay in the aerobic range for at least twenty minutes, you need to work harder.

It may require much more attention to detail and instruction. If you do these exercises in a desultory or sloppy manner, they might not be aerobic at all. They must be done carefully and correctly to be useful aerobically.

It may require positions that overstress the knees—for example, holding a lunge position over one leg. This kind of isometric exercise places a great deal of pressure on the knee. For some people it may be too much.

STRETCHING VIDEOTAPES

Advantages

Stretching can improve flexibility for other activities. That's the primary benefit of stretching, really—that and preventing tired muscles from tightening and going into spasm. By itself and for itself, stretching may be of little use.

It can be used as a warm-up or warm-down for other activities.

It can be used as an alternative exercise on days you don't do regular aerobics.

Disadvantages

It must be done with caution. Overstretching—especially to music—is a real problem. It can lead to injuries. So can bouncing into stretches. If you stretch, be sure to stretch slowly and gently.

It requires precise adherence to instructions. There's usually a right way and a wrong way to stretch. Any good stretching tape should offer specific instructions, both in the narrative and in the accompanying pamphlet.

Stretching has limited benefits. It will not result in increased strength, for example, nor will it slim you down or change your body configuration or provide an aerobic workout. What it will do is increase your flexibility, which may or may not be beneficial, depending on the other activities that you do.

WEIGHT TRAINING OR STRENGTHENING VIDEOTAPES

Advantages

They can help increase muscle strength and tone—especially in muscles used in the activities of daily living that might not be dealt with in other programs.

They can improve your appearance. In contrast to fat, muscles can be shaped and toned. They generally look more attractive than fat. However, you might not lose weight in the process—you might even put on a few pounds. Muscles weigh more than fat.

You can alternate them with standard aerobic programs. In fact, it can be a good strategy to do weight training every other day and aerobic exercise every other day. That way, you gain the benefits of both while not burning out on either. Variety in exercise is important—physically and psychologically.

You can use them at home with a minimum of equipment. There's no more convenient way to weight train. It saves you the trouble—and cost—of going to a health club.

They offer privacy. If you're self-conscious about your lack of fitness, weight training tapes offer complete privacy as well as competent instruction. In fact, they might provide you a means to get in good enough shape to have the courage to go to a health club.

Disadvantages

They're often not well balanced. Weight training tapes tend to spend a disproportionate time on the upper body. Upper body muscle development is usually more noticeable than that of the lower body, of course, and often people are fully as interested in how they look as how strong and fit they are—if not more. So it's understandable that these tapes might emphasize upper body development. But if it's total body balance you're after, you might not be satisfied with them.

They often don't start gently enough for beginners. It's important to begin any new activity gradually, and it's especially important with weight training. Lifting too much too quickly can lead to injury, and these tapes tend to start off beginners with too much weight.

They often don't progress effectively. Instead of starting light and working up to heavier weights, these tapes tend to start relatively heavy and become heavier. That's fine if you're already used to lifting, but for beginners, who must develop strength and experience, the progression in these tapes can be too abrupt.

Some require too much equipment to be practical for home use. Many people simply don't have the assortment of barbells and dumbbells that some tapes require.

The music is often too fast to allow correct execution of the exercises. It's fun to exercise to music, true, but if the music hurtles along at such a pace that you can't lift slowly and deliberately, better turn off the sound. When people lift quickly they tend to bounce into their lifts. That decreases the benefits of the lift and often leads to injury.

They often don't explain which muscles you're strengthening. Nor do they suggest what these muscles are used for in normal or athletic activities. Lifting for general body bulk is one thing, but if you're lifting toward a specific end, it's important to know the effect of each lift.

They often don't suggest how much weight you should lift in the beginning. Every individual is different and should be treated as such. It's important to know how much weight is appropriate for you, specifically, not how much is good for most people. Lifting too much can lead to injury.

They often promise the impossible. Weight training can be effective exercise, but it can only do so much. To suggest that, for example, a triceps strengthening program will get rid of loose skin at the back of the arms or a hamstring strengthening program will make flabby thighs vanish is simply not true. These exercises won't hurt, certainly, but they won't work miracles.

They often ignore potentially dangerous positions of the back during exercises. One of the most common mistakes involved in weight training, and one particularly likely to lead to injury, is arching your back while lifting. Yet often these tapes fail to caution you against the position. A word to the wise: keep your back flat when lifting weights.

They often have had little medical or scientific input. The caution we offered at the beginning of this section still applies: make sure your tape has been approved by a recognized authority or scientific organization.

DANCE VIDEOTAPES

Advantages

They may provide an aerobic workout. If so, dance videos can be a particularly enjoyable way to do your aerobic workout.

They provide variety. As any dedicated exerciser knows, varying your workouts is good for the mind and body. It helps keep you fresh and interested.

They provide the challenge of learning new choreography while exercising. In other words, they engage your mind as well as your body. Doing the same exercise over and over can become mind-numbing at the same time as it's body-enhancing. Being challenged to learn new moves can increase your interest and therefore your commitment.

Disadvantages

They often don't provide an adequate warm-up. It's important to warm up before exercise, especially for the nonexerciser. Cold, tight muscles are more easily injured than warm, loose muscles.

They often don't provide an adequate cool-down or postexercise stretches. It's important to cool down and stretch after exercise. The cool-down allows your heart rate to slow down gradually, and if you don't stretch and relax your muscles after a workout, you risk tight, sore muscles the next morning. Again, muscles that function best and feel best are loose, relaxed muscles.

They often don't provide breaks to take your pulse. The only way to know for sure if you're doing an aerobic workout is to take your pulse from time to time and figure out your heart rate. With these tapes, you often have to push PAUSE to take your pulse, then start the tape going again.

They often don't provide alternative exercises for beginners or the less fit. It's all well and good to be fit and flexible enough to do many of the movements in these tapes, but many people aren't yet. These tapes give short shrift to the less advanced viewer.

They may be too vigorous for aerobic exercise. How can exercise be too vigorous? Well, it depends again on what your exercise goals are. If it's cardiovascular fitness you want, exercising too hard can go beyond aerobic exercise to anaerobic exercise, in which your body can't get enough energy from breathing and must resort to its stored supply. Anaerobic exercise has its own benefits, but cardiovascular fitness and fat-burning capabilities aren't among them.

The choreography may be too complicated to learn easily. If so, you may not get an aerobic workout for the time it takes you to get the hang of it.

Fitness Facilities

The ads scream out at you from newspapers and magazines. Gorgeous people with gorgeous bodies smile at you, as if to say, "Join us, and you can look like this too." And not only that, but you'll be healthier and happier and your sex life will improve. Indeed, fitness clubs have been proclaimed the singles bars of the decade—a place to meet people who are in such good shape that you'll be glad you did.

Well, it may be asking too much of fitness facilities to follow through with all these claims, but there's no doubt that they can provide an environment conducive to fitness training. So might as well run right out and join up, right? Perhaps so—millions of people have. But it's not quite so easy as all that. In the first place, you're not going to find every service in every fitness facility. There are various types of fitness facilities, each with different emphases, each with different advantages and disadvantages. Before signing on, you need to know what your fitness goals are.

For example, there's no point in joining a weight training facility if you want to play tennis or swim. On the other hand, if it's muscle development you're after, you won't get it in an aerobic dance class. On a more subtle level, if you're a triathlete, say, and you're interested in weight training for endurance, you probably don't want to sign up at a free-weight gym. Conversely, Nautilus® training alone might not build show muscles.

So the first thing to do is decide what your fitness goals are. Knowing that, you can search for the facility that will best help you achieve those goals. What follows is a description of the various kinds of fitness facilities, some advantages and disadvantages of each, and what sorts of general things to be aware of no matter what kind of facility you choose. Forewarned is forearmed.

WEIGHT TRAINING FACILITIES

There are three types of weight-training clubs:
• Clubs that specialize in weight-training machines, such as Nautilus, Universal®, and Hydra-Gym®.
• Clubs that specialize in free weights—that is, dumbbells and barbells.
• Clubs that offer a combination of the two approaches.

Advantages

They offer a large variety of equipment. Since weight training is all these clubs offer, they don't have to devote space and resources to other kinds of equipment and activities.

They attract serious weight lifters. It's a pleasure to work out with other people seriously doing the same thing. It helps provide motivation and allows the sharing of expertise.

Disadvantages

Serious weight lifters can be intolerant of beginners. It's the other side of the coin: as useful and inspiring as it can be to work out with dedicated people, it can also be uncomfortable and threatening. Sometimes accomplished people don't like to work out with beginners. Sometimes extremely fit people are intolerant of unfit people. And sometimes the staff will expect prospective members already to be familiar with the equipment and know how to use it.

So it can sometimes take guts for a novice to walk into a serious weight lifting club and begin working out. Check out the feel and atmosphere of any weight lifting facility before joining. Be sure the staff is friendly and willing to help you get started.

Women may feel out of place. The traditional separation of sexes in these facilities is changing, of course, but still male weight trainers probably outnumber female. Some women may like that imbalance; others may not feel comfortable.

There are three general types of weight training machines—we'll discuss their particular advantages and disadvantages in a moment. You can also train with free weights, but weight training machines have two distinct advantages.

You don't have to worry about dropping weights. Anyone who has ever lifted barbells that are too heavy knows the sinking sensation of losing control and feeling the weights begin to slip away. The danger of dropping weights is one very good reason why people who lift free weights should always work out with a partner.

With weight training machines, you may lose control as well, but even if you do drop weights the only consequence may be an embarrassing clatter as they fall back into their stack. You don't have to risk injury from a weight falling onto your body.

Weight training machines require less instruction in technique than free weights. You're placed in the machines in such a way that it's almost impossible to lift incorrectly, thus lessening the risk of serious injury.

Almost impossible, that is. There's one mistake that virtually anyone who uses weight training machines (not to mention free weights) makes at one time or another. It's the primary cause of weight-training injuries: arching the back.

Don't arch your back while lifting. Keep your back flattened into the bench or back support.

Eccentric Cam Machines

The most familiar example of this type of weight training equipment is the Nautilus machine. Take a close look—you'll see that part of the drive train of the machine consists of an elliptical plate. That's the eccentric cam. It's an ingenious design, allowing the practical transfer of weight from the machine to you to be appropriate throughout your entire range of motion.

To explain: muscles are weakest when they're fully extended or fully contracted—in other words, at the extremes of the range of motion. With your arm completely straightened, you can't generate as much power as when your arm is halfway bent. Bend your arm all the way and you become relatively weak again.

The same is true of your legs—notice how much easier it is to get up from a half squat than a full one.

The eccentric cam varies the amount of weight the machine transfers to you. When your arm is straight or completely bent, the weight is relatively light; when you're strongest, at the midpoint of your range of motion, the weight is heaviest. So the effect is constant. Rather than feeling relatively heavy at the extremes of motion, the weight feels the same all the way through the range of motion.

The advantage of the eccentric cam is that *it* allows you to lift throughout your range of motion. It used to be that people did the bulk of their lifting through the midrange, because it was too tough to handle the extremes. The result was a tendency to become muscle-bound. Eccentric cam machines have changed all that.

For example, let's say that you can lift 150 pounds on the leg extension machine. Were it not for the eccentric cam, the weight would feel especially heavy at the beginning of the lift, relatively manageable during the middle portion, and then heavy again at the end. But the action of the cam transfers only part of the entire 150 pounds to your legs at the beginning and end, when you're weakest, and the full weight during the middle portion of your lift, when you're strongest. You don't have to lift only in the midrange of motion.

So you're able to work your muscles, and thereby become stronger, during the entire range of motion. Theoretically, this action decreases the likelihood of becoming muscle-bound. It forces you to stretch before and after your lift. And it reduces the risk of injury.

There are several disadvantages. The weight increments are often too large. In most machines the increments are at least ten pounds. That might be fine if you're lifting one hundred pounds or more—a 10 percent increase provides a safe and effective progression. But if you're just beginning, or aren't particularly strong, and are lifting ten or perhaps twenty pounds, a ten-pound increase is a huge jump. Such a forced progression can lead to injury.

Nautilus offers saddle plates that fit over the top of the weight stacks. These supplementary plates range from 1¼ pounds to 7½ pounds, thereby offering a saner, safer lifting progression. (They can sometimes be hard to find, however. Make sure your fitness facility has a full set.)

Small people may not fit into the machines. There are smaller versions of Nautilus and other machines, but they're not nearly as widespread as the standard size. If you're not large enough for these machines, all sorts of problems can result. The bar or handle of the machine may fit you at an inappropriate spot on your body. For example, a short person working on a hip adductor machine, in which the pad should touch above the knee, may find it makes contact below the knee. That can place the force of the lift across the knee joint, where it shouldn't be, rather than along the thigh muscles, where it should. It's dangerous to stress joints that way.

You can lose control and hurt yourself. True, you don't risk dropping a weight, as you do when lifting free weights, but once you've lifted you still have to be able to control the weight. If you lift it partway and then lose control, the falling weight may force you to stretch beyond your comfortable range of motion. That can lead to injury.

Pulley/Weight Stack Machines

The most common examples of this type are the Universal weight training machines. In contrast to the eccentric cam type, Universal machines transfer weight by means of a direct pulley. So the weight essentially "weighs" the same throughout the range of motion—there's little compensation for the varying strength of the person using the machine. A fifty-pound weight, therefore, feels heavier at the beginning and end of the lift and lighter during the middle portion, when you're stronger.

The advantage here is that you can still increase your strength. Even though these machines may force you to emphasize the mid-range of motion, they still help you grow stronger. They provide effective weight training.

On the other hand, these machines may encourage improper lifting. Because these machines don't compensate for your tendency to be stronger in the midrange of motion and weaker at the extremes, a weight that might be appropriate for the midrange is likely to be too heavy at the beginning and end. So people tend to bounce into their lifts, using the rest of their body as much as possible to get them through the difficult beginning and ending parts of the exercise. That can lead to injury.

Or they tend to use weights that may be suitable for the extremes of motion but are not heavy enough for the strongest portion, the midrange. So they don't work their muscles at the same rate all the way through.

Either way, the workout suffers.

You can lose control and hurt yourself. As with eccentric cam machines, once you've lifted you have to be able to control the weight. If you lift partway and then lose control, the falling weight may force you to stretch beyond your comfortable range of motion. That can lead to injury.

Hydraulic Weight Machines

These machines, like those made by Hydra-Gym, approximate the effect of the eccentric cam machines by the use of a hydraulic, shock-absorber type of mechanism. The harder you push, the more fluid or air passes into the shock absorber, increasing the resistance. The less you push, the less fluid or air, and therefore the less resistance.

So at the beginning of your lift, when you're weakest, the machine offers little resistance. In the middle of the lift, when you're applying the most force, the machine in effect pushes back. At the end of the lift, the machine eases up again, allowing you to finish the lift while still working your muscles appropriately.

The machines allow you to lift throughout your range of motion.

Like eccentric cam machines, they keep appropriate resistance against your muscles from beginning to end.

They accommodate restricted lifting. If you have an injury that doesn't allow you much range of motion, hydraulic machines accommodate themselves to your restrictions. If you can lift through only half of your range of motion, for example, these machines will supply resistance only during that half.

They demand less control. Since you're not working with weight, as such, but the resistance of hydraulic fluid, when you stop pushing the machine stops pushing back. So, in contrast to the other types, there's no risk of hurting yourself when you lose control.

But, when you stop moving, with most machines the resistance disappears. The advantage in one sense is a disadvantage in another. When you stop lifting, the weight—or, in this case, resistance—disappears. So you can't do isometric training by stopping lifting and holding the weight, as you can with the other machines.

Free Weights

Free weights, dumbbells and barbells, have been around for a long time, of course—before there were such things as weight training machines. They're the archetypal weight lifting equipment, the kind people associate with body building. Power lifting involves free weights, as does the sport of weight lifting as performed in the Olympics and elsewhere. It's elemental exercise, weight training reduced to its essence: person lifts heavy weight.

These days, with the ascendency of weight training machines, free weights have lost their place as the dominant weight training equipment, but, chromed and offered in designer colors and shapes, free weights are finding their way into settings that were unheard of not too long ago. No longer reserved to power lifting gyms, free weights are available in all types of fitness facilities and are used by all kinds of people.

The good news is that you can use free weights to strengthen virtually any muscle in the body. There's really no limit to the ways in which you can utilize free weights. In contrast to using weight training machines, you can change your own body position when working with free weights to exercise any muscle group. You can work with one arm or both, one leg or both, and you can easily vary the amount of weight from side to side. There's no more flexible weight workout possible.

Free weights offer an almost limitless range of weights. You can work with dumbbells weighing less than a pound as well as barbells weighing hundreds of pounds and everything in between.

Free weights may offer a more functional way of lifting. Rather than being artificially supported by a machine, when you use free weights your body must support itself, just as it does in everyday living. When you do an overhead triceps curl, for example, you must use your shoulder and back muscles to maintain the proper position for the exercise. So the triceps curl strengthens those parts of your body as well as your triceps. Some people feel that working with free weights offers the most natural weight training possible.

There can be a few problems. Free weights can be dangerous. As free weights are just that—free—it's possible to drop them, on yourself as well as on others. People who work with free weights must take the utmost care. It's always a good idea to work out with a partner.

Free weights offer a relatively high risk of injury. Because the weights are not restrained by a machine, it's relatively easy to lose control while lifting, forcing another muscle group to take over. If those alternate muscles are weaker than the muscles you should be working with, they might not be capable of lifting the amount of weight you're using or handling the position in which you're lifting. The result can be injury.

Free weights may induce improper lifting. As with the pulley weight machines, what you lift is what you get. If your barbell weighs one hundred pounds, it'll weigh that at the beginning of your lift, during the midrange, and at the end. But you're weakest at the extremes of your range of motion and therefore might not be able to handle the weight at those extremes. So free weights may encourage lifting through a limited range of motion.

The old cliché of the muscle-bound weight lifter comes from this characteristic of free weights. If you lift only through a limited range of motion, you build muscles only in that range. Muscle-bound people lack flexibility and fluidity—a result of a limited range of motion in their weight training.

GENERAL FITNESS OR ATHLETIC FACILITIES

These facilities generally offer a number of services:
• Weight training
• Sports such as tennis, basketball, racketball, handball, and swimming
• Aerobic exercise classes
• Shopping (pro shop, sports clothing shop, etc.)
• Food and beverages

Advantages

More variety. These facilities offer more services than any other. Whether your preference is weight training, tennis, or the

Friday-afternoon happy hour, you can most likely find it here—not in the same depth and backed by the same expertise as elsewhere, perhaps, but it'll be here. These facilities also may offer services such as physical therapy, nutrition advice, and fitness assessment.

A more nearly equal mix of males and females. Membership in weight training facilities is overwhelmingly male; it tends to even out in fitness and health clubs. Which may be one reason why they often offer . . .

More social activity. If the social aspect of fitness interests you, these generalized fitness facilities tend to offer more of it than strictly weight training clubs. They may even promote outside social activities, such as travel and attendance at special sporting events.

They may provide family-oriented services. While you might not take children to a weight training facility, generalized fitness clubs sometimes offer kids' fitness equipment and classes as well as child care.

They offer more amenities. Hot tubs, Jacuzzi, massage, steam room and sauna, suntan room, hair salon, fancy locker rooms—these facilities may offer some or all.

They may offer special membership plans. These are the clubs that often aggressively go after prospective members by offering such enticing membership options as a free month's tryout or a membership for two for the price of a single membership.

Disadvantages

Individual fitness aspects may lack the depth of more specialized clubs. It's an old story—the more you branch out, the thinner you must spread yourself. While these facilities may offer a little of just about everything, they may not offer a lot of any one thing. Often that translates into instructors who are less well trained than they might be at a more specialized facility and more part-time instructors—aerobic exercise teachers, for example—who may not be available at all times.

Less extensive weight training equipment. If your interest is weight training, be sure that a generalized fitness facility offers the variety of equipment you need.

Activity areas may be less specialized. What that may mean, for example, is that one area may have to double as basketball court and weight room and aerobic exercise room. Assuming that the weight machines don't get in the way, that may not necessarily seem to be a problem—except that the weight room may have a firm, unyielding, concrete slab underfloor, while aerobic exercise demands a more flexible, springy floor. If the area is not suitable to the activity, injuries can result.

They may be crowded during peak times. Mornings before work and evenings after work can resemble rush hour at popular general fitness clubs. Too many people can take away from both the fun and the efficiency of your workout.

They may be too crowded for adequate supervision during peak hours. It's one of the real problems of fitness facilities. Supervision can be crucial in weight training, for example, especially when it comes to free weights. It's also important in using cross-country skiing machines and treadmills. But if there are simply too many bodies for any number of instructors to keep track of, such supervision can be sadly lacking. The result can be injury.

AEROBIC EXERCISE OR DANCE FACILITIES

These are the studios that specialize in aerobic exercise and dance classes. They may or may not offer weight training equipment and probably don't offer sports facilities of any kind. They may or may not have dressing rooms or showers. They may offer shopping and eating.

Advantages

More full-time instructors. Here's where you encounter the people who make their living—or at least a chunk of it—by teaching aerobic exercise. That means instructors may be available just about whenever you need them.

More extensively trained instructors. Because these people don't have to be jacks-of-all-trades, they can concentrate on their own. You can usually trust the instruction you'll receive at these facilities.

A greater variety of aerobic programs. These might include regular aerobic exercise classes at various levels—beginner, intermediate, advanced, senior citizen, pregnant women, etc.—non- or low-impact aerobics, dance classes such as jazzercise, stretching classes, and muscle toning classes.

Classes offered throughout the day. While general fitness facilities might offer classes at peak times only, aerobics studios generally have more classes and at a variety of times.

Disadvantages

The program is one-dimensional. Specialization has its rewards and drawbacks. Aerobic exercise can be a very effective way of realizing cardiovascular benefits, but some people prefer a greater variety of exercise activities. You won't find that here.

Men may feel out of place. Aerobics studios serve many more women than men. Aerobic exercise appeals more to women than men, and at these studios the proportion is often exaggerated.

The amenities vary. If it's luxurious dressing rooms you're after, for example, you may not find them here. In fact, the facilities might be completely inadequate during all but the slowest times. People often come to aerobics studios already in leotards and leave afterward to shower and change at home.

Location

Is the facility near home or work? No matter how complete it is, if a fitness facility isn't conveniently located, it might not be worth joining. The idea is to spend your free time working out, not traveling to and from the fitness club.

For example, to exercise during your lunch break you must be able to get to the facility, change clothes, exercise, shower, dress, and get back to work. If the facility isn't conveniently located, the nonexercise portion of the hour might take up more time than the actual workout.

And you want the facility to be well located with respect to when you're able to go there. For example, if it's a downtown facility, located near work, it might be very crowded during the times when you're able to exercise—noon and early evening, say. Whereas if you find a facility located near home, you might be able to go there on weekends or later in the evening and thereby miss the crowds.

Does it have adequate parking? The only way to know for sure is to visit the facility during peak hours. In fact, before buying a membership at any exercise club you should visit during the most crowded time of day. Any place can look inviting during off hours. You learn much more when the club is busy.

Is the area safe? And is it safe after dark and on weekends, in particular?

Hours

Do the hours correspond with your workout time? Some facilities close or greatly reduce staff during off hours, and that might be when you want to use the club.

Are the hours good for your family? In some clubs children simply aren't welcome. In some they are but only during off hours —and that's when kids are in school, anyway.

Physical Facilities

Does it offer the kind of workout equipment you want? No use joining an aerobics club if it's weight training you're after.

Are the locker rooms adequate? Are the lockers themselves big enough to hold your clothes—long enough for a dress, wide enough for a sports coat? Is there enough room to store a heavy coat or winter jacket? Are there enough benches to serve the number of lockers? One bench per fifty lockers will cause problems during peak hours. Are there enough showers to handle the crush? Is there enough changing room? Does the facility supply shampoo, razors, hair dryers, cologne? Can you get in, exercise, and get out quickly? It can mean the difference between doing a lunch-hour workout or not.

Is there a convenient place to lock up valuables? Or do you have to run all the way to the front desk?

Is the facility clean? To find out, examine the club during or after peak hours. Or take a look during the hours you'll be using the facility.

Is heating/air conditioning adequate? Remember, you'll be sweating during exercise, and excessively high temperatures can make your workouts miserable. What may seem pleasantly warm during a visit can be intolerable during a workout.

The same goes for water temperature in a swimming pool. What may feel comfy when you're splashing around in the shallow end can be oppressive when you're working out. Ideally, the pool should feel a bit chilly when you first jump in. It'll feel warmer soon enough.

Is the parking lot adequate and well lighted? Is it secure and safe? Is it shared with other businesses? Is there somewhere else to park if the lot is full?

Do you have to wait in line during peak hours? If the check-in desk or towel-claim area can't handle the crowds, you may not have time to get in your workout.

Can you readily schedule specific activities? For example, can you reserve a racketball court anytime or just on the first Tuesday of the month? Can you schedule days or weeks in advance or just on the day of use? Can you schedule by phone?

Does the snack bar serve what you want to eat? For example, health food and vegetable juices aren't everyone's fare. If you don't like what's available, you may find yourself missing meals (which, of course, may not be a bad idea for some of us).

Are there meeting or seminar rooms available? Or, for example, are aerobics classes canceled from time to time so that the diet expert can have somewhere to lecture?

Is equipment well maintained? Are dumbbells and barbells picked up and put in racks according to weight? Are seats and pads ripped? Are instructions clearly visible on *each* machine?

Are there enough phone lines so that you can easily call in or out? Can you be reached in case of an emergency?

Is there child care or baby-sitting available? These services can determine whether a single parent, for example, is able to work out or not.

Personnel

Is someone always at the front desk? Can he answer your questions about prices, scheduling, hours, reserving courts, etc.?

How well trained are the instructors? Are they certified? By whom? Are they CPR-trained with current cards? *CPR training is absolutely necessary.* Do they take continuing training classes? Do they have American Red Cross First Aid training? Is a certified athletic trainer available? Do lifeguards have Water Safety Instructor certificates?

Are most of the employees full time? How long have they worked there? Are they conscientious about their jobs, and do they care about the members? Are they friendly and agreeable?

Traditionally these are poor-paying jobs and turnover is high. Facilities often cut costs by hiring predominantly part-time employees to avoid paying benefits.

If the facility has a weight training room, is an instructor always available? Are there enough instructors to handle the load during peak hours? Instructors should supervise, offer suggestions, correct someone who is using the equipment incorrectly. The primary cause of injuries in weight training is improper technique. And improper technique is usually the result of inadequate instruction and supervision.

If the facility offers aerobic exercise classes, is the instruction effective? Do the instructors correct students' bad habits? Do they instruct as well as demonstrate? Are they available after class to answer questions? Do they give alternate exercises to those unable to do a regular workout?

If the facility offers racketball or tennis, are the instructors professionals? Do they belong to professional associations, or are they merely reasonable players working a part-time job? Are they available during the hours you need them? Are courts available for lessons during peak hours?

Costs

Is there a one-time initiation fee? Can it be transferred or sold?

Is there a short-term membership? Often a short-term membership is a good initial option. If it turns out that you want to stop using the facility after a couple of months (often the case), then a $90 three-month membership, for example, makes more sense than a $250 annual membership, even though the year-long membership is cheaper per month. Often the cost of a short-term membership can be applied to an annual fee if you want to upgrade.

Can you bring guests? How much does it cost? Is there a limit on the number of guests you can invite? Some clubs discourage guests by charging exorbitant guest fees—they'd rather that everyone who uses the facilities join up. Others encourage guests by moderate fees and special no-fee days. If bringing friends is important to you, better find out in advance.

What does your membership cover? Locker? Towels? Parking? Laundry (for workout clothes)? Aerobics classes? Court use?

If you're interested in aerobics classes, for example, but you must pay extra for them, then perhaps this isn't the facility for you.

Have annual rates been steadily increasing? The answer is probably *yes*. By how much?

How long has the club been operating? If it folds, a not uncommon occurrence in this business, will you get your money back?

Will your membership allow you to visit other clubs? At no cost?

Will you be assessed for improvements?

PART TWO
Working Out

4 How to Train for Your Favorite Sports Activity

et's recap where we've come so far. First, you've assessed your condition to find out where you're weak and what you'd like to work on. Next, you've brought yourself up to a balanced level of fitness, primed and ready to go. Third, you've taken a look at the fitness possibilities so as to match your goals to the best methods of achieving them. You've set the table and served the appetizers, now to the main course—how to train for your favorite sports activity. If you want to do better in your favorite sport, supplement it with other exercise, or find an alternative way of staying in shape while you're out with an injury, this is the chapter for you.

It's an approach to fitness that's relatively new. Not so many years ago few athletes used techniques such as weight training and aerobic conditioning to train for their sport. In baseball, for example, it was thought that lifting weights only served to tighten and thicken muscles, not to improve their performance. And running was something you did under duress. Old-timers' games are replete with veterans who did little to maintain or improve their general condition, and if you ask them, they'll tell you they regret it now.

Those days are gone. Now athletes in all sports do supplementary exercise to become even better athletes. Baseball and football players work out all year round, lifting weights as well as participating in quickness-enhancing sports such as racketball and basketball. Some even do ballet. Perhaps no well-known performer exemplifies this approach more successfully than tennis champion Martina Navratilova.

"Martina is successful because she's realized that it takes more than just playing tennis to play superbly," says Garrick. Although blessed with great athletic ability, Martina didn't begin to dominate her sport until she fully developed her ability by supplementing tennis playing with other kinds of exercise, such as weight training. She conditions herself off the court while honing her game between the white lines.

For years the combination proved to be virtually unbeatable. Martina has provided an example that other tennis pros have followed. For example, her longtime rival Chris Evert similarly took to off-court conditioning, with the result that she has played some of the best tennis of her career—and at an age when the quality of one's game is expected to decline.

You, too, can become more successful—and have more fun—in your favorite sport. This chapter will suggest how. These suggestions won't turn anyone into Martina Navratilova or Chris Evert, of course, but they sure can help you do as well as possible in your activity. And you can rest assured that your *approach* is the same as that of these exceptional athletes. That we can guarantee you.

A few tips: In the case of running, walking, swimming, cycling, and aerobic dance—all activities that themselves provide a means of training for other sports—we've provided brief suggestions as to how you might get started and stay involved. But if you want to learn advanced running or swimming technique, for example, the thing to do is take a lesson or consult any number of books and articles dealing with the subject. The same goes for learning how to play tennis or golf or how to ski.

This book is not a how-to-play-tennis or how-to-swim book. There are ample resources available for that. We have other fish to fry—that is, teaching you how you can train for these activities and thereby perform them better and enjoy them more, and what you can do to stay in shape if an injury keeps you away.

The chapter is divided into sections that deal with ten of the most popular sports/fitness activities: tennis, golf, running, walking, swimming, alpine skiing, cycling, aerobic dance, weight training, and stretching.

Each section begins with some general comments about the nature of the activity and what kinds of supplementary exercises will help you to perform better.

Next are recommendations of specific aerobic exercises you can do to supplement your activity. For example, the section on tennis (see page 111) recommends running, cycling, aerobic dance, and working out on a cross-country ski trainer—with advantages and disadvantages of each—as good aerobic exercises that will help your game.

Which one should you do? That depends on you. Pick the exercise that is most convenient and accessible for you, the one that you most like doing, and the one that is most appropriate for you given your particular body and history of injuries. For example, if you've suffered from knee injuries or ankle problems, running and aerobic dance might not be the exercises for you. You'll probably want to cycle instead. If you live in an area where inclement weather is a strong consideration, you might want to stick to indoor aerobic exercises such as aerobic dance, riding an exercise bike, or using a cross-country trainer. And, of course, all these considerations may mean little if none of these exercises is available to you. If you don't have access to an exercise bike or a cross-country ski trainer, and there are no aerobic dance classes in your area, running may be the exercise for you—by default if for no other reason.

Each section ends with recommendations for strengthening and stretching exercises that will supplement your favorite sports activity, along with page numbers showing where in the next chapter you can find the exercises and how to do them. Again, let's look at the tennis section as an example. Beginning on page 115 we direct you to exercises that will strengthen your wrist and forearm; upper arm and elbow; shoulder; trunk; hip, knee, and thigh; and calf and ankle—all areas important in playing tennis. And we further nail it down for you by suggesting which of these areas you should concentrate on as the most important for your game—the wrist, shoulder, thigh, and ankle.

So tailor the recommendations to fit your particular situation. That's what *Be Your Own Personal Trainer* is for: to provide a personalized program just for you. In effect, this chapter offers a sumptuous menu of exercise dishes. Your job is to consider your goals and our recommendations and order as you see fit. We won't *tell* you which exercises to do, as any particular approach might be right for some but would do a disservice to others. The idea all the way through this book is to do what's right for *you*—no one else. And to do that, we will work *with* you to provide you the safest, most effective, most enjoyable fitness program possible.

Tennis

Marc is fifty-three years old. His passion is tennis—he plays three times a week. He took it up a year ago after having been a runner for most of the years before that. He quit running because his lower back increasingly bothered him due to all the pounding and jarring. Tennis is not nearly so hard on his back, but since he has stopped running he has noticed a falloff in endurance. At the end of a couple of sets, even doubles, he's bushed. And besides that, he has trouble rearing back to serve the way he'd like. He's determined to do something about both problems.

"Well," Garrick says, "I hate to be the one to break it to you, but I suspect you're just plain out of shape."

"I'm not surprised," Marc says.

"I think you've lost conditioning since your running days," Garrick says. "The thing is, we fall out of shape at least twice as fast as it took to get in shape in the first place. You could use some aerobic conditioning."

"I don't want to start running again," Marc says. "My back won't stand for it."

"Right," Garrick says. "Running or even walking isn't the thing for you. We'll set you up with another aerobic activity. Cycling is a good one."

"But what about my game?" Marc says. "I'm tired of powder-puff serves."

Garrick laughs. "We'll get you on a strength and flexibility program, too. Do you belong to a fitness club?"

"No," Marc says, "but my tennis club has weight machines and some exercise bikes."

"Good," Garrick says. "You're about to make the most of your membership dues."

Strength? Tennis isn't usually thought of as a strength sport. Endurance, yes—certainly you don't want to run out of gas on the court—but many players might describe tennis as first and foremost a game of finesse. Agility, coordination, touch—these are at least as important as how much muscle you have. Just look at John McEnroe.

Well, finesse is undoubtedly important, but strength, too, is crucial in tennis, in a couple of ways that aren't always appreciated. The first has to do with the common lament of recreational players: they just aren't able to play as much as they'd like. For many people, playing opportunities boil down to a day or two on the weekends and maybe, just maybe, another day during the week once in a while. That's simply not enough to maintain conditioning. You need to play at least three times a week—three times *every* week—to keep your muscles strong and supple.

The point is that muscles expected to do the same task in the same manner over and over—serve a tennis ball, for example—must have enough strength and endurance not to tire out before you're ready to walk off the court. Weak muscles, muscles not used enough to develop the strength they need, tend to react slowly, fatigue easily, and tighten up. When that happens, the consequences can be more severe than simply getting tired—it can mean an injury. The process works this way.

Tennis players talk about "getting in a groove." What that means is that the muscles responsible for the repetitive motions in tennis are working together perfectly, each one playing its role in harmony with the others. But when these muscles begin to tire, your body must enlist other muscles to help out so that you can continue serving and hitting forehands, backhands, and volleys. The problem is that these secondary muscles—secondary to the task at hand, that is—aren't used to doing what the primary muscles are designed to do. And they don't do it very well.

So, number one, your game suffers. Well, that's life. There's always next time. But, number two, these newly enlisted muscles forced to do tasks they're not accustomed to can easily become injured—as can your tired, tight primary muscles. And an injury is not as easy to shrug off as a bad set. Play badly and you can always come back the next time, rested and fresh. But an injury will stay with you.

You just can't overlook the problem of tennis injuries. From tennis elbow to pulled muscles to tendinitis and sore joints, many adult tennis players are always nursing injuries. And that fact leads to the second major advantage of strength in tennis: strong muscles are less likely to be injured. So strength in tennis, as in any sport, is a double asset. It helps keep you playing long and well and it helps keep you from being injured—for the first time or again (and again and again).

The idea of being able simply to play yourself back into condition after an injury is just plain wrong. Attempting to do so will most likely result in playing yourself into a recurrence of the injury or a new injury altogether. You have to rehabilitate injuries, and that means conscious, formal stretching and strengthening. And if the injury is of any consequence, that period of rehabilitation should continue much longer than most people think—for at least a month after you return to your full normal tennis activities.

To exercise for tennis, there's nothing that will help you with your game as much as actually playing. Learning effective stroke technique, working on hitting the ball, getting into position, running up and down the court—all these are better for your game than any amount of lifting weights or stretching. But combining playing with supplementary exercises is even better. And when you just can't play for one reason or another, doing your best to stay in shape through other kinds of exercise is a great idea. Pursued in this spirit, supplementary exercises can make a significant difference in the quality of your game.

We've separated these exercises into two categories: aerobic exercise and muscle work. Aerobic exercise primarily helps develop stamina, wind, endurance—a healthy cardiorespiratory system. Many recreational tennis players run out of gas in the third set of a hotly contested match, and it's tough to concentrate on hitting the ball if all your attention is directed toward getting enough oxygen. Good aerobic conditioning can alleviate the problem.

Muscle work involves strengthening and stretching. Again, strength and flexibility enable your muscles to continue to do the tasks they're designed to do throughout the match, and so avoid injury. For suggestions as to how to do the exercises to follow, simply turn to the appropriate section of the book (page numbers are given in parentheses).

If you're not rehabilitating an injury, an effective supplementary workout for tennis might combine:
• an upper and lower body aerobic conditioner, such as aerobic dance, and
• strengthening your wrists, shoulders, thighs, and ankles, primarily.

Aerobic Exercise

RUNNING

Advantages

It uses the same muscles you use to run on the tennis court.
Many people already run and so have worked through the early high-risk injury period.

Disadvantages

You may be limited by inclement winter weather during the period when you should be preparing for the new tennis season.
It is hard on previously injured joints—especially the hip, knee, and ankle. These are the joints most frequently involved in early degenerative arthritis during midlife and later years.
Running injuries are essentially the same as tennis injuries involving the lower body. So if you want to get in shape for tennis, you might want to do an activity that won't produce injuries that hinder your play.
It does nothing for the shoulders and arms.

CYCLING

Advantages

With an exercise bike, it can be done in any weather, day or night.
Cycling primarily exercises the quadriceps muscles in the thigh, one of the most important muscles in tennis.

It is probably safer than running (when using an exercise bike, that is).

You can control the quality of the workout by setting and varying resistance.

Disadvantages

It may cause knee problems. (Be sure to follow our seat and feet position recommendations. See page 157.)

It can cause quadriceps muscles to become tight as a result of the hip-flexed, sitting position. Be sure to stretch well afterward.

It does nothing for the upper body.

CROSS-COUNTRY SKI TRAINER

Advantages

There is not as much stress on knees as in cycling or running.

You can do the exercise regardless of weather or time of day.

It exercises the upper and lower body.

Disadvantages

The equipment is relatively expensive and difficult to find at fitness facilities.

It demands special attention to proper technique.

AEROBIC DANCE

Advantages

Aerobic dance exercises the upper and lower body.

You can do the exercise regardless of weather and time of day.

It enhances your ability to move in many directions, as on the tennis court.

It combines aerobic exercise with stretching and strengthening.

Disadvantages

It requires more gradual start-up than some other aerobic activities.

It can produce injuries similar to those of tennis.

Muscle Work—Strengthening and Stretching

As sheer power isn't as important in tennis as continuous strength and tone, the emphasis in these exercises should lean toward endurance rather than pure strength. Follow the *endurance* prescriptions for the exercises to follow.

The most important areas to strengthen for tennis are the wrist, shoulder, thigh, and ankle. We'll mark the specific exercises with an asterisk (*).

- Wrist/forearm
    *Wrist extensors (page 315)
    Gripping muscles (page 320)
- Arm/elbow
    Triceps (page 295)
        Give particular emphasis to stretching.
- Shoulder
    Trapezius (raising exercises) (page 284)
    *Rhomboids and lats (pulling exercises) (page 277)
    *Deltoid (raising exercises) (page 284)
- Trunk
    Back flexibility (page 262)
    Stomach strengthening (page 247)
- Hip/knee/thigh
    *Quadriceps (knee extensions) (page 209)
- Calf/ankle
    Calf (page 187)
    *Ankle (inversion/eversion strengthening, especially with any history of ankle sprains (page 197)

Golf

Jack turned sixty-five years old on Labor Day. He celebrated his retirement by playing eighteen holes. He plays four times a week, walks the entire course, scores in the eighties. A week ago he spent a Saturday morning cutting the hedge around his house with an electric trimmer. His right shoulder felt tired by the time he was done, awfully sore on Sunday morning, and by Monday he couldn't raise his arm halfway to his shoulder, much less swing a golf club.

Garrick peers at him over his half-glasses. "Not exactly the smartest thing you've ever done."

Jack laughs. "Think of the money I saved by not hiring someone."

"Far be it from me to advise against frugality, but do us all a favor—next time, hire someone."

"So what do I have to look forward to?" Jack asks. "Long hours of boredom?"

"Well, you should stay away from the golf course for a while. There really isn't much we can do for you until the shoulder's comfortable. Then we can help you rebuild and restrengthen it. But for now it means not using it. It might even be a good idea to put your arm in a sling for a few days." Garrick notices Jack's expression. "Don't worry, we'll keep you busy in the meantime. Do you have access to an exercise bike?"

"I have one in the TV room."

"Do you watch the evening news?"

"Religiously."

"Try cycling while you watch the news. You might even try walking around the block instead of the course for a while."

So now Jack cycles. He has also taken up walking while he waits for his shoulder to heal. Exploring the neighborhood isn't the same as hiking the rolling hills of the golf course, club in hand, but he's getting acquainted with folks he never knew before. Anyway, his wife reminds him, he always did enjoy visiting with his golfing buddies more than knocking that little ball into the hole. Besides that, he's getting a good aerobic workout, and he's certainly up on the evening news.

Golf receives a lot of abuse from the fitness establishment because it's perceived as being nonaerobic, of little value as far as fitness conditioning is concerned. There's truth in that—golf offers little in the way of an aerobic workout. It just doesn't take much effort to swing a golf club every once in a while. But physical conditioning involves both effort and time, and while the aerobic effort in swinging a golf club may not be much, it continues over a relatively long time. Even minimal effort over a long enough time can produce a conditioning effect.

Combine the effort of swinging the club with that of walking over hill and dale for a few hours, and the conditioning benefits of golf are increased many times over—even if that walking is punctuated by frequent pauses to check your lie, hunt for the right club, wait for the party ahead of you to get out of the way, and hit the ball. Carrying or pulling a golf bag substantially adds to the effort involved, increasing the value of a golfing workout. (On the other hand, the use of a motorized golf cart—mandated on many courses —robs golf of much of its fitness benefit.) In any case, few would dispute the notion that playing golf is better than doing nothing.

Like tennis, golf is a precision sport that requires the repetitive grooving of specific muscle activity patterns. To hit the same stroke over and over and over, your muscles must work together in precisely the same way time after time. Ben Hogan called this grooving "muscle memory." Although pure power is important—

men hit the ball farther than women, after all—accuracy and consistency are more important. For example, the longest hitters on the men's and women's tours are rarely the best golfers. Hogan, in his day, was a good example of that.

As with other precision activities—serving a tennis ball, for example—strength and endurance are particularly important in golf, because only when your muscles are strong are they capable of performing the same tasks in the same way again and again. As muscles grow tired, they begin to function differently from before, or not at all. If you continue to play, your body must call in other muscles to help out. But those newly enlisted muscles just aren't designed to perform tasks better suited to your tired primary muscles. They do the best they can, but the result is invariably a falloff in the quality of your game and a heightened risk of injury.

In golf, those injuries are most commonly back problems. All that twisting, especially with long shots, places stresses on the back that the muscles simply don't encounter in everyday living. It's important that your back muscles be strong and supple, and that may mean some building up.

Golfers also suffer shoulder and elbow problems. Your shoulders and arms must provide a rigid, stable chain for the transmission of force from the legs and trunk if you're to get off those 250-yard drives. To do so, those muscles, too, must be strong.

If you're not rehabilitating an injury, an effective supplementary workout for golf might include:
• an upper and lower body aerobic conditioner such as aerobic dance or walking, and
• strengthening your shoulders and back, primarily.

Aerobic Exercise

Regardless of whether golf is an effective conditioner or not, you need at least a modicum of aerobic fitness to play the game well. Even if you use a golf cart, you may find yourself climbing up and down hills and doing some walking. If climbing a small knoll toward your ball makes you breathless and weak in the knees, good luck with your next shot. Those precisely coordinated muscle movements necessary to hit the ball just right may be badly out of kilter.

An aerobic exercise program for golf should establish enough conditioning so that any fitness inadequacies don't interfere with your concentration and swing, and it should enhance whatever conditioning naturally occurs during the game. And at least some of the exercises should strengthen the back and the rest of the upper body at the same time.

ROWING MACHINE

Advantages

It exercises the upper body—shoulders, arms, and back.
It is adjustable to your current level of fitness.
Machines are readily available—to buy or at fitness facilities.

Disadvantages

Rowing may require some effort to learn to do properly.
It may worsen (or cause) golf-type injuries to the elbow, shoulder, and back.

CROSS-COUNTRY SKI TRAINER

Advantages

It offers upper and lower body workout.
It is adjustable to your current level of fitness.
It requires only limited hip and knee motion—especially good for aging people and people with previous injuries.

Disadvantages

Ski trainers are not readily available in fitness facilities and are expensive to buy.
They do not offer an especially good workout for back muscles.
It is relatively difficult to learn how to use the machine properly.

AEROBIC DANCE

Advantages

It is good flexibility exercise for shoulders and arms (and modest strengthening).
It provides good stomach and back strengthening and a flexibility workout.
It is a form of exercise readily available through classes and tapes.
It doesn't usually cause the kinds of injuries golfers suffer.
It offers good general conditioning.

Disadvantages

It requires gradual working into a program.
It requires a great deal of time for relatively few exercises that directly help golf.

RUNNING

Advantage

Running is one of the most available and inexpensive exercise activities.

Disadvantages

You have to start gradually.

The injuries common in running—such as knee problems and ankle sprains—are also common problems in golf.

It does not exercise the shoulders and arms.

It does not exercise the stomach and back—in fact, running sometimes causes back injuries.

CYCLING

Advantages

Cycling generally causes few golf-type injuries.

You can adjust it to your level of fitness.

Disadvantages

It does not exercise shoulders and arms.

It does not exercise back and stomach—in fact, it may even worsen back problems.

SWIMMING

Advantages

Swimming offers a good workout for the shoulders and arms (exercising many of the same muscles used in golf).

Swimming may be particularly available to golfers, many of whom have access to golf club pools.

It probably won't make knee or hip problems worse.

Disadvantages

It does little for the back. New swimmers might even have back problems.

It requires instruction—and may be particularly difficult to learn as you grow older.

Muscle Work—Strengthening and Stretching

The main goals here are strength and flexibility. Endurance is not a major problem in golf, except, perhaps, for the back. Follow the *strength* prescriptions for the exercises to follow.

The most important exercises for golf involve the shoulder and back. We'll mark them with an asterisk (*).

- Wrist/forearm
  These muscles are important to provide a stiff, stable wrist during the stroke.
  > Wrist extensors (page 315)
  > Wrist flexors (gripping muscles) (page 317)
- Arm/elbow
  > Triceps (for elbow stability) (page 295)
- Shoulder
  > *Deltoid (raising exercises) (page 285)
  > *Rhomboids and trapezius (pulling exercises) (page 277)
- Trunk
  > *Back (page 257)
- Stomach (with particular emphasis on oblique muscles) (page 247)
- Hips and legs (page 222)

Golf Tips

Lessons from a professional are essential. Lessons enable you to become a good golfer and help you avoid injury.

Practicing at a driving range is probably necessary. In the usual round of golf, even one requiring a hundred strokes, you don't hit any single shot often enough to groove your swing.

Among beginning golfers, the driving range may be a more frequent source of injury than the golf course. In one hour at the driving range, it's possible to hit more shots than you would in a month of weekend golf. And because the long shots in particular exercise large, powerful muscles not used extensively in everyday living, there's a good chance of tiring, tightening, and even overstretching and tearing these muscles.

It's a good idea to change clubs every fifteen to twenty shots. Start with a midrange iron to warm up. Then go to the driver, and follow with a short iron. The irons, especially the shorter ones, require a different swing than the woods. Alternating clubs allows your muscles to rest, reducing the risk of fatigue and possible injury.

Unlike many precision activities, golf will often allow you to continue a certain amount of playing even when you're injured. For example, it's usually possible to practice putting even with a sore shoulder or knee. Using a pitching wedge may be possible even though driving the ball causes pain.

Running

Sandy is twenty-six years old and in her first year of residency at a San Francisco hospital. If you can get her undivided attention long enough, she'll tell you that she likes medicine, but she considers herself little more than a slave. On call thirty-six hours at a stretch, making rounds with her eyelids drooping, nodding off during meetings, at the mercy of whoever is attending on the ward, she feels her life is no longer her own. So when she's not working —and is awake—she runs.

Sandy runs whenever she has the chance. She runs up and down hills, on level ground, around and around the high-school track, and through the neighborhood at five-thirty in the morning, accompanied only by barking dogs and the rising sun. Her favorite course is along the Bay from the Marina to the base of the Golden Gate Bridge. Besides medicine, running is her raison d'être. She wouldn't stop running if you paid her, and she wouldn't consider doing any other activity—at least, not seriously. As far as she's concerned, medicine is her career, but running is living—anything else doesn't count.

"How did you survive it?" she asks.

"Residency?" Garrick says. "One day you'll look back on it with nostalgia."

"You must be kidding."

"Well, maybe I am, a little."

"If I didn't run I'd go crazy."

"I don't mean to butt in," Garrick says, "but you might think of varying your exercise a bit. There are activities that are easier on the body, you know."

"But I like to run."

"Aha."

"And nothing else gives as good a workout."

"Well, maybe."

"So I'm not about to change."

"In that case," Garrick says, "I think you ought to keep on running."

Sandy laughs. "You know just how to handle me, don't you."

"The way to handle you, m'dear," Garrick says, "is to let you do whatever you want to do. I learned that a long time ago."

Most runners are loath to consider any alternate activity good training for their sport, and they may be right. There's simply nothing better for running than running. So why do anything else? Because sometimes—whether due to inclement weather, work-related commitments, or injury—it's simply not possible to get out and run. And that can be a real problem, because running is an endurance activity. You have to keep up regular and frequent workouts, at least three per week, or your running, and therefore your conditioning, suffers.

Consistent workouts are necessary for the recreational runner and particularly crucial for the serious, high-mileage runner. As a general rule, the nearer you function to your maximum performance, the more likely you are to be injured by changes in your training regimen. Someone who runs fifteen miles a week may be able to pick up pretty close to where he left off after a ten-day layoff; a seventy-mile-a-week runner will most likely have to cut down and build back up following a similar time away. So how can a runner deal with enforced layoffs? The answer is to do alternate training.

Alternate training can be particularly important if the reason for your layoff is injury. And with runners, it well may be. Of all the popular fitness activities, running presents the highest risk of injury. If you run anywhere near thirty miles a week, the likelihood of suffering an injury serious enough to send you to a doctor is one in four. And the rate increases as you increase mileage.

Some runners attempt to run through injuries. *Not* a good idea. If you can't run right, you shouldn't run at all. Attempting to run through an injury will usually result in either worsening the injury or causing a new one—or both. The thing to do in such cases is to try alternate exercise. Besides, some of these exercises might be useful in preparing you to run on different types of terrain.

Because running is primarily an aerobic activity, there's no better aerobic conditioner for runners than actually running. It uses the proper muscles in the right sequences. And maintenance of aerobic capability is the single most important task for a runner. Running out of gas during a workout or a competition is more likely to compromise a runner's goals than is the failure of any particular muscle group (in contrast to tennis, say, in which a problem with the muscles that extend the wrist or rotate the shoulders can completely wipe out your game).

Running also provides impact, which is at once a major reason for the high injury risk in running and a basis for any aerobic training program for running. Because running is an impact, weight-bearing activity, not only the muscles but the bones in the legs must adapt and become strong. You might be able to keep your running muscles in reasonable shape by doing non–weight-bearing exercises, but unless the bones of your legs bear weight and undergo impact, they won't be strong enough to withstand the rigors of running. The danger here is the very real possibility of stress fractures.

Supplement your running by strengthening your trunk, thighs, and lower legs, primarily.

Aerobic Exercise

TREADMILL RUNNING

Advantages

It involves running and so exercises the running muscles. It also provides some impact, but not as much as running on a hard surface.

It's available regardless of the weather.

It can be controlled more precisely than actual running. You can add "hills" by increasing the tilt of the treadmill and determine speed by varying the speed of the treadmill.

You can easily monitor pulse rates by devices often attached to the treadmill.

Disadvantages

It's boring.

Your running gait on a treadmill may differ slightly from your gait when actually running.

It takes some time to learn to use a treadmill.

It may not prepare your body for the demands—especially those on the ankle—of the variations of terrain encountered in actual running.

Treadmills may not be readily available in fitness facilities, and they're expensive to buy.

SWIMMING

Advantages

It can be a good aerobic activity.

As it's non–weight-bearing, swimming is a good activity to do when recovering from an injury. Sometimes it's the only aerobic activity possible.

The workout afforded the shoulders and arms is a good complement to running, which exercises virtually none of these muscles.

Disadvantages

Because swimming is primarily an upper body conditioner, its benefits aren't wholly transferable to a lower body activity like running.

It does little to strengthen or maintain the muscles used in running.

It involves neither weight-bearing nor impact, therefore does not strengthen muscles and bones for running in particular.

It requires instruction—you have to be able to swim well to realize a good aerobic workout.

CYCLING

Advantages

It's a lower body conditioner, exercising most of the same muscles (especially those of the thigh and buttocks) used in running.

It's a nonimpact activity and so lends itself to recovery from impact injuries such as stress fractures and shin splints.

Most people already know how to ride a bike (as opposed to swimming, for example).

It doesn't demand precise technique.

Exercise bikes can be adjusted so as to increase or decrease the difficulty of the exercise. You may adjust it to compensate for injury limitations. For example, if you've sprained your ankle, place the pedal directly beneath your heel and adjust the seat height so you can just reach the pedal. You can then cycle with no ankle motion. As your ankle heals and motion returns, place the pedal farther forward on your foot and raise the seat accordingly. As needed, you can alter the seat height until it's comfortable for your hip or knee, or rotate your foot on the pedal until it's comfortable for your knee.

You can use exercise bikes regardless of the weather.

Disadvantages

As cycling is a nonimpact and only partially weight-bearing activity, it does little to prepare the feet and lower legs for the rigors of running.

Because it's done sitting down, cycling tends to tighten the muscles that flex the hip. Therefore, cycling requires more stretching before and afterward than does running.

Some of the knee problems associated with cycling are the same as those of running.

CROSS-COUNTRY SKI TRAINER

Advantages

You can use it regardless of the weather.

It exercises many of the same leg muscles used in running.

It's a weight-bearing activity and so offers more protection than cycling and swimming against injuries such as stress fractures and shin splints.

It exercises the upper body as well as the lower (not particularly important for running but good for general conditioning).

It can be adjusted so as to increase or decrease the difficulty of the exercise.

Disadvantages

It requires instruction in order to use properly.

It's not an impact activity and so might not strengthen muscles and bones effectively for running.

Cross-country ski trainers are relatively expensive to buy and generally unavailable at fitness facilities.

AEROBIC DANCE

Advantages

You can do it regardless of the weather.

You can do it at home by using videotapes.

It provides a higher level of general conditioning than running.

It provides as good an aerobic workout as running.

It's an impact and weight-bearing activity.

Disadvantages

Aerobic dance exercises everything a little but nothing a lot. Therefore, it doesn't necessarily strengthen the muscles used in running.

The actual aerobic portion of typical aerobic classes is only twenty to thirty minutes. So even though you might spend an hour in class, your aerobic workout is appreciably less than that of running for an hour.

The injuries commonly suffered in aerobic dance are similar to those suffered by runners.

POOL RUNNING

Pool running involves either running in waist-deep water or running in deep water while being held afloat by a life jacket or water ski vest.

Advantages

Since weight bearing is either minimized or eliminated completely, it's a good activity to do while you're recovering from impact injuries.

It requires little skill.

It uses many of the same muscles as running. (And more—you have to push your legs down against the water as well as bring them up.)

It provides a good aerobic workout.

Disadvantages

It can be hard to find pool time for nonswimming activities.

It does not prepare bones and muscles for the impact of running and the necessity of bearing weight.

Due to the resistance of the water, it can be a tough workout. It may take some building up to.

JUMPING ROPE

We include jumping rope because many people seem to think it's a good substitute exercise. But because of the high impact involved in jumping rope and the high risk of injury, we don't recommend the activity.

Advantages

It's a weight-bearing, impact activity—similar to running.

You can do it indoors, regardless of the weather.

It requires little equipment.

Disadvantages

It produces more impact than running, because none of the energy goes into forward motion.

It may be more likely to produce impact injuries than running, and these injuries are nearly identical to those of running: knee problems, shin splints, stress fractures.

It requires skill. The more variety in your jumping—forward and backward, side to side, alternation of legs, etc.—the greater the safety of the activity. (Variety may be a reason that professional boxers, who do a great deal of rope jumping, are rarely injured because of it.)

MINI-TRAMPOLINE

Advantages

It softens impact.

You can do a near-running motion, thus exercising the same muscles used in running.

You can do it indoors, regardless of the weather.

Disadvantages

The equipment can be costly.

It requires skill and practice.

It's hard to maintain a good aerobic workout because the rebound effect is so strong that you're in effect using your muscles only half the time. As a general rule, you have to almost double your running pace to realize the same aerobic workout as that afforded by a comparable time running.

ROWING MACHINE

Advantages

You can easily adjust the work load and monitor progress.

It's a good aerobic conditioner. The use of the shoulders and arms is a good complement to running, which exercises virtually none of these muscles.

As rowing is nonimpact and only partially weight-bearing, you can do it when suffering from running injuries.

It may help prepare for running hills because of the emphasis on strengthening the muscles in the buttocks that extend the hips.

Disadvantages

It may result in knee problems similar to those of running.

The muscle use doesn't parallel that of running.

It can be hard for people with back problems.

As it's nonimpact and only partially weight-bearing, it will not prepare the bones and muscles for running.

The heavy aerobic reliance on shoulders and arms does not transfer directly to running.

STAIR CLIMBING MACHINE

Advantages

This generally exercises the same muscles used in running, with an emphasis on the muscles used to climb hills.

It's adjustable and allows you to monitor your progress precisely.

Some stair climbing machines engage the upper body as well as the lower, providing more complete conditioning.

It's low-impact.

Disadvantages

It may cause or accentuate the knee problems seen in running.

Climbing machines are not readily available in fitness facilities and are expensive to buy.

They're nonimpact and so don't prepare your body for running.

Muscle Work—Strengthening and Stretching

In general, muscle exercises for running should emphasize endurance rather than strength. So unless you're rehabilitating an injury that has resulted in a substantial loss of strength, use the endurance prescriptions for the exercises to follow. If you do need to rehabilitate an injury, follow the prescriptions for overcoming a specific weakness.

The most important exercises for running involve the trunk, thighs, and lower legs. We've marked them with an asterisk (*).

• Shoulder/arm

For purposes of running, there's no need to exercise the shoulder and arm—unless you've suffered an injury that restricts your arm swing while running. An altered or limited arm swing can result in a change in both posture and running gait, robbing you of running efficiency as well as contributing to injuries such as back strains.

Deltoid (and rotator cuff) (page 284)

Weakness in this muscle is the most likely to restrict arm swing and shoulder motion.

Rhomboids and trapezius (page 277)
> These muscles counteract the tendency toward being round-shouldered and having upper back pain while running.

- Trunk (page 257)
Running may cause low back pain, as well as worsening existing back problems. If your running causes any *radiating pain, numbness or tingling, sharp pain with coughing or sneezing, or weakness, see a doctor immediately.*

- Stomach (page 247)
Stomach exercises are especially recommended for people with protruding stomachs, as the condition increases your tendency to overarch your back.

- Hip
  Hip extensor muscles (buttocks) (page 229)
  > It's a good idea to condition these muscles in preparation for increased hill running.

- Knee
  *Quadriceps (page 201)
  > Strengthening the quads is a good idea for any runner. Knee problems are the most common running injuries. Although they may seem to be a result of improper training, they're usually caused by increasing distance or speed before the quadriceps muscles are strong enough. (page 38)
  >
  > In addition to traditional quad exercises, cycling does a good job to build strength and endurance, while providing aerobic conditioning as well.

  Hamstrings (page 216)
  > Hamstring strengthening is especially important—more than stretching, even—following a hamstring strain.
  >
  > Running backward does a good job of conditioning your hamstrings. Be sure to do so on absolutely level ground with no obstacles.

- Calf/ankle
  *Gastrocnemius/soleus (page 187)
  > Strengthening and stretching these calf muscles is especially important when preparing to run hills.

  *Front of the lower leg (page 197)
  > Strengthening the muscles in the shin area is especially important in preparing to run hills and as a way of preventing shin splints.

Running Tips

The only equipment necessary for running is a comfortable *pair of running shoes*. You don't have to buy the most high-tech, expensive racing model, but rather a middle-of-the-line shoe from a known brand line.

You can safely ignore all *running shoe advertising claims relating to safety or injury prevention*. There's absolutely no scientific evidence substantiating any claim of any particular shoe as being capable of preventing injuries.

The only way to determine which shoes are best for you is to try them on. Feet swell during the day, so it's best to shop at the time of day when you usually run. Wear the socks you wear while running and walk around the store for at least fifteen minutes. If the shoe doesn't feel good in the store, it's unlikely it'll feel better later—shoes don't break in.

When you're beginning, run on level ground. Don't add hills until you've established a stable, comfortable running base. Twenty minutes three times a week is the amount of running time necessary to realize aerobic benefits.

Run on streets or sidewalks rather than soft ground. Contrary to popular belief, running on soft surfaces is more likely to result in injury than is working out on less resilient surfaces. Soft ground is often irregular, with ruts and sprinkler heads. And, with their cushioning, current running shoes are designed to make hard surfaces feel soft to the stride.

Synthetic tracks are generally poor for distance running. Even though these surfaces may feel springy, they actually have relatively little give and may alter your running gait.

Be careful of running on high-school or college tracks. While the tracks do provide nice level surfaces, and you'll have the company of other runners, over half of the track consists of turns. Even when you're running slowly, you lean into turns. The effect is similar to that of traversing a hill—your outer leg becomes "longer" and your inner leg "shorter." For someone not trained, a steady diet of that kind of strain can result in injury.

If you must run on a track, change your direction—clockwise and counterclockwise—at least every three or four laps, even more often if you begin to hurt.

Be particularly careful if you're beginning or resuming running. Here's a basic program designed for the beginning runner or the person who has been unable to run because of an injury and wants to get back into it. If you feel the need, you can speed up the progressions, so long as you remain comfortable and pain-free. But don't change your schedule by more than five minutes from day to day. If in doubt, go too slowly rather than too quickly.

Walk-to-Run Program

Day	Rapid Walk	Jog	Run
	(Times in Minutes)		
1	5	—	—
2	7	—	—
3	9	—	—
4	12	—	—
5	15	—	—
6	17	—	—
7	20	—	—
8	17	3	—
9	15	5	—
10	12	8	—
11	9	11	—
12	6	14	—
13	3	17	—
14	—	20	—
15	—	15	5
16	—	13	7
17	—	10	10
18	—	7	13
19	—	3	17
20	—	—	20

Walking

Marcy, a receptionist at a San Francisco hospital, is forty-two years old and overweight. Between the hospital and the parking garage is (what else?) a steep hill. Marcy's unable to climb the hill without arriving at the elevator panting and perspiring, her clean, ironed blouse looking as though it's been through a wringer, and her heart pounding.

"God forbid the elevator should ever break down," she says. "I know that as bad as I feel now, it's only going to get worse— unless I do something about it."

"You're wise," Garrick says. "You're getting to an age where the combination of extra weight and poor cardiovascular condition is not a good thing.''

The problem: Marcy is simply out of shape. The main tip-offs are her elevated heart rate and loss of breath. She needs aerobic conditioning and weight loss in general and strengthening of her lower body in particular.

''If I were you,'' Garrick says, ''I'd take up walking.''

''Walking?'' Marcy says. ''I didn't know you could get aerobic exercise by walking.''

''It depends how you do it,'' Garrick says. ''It can be one of the best ways to do aerobic exercise, and it's a particularly good way to begin. Are you game?''

''I know I have to do something,'' Marcy says. ''This sounds pretty painless.''

Walking is the safest, least expensive, and most readily available form of aerobic exercise. It affords as good an aerobic workout as any other activity and requires no particular skill—at least at the beginning. The only equipment you'll need is a pair of comfortable shoes. Usually, running shoes will do just fine. There's little evidence that walking shoes are any better than a pair of good, flexible running shoes. Do stay away from court shoes and sandals, however. Because of their lack of cushioning and relatively low heel, they're not suitable for aerobic walking.

Walking is not only an aerobic exercise in itself, it's the first stage in beginning or returning to virtually any running or jumping activity. You should be able to walk rapidly and comfortably before going on to run.

Walking is remarkably free of injury—but not totally. Walking injuries, when they do occur, are similar to those caused by running. The most common ones involve knee problems and are often the result of walking hills. Walking hills can also result in shin splints and a variety of foot complaints. And walking in the sand may lead to injury, as, whether or not you wear shoes, your foot tends to sink in the sand. The result can be ankle injuries.

Sometimes walking problems are the result of the common attitude that walking is not really an athletic endeavor at all. ''I can wear any old shoe—I'm just walking.'' ''I know I could never run with my bad knees, so I'm just walking.'' Well, easy on the body though it may be, walking—especially rapid walking—*is* exercise and should be approached accordingly.

Because walking is the easiest and most available aerobic activity, alternate exercises can be pretty much beside the point. If you're too injured to walk, what activity can you turn to? You certainly can't run. Besides, walking itself is the activity many people use to work up to other aerobic activities.

So if you're simply looking for alternate exercise to supplement your walking, the options to follow may do you some good. If your problem is injury, every one of these exercises will have significant disadvantages. You just have to do the best you can.

Supplement your walking by strengthening your thighs and calves, primarily.

Aerobic Exercise

POOL WALKING

Pool walking involves either walking in waist-deep water or walking in deep water while being held afloat by a life jacket or water ski vest.

Advantages

Since weight bearing is either minimized or eliminated completely, it's a good activity to do while you're recovering from impact injuries.

It requires little skill.

It uses many of the same muscles as walking. (And more. Because the effect of gravity is virtually eliminated, you have to push your legs down against the water as well as bring them up.)

It provides a good aerobic workout.

The water provides resistance, which thereby enhances muscle strength and development. You can alter the resistance by your speed of walking. Fast means more resistance—slowly lessens resistance.

Disadvantages

It can be hard to find pool time for nonswimming activities.

It does not prepare bones and muscles for the impact of walking and the necessity of bearing weight.

Due to the resistance of the water, it can be a tough workout. It may take some building up to.

CYCLING

It's best to use an exercise bike, as you can better control your workout. It's also much safer.

Advantages

It's nonimpact.

You may make adjustments to compensate for injury limitations. For example, if you've sprained your ankle, place the pedal directly beneath your heel and adjust the seat height so you can just reach the pedal. You can then cycle with no ankle motion. As your ankle heals and motion returns, place the pedal farther forward on your foot and raise the seat accordingly. As needed, you can alter the seat height until it's comfortable for your hip or knee, or rotate your foot on the pedal until it's comfortable for your knee.

You can control your level of training by adjusting resistance.

Disadvantages

Cycling requires more knee and hip motion than walking.

Sometimes cycling results in similar injuries—knee problems in particular—as those in walking.

CROSS-COUNTRY SKI TRAINER

Advantages

The ski trainer requires no more hip or knee motion than walking.

It's nonimpact.

You can adjust the machine for an appropriate workout.

It generally emphasizes the same muscles as walking.

It offers workout for the upper body and arms as well as the legs.

Disadvantages

It requires instruction and practice.

It's not readily available in fitness facilities and is expensive to buy.

AEROBIC DANCE

Advantages

With a variety of aerobic dance programs available—nonimpact, low-impact, etc.—you can often work around injuries that may be a problem in walking.

You can avoid the steps and exercises that bother you and still get a good aerobic workout.

Good instructors may be able to provide alternate exercises that allow you to get a good aerobic workout despite injury problems.

In addition to aerobics, good aerobic dance programs provide strengthening exercises during the floor portion of the class. These exercises tend to use many of the muscles important in walking—especially those involving the hips and trunk.

It's readily available through classes or videotapes.

Disadvantages

Injuries common to aerobic dance are similar to those suffered in walking.

It requires a gradual start-up even for accomplished walkers, as many more muscles are exercised in aerobic dance.

SWIMMING

Advantages

It's non–weight-bearing and nonimpact.

The injuries suffered by swimmers usually pose no problem to walkers.

Disadvantages

There's little strength carry-over from swimming to walking. Swimming will not keep your legs in shape for walking.

The aerobic effect of swimming is concentrated in the upper body—it won't transfer completely to walking.

It requires instruction and proper technique.

If you walk because of joint stiffness that won't let you do other activities, swimming may be difficult. It requires a great deal of shoulder mobility.

ROWING MACHINE

Advantages

It's nonimpact and non–weight-bearing.

You can adjust the machine to provide a proper workout intensity.

It exercises the muscles that extend the hips, the same ones used in walking hills.

You can partially adjust the machine to compensate for lack of motion in your hips and knees.

Disadvantages

Even though you use your thigh muscles, the activity doesn't precisely exercise the muscles used in walking.

It requires reasonable conditioning of back and shoulder muscles.

STAIR CLIMBING MACHINE

Advantages

They emphasize exercising the legs.

You can adjust your workout level.

You can monitor your progress more accurately than when walking.

The exercise can provide specific conditioning for walking hills.

It's a low-impact exercise.

Disadvantages

It may result in the same knee problems encountered in walking.

The machines are not readily available in fitness facilities and are expensive to buy.

It's a weight-bearing exercise.

Muscle Work—Strengthening and Stretching

Muscle work for walking should emphasize endurance rather than pure strength. Follow the *endurance* prescriptions unless specific muscles need restrengthening because of injury. In the latter case, follow the prescriptions for *overcoming a specific weakness.*

The most important exercises for walking involve the thighs and calves. We've marked them with an asterisk (*).

• Wrist/elbow/shoulder (page 294)
  These muscles may require work to provide a good arm swing while walking.
• Trunk (page 247)
• Neck (page 263)
  Neck strengthening can be important because often people walk with their head thrust forward, which can result in aching muscles in the back of the neck. (Particularly true when climbing hills.)
• Back and stomach (page 247)
  Walkers, especially overweight walkers, often suffer back pain. (Indeed, some people walk because back pain keeps them from other, higher-impact activities.)

- Hip
  Hip muscles are often weak in people with the beginnings of degenerative arthritis in the hips or knees.
  > Hip extensor (buttock) muscle (page 229)
  > > Important in climbing hills.
  > Hip flexor muscles (page 225)
  > > Be sure to stretch and strengthen, as these muscles tighten up because of back and hip problems.
  > Adductor and abductors (pages 239, 235)
- Knees
  > *Quadriceps (page 201)
  > > A weak quadriceps muscle is the most common cause of knee complaints. Isometric quad sets (page 201) are an especially good preventive exercise.
  > Hamstrings (page 216)
  > > Pay particular attention to stretching, because the hamstrings tend to tighten with age, and walking provides little extra flexibility.
- Calf/ankle
  > *Calf (page 187)
  > > Calf stretching and strengthening is important for walking hills and walking in sand. It's also important because wearing high heels tends to make calf muscles short and tight, which can lead to Achilles tendinitis.
  > Front of the lower leg (page 198)
  > > Helps to avoid shin splints, especially when walking hills.
  > Ankle (page 197)
  > > Strengthening these muscles can help alleviate weakness from prior ankle sprains and prepare you to walk on soft or irregular surfaces.

Walking Tips

The most important (and only necessary) equipment is a pair of comfortable *walking shoes.* If you already have comfortable running shoes, they'll probably do. Be careful of low-heeled court shoes or sandals unless you usually wear this kind of footwear.

Always start on level terrain. If necessary, drive somewhere that's level. In contrast to running, a local high-school or college track is a good place to start.

Work toward twenty-minute time *blocks, not distances.* Twenty minutes three times a week is the minimum necessary to achieve an aerobic workout.

Stroll to Walk Program

Progress as quickly as is comfortable, but you should never make more than five minutes' change from session to session. Time is in minutes.

Stroll	Brisk Walk
20	—
15	5
13	7
10	10
7	13
4	16
—	20

Your pace should be as brisk as is comfortable. Freely swing your arms and keep your body upright rather than bent forward. If you walk as fast as you can without being so breathless that you can't carry on a conversation, you're probably going at an aerobic rate.

Always add changes such as hills early in the exercise period, when you're fresh and strong. For example, walk hills for the first five minutes, then level ground for fifteen minutes. Next time walk hills for seven minutes, level ground for thirteen minutes, and so on.

Once you've established a comfortable twenty-minute walking base, you can add other changes—wrist weights, for example, or an exaggerated arm swing. Remember to add the changes at the beginning of the workout in the pattern we've already suggested: changes in the first five minutes, usual workout in the next fifteen minutes; changes first seven minutes, usual workout next fifteen minutes, and so on.

Swimming

Rick, fifty-four years old, used to be a runner. But after a steady diet of stepping into chuckholes in the morning twilight, skinning his elbows and knees in the process, and suffering a sore lower back that continually grew worse, he decided that there must be something else he could do to help control his weight and keep him in reasonable shape.

"How about swimming?" Garrick said.

"Swimming?" Rick laughed. "I can't swim a lick."

"Seriously?"

"Seriously. I used to play around in the water when I was a kid, but I don't think I could swim as much as a lap without stopping."

"Okay," Garrick said. "Let's try something else. Cycling provides a good aerobic workout, and it's probably even better for controlling your weight. Why don't you—"

"Wait a minute," Rick said. "I always liked the water. I could use the pool before I go to work. I think that's a great idea."

"But you can't swim."

"A minor problem."

Garrick laughed. "I love a person who likes challenges. But do me a favor—take care of yourself, okay?"

"Don't worry about a thing. I'll let you know how it's going."

So Rick turned to swimming. And he wasn't kidding—when it came to moving through the pool in a controlled, purposeful fashion, Rick was helpless. But, determined and tenacious as always, he decided he'd take some lessons and get this show on the road.

His instructor worked on his stroke and his breathing, endured his constant questioning, and finally came up with an inspiration— she told him to buy a pair of swim fins. The problem was that Rick wasn't strong enough in his arms and shoulders, and also couldn't kick well enough to keep his feet from dragging on the bottom while he swam. By using fins, he could generate enough momentum to help provide forward motion and at the same time keep his legs and feet near the surface of the water.

It was the beginning of a success story. Rick persisted, and ten months later he was swimming almost a mile and a half using his fins. He was doing so well that he decided to chuck the fins and try it unassisted. At first he dropped back to about a half mile, but now he's back up to a mile three or four times a week. He still uses the fins once in a while, but only when trying to learn how to breathe on both sides.

In the process, his formerly weak shoulders grew from forty-two to forty-seven inches and he gained twenty pounds—swimming is not a good way to lose weight—most of it muscle (he put on only an inch around the waist).

"My object was to have good muscle tone and get rid of a saggy, baggy gut," Rick says. "Now I want to take off the extra inch around the middle. What would be a good exercise to supplement my water time?"

Garrick laughs. "The curse of people hooked on exercise: they want to do more. We'll get you started on a cross-country ski trainer. That ought to do the trick.''

Swimming may be the most popular recreational exercise of all, and with good reason. For many people, there's no more refreshing, enjoyable, and exhilarating activity than jumping in the water. At least, that's the opinion of swimming devotees and of a great many kids, devotees or not. There's simply something terrific about being in the water.

But playing in the water is a far cry from working out in the water. As with any fitness activity, workout swimming demands discipline and commitment. It also demands a pool, and finding one suitable for lap swimming, especially in crowded cities, can be a challenge. Along with golf, skiing, and, to a lesser extent, tennis, swimming is one of the least accessible of the popular sporting activities.

It's also one of the best. It provides a good aerobic workout without the pounding and jarring of gravity-based activities. In fact, swimming is often suggested as an aerobic maintenance program for athletes—usually those with leg injuries—in other sports. And, as Rick discovered, it does a great job of strengthening the upper body.

There may be an ironic disadvantage to swimming, however. Because water supports your body weight, bones aren't encouraged to stay as strong as they might otherwise. It's the old story: if you don't use it, you lose it. If bones don't have to bear weight and endure impact, they don't maintain strength accordingly. The problem is the same as that of astronauts who have returned to earth to find that they've actually lost bone and muscle mass during their time in gravity-free space and aren't even able to walk when they step onto land.

Further, although swimming does a terrific job of conditioning the upper body—particularly the shoulders—it does next to nothing for the legs. It does little to maintain the conditioning of the quadriceps, for example, the very muscle that causes so many major problems when allowed to weaken. As an alternative conditioner for injured athletes from other sports, then, swimming may not be as desirable as many think. Perhaps the best course of action for the injured or healthy athlete is to do what Rick is contemplating: combine swimming workouts with others that provide lower body conditioning and weight bearing.

The injuries involved with swimming, as you may suspect, center around the shoulders. There's virtually no other activity that requires as full and frequent shoulder motion as swimming—and sometimes it's simply too much. "Swimmer's shoulder"—tendinitis of the shoulder—is aptly named. Shoulder problems are particularly likely for adults who come to the activity later in life.

Swimming also can worsen injuries common in other activities, such as low back pain, little league elbow, and knee and ankle problems. And there are the everyday minor hazards of swimming: eye irritation, ear infection, etc. But compared to fitness activities such as running, and other noncontact competitive sports such as track and field and tennis, the injury risk in swimming ranks low indeed.

It's hard to find a good supplementary conditioning program for swimming, because no other popular fitness activity parallels swimming's use of the arms and shoulders. Specific shoulder strengthening programs are a possibility, but you must approach them carefully. If you don't do the exercises correctly and inadvertently reduce your range of motion and tighten muscles, you'll hurt your swimming more than if you let your muscles remain weak.

Sometimes people try to enhance their training by making their swimming more difficult. Just as a runner trains on hills in order to increase leg strength, a swimmer may increase resistance in the water to build up strength. Wearing vests with water-catching pockets, using paddles that impede your stroke, using a pull-buoy or partially inflated inner tube to provide resistance while you stroke, even wearing swim fins—all these techniques can build up strength and endurance.

But be careful. Making an exercise more difficult by artificial means actually changes the nature of the exercise. Using hand paddles changes your stroke. You start using your muscles in a slightly different manner, providing overloads, or new loads, in unaccustomed places. The result can be injury. Techniques that may be extremely effective for young, competitive swimmers can turn into a hazard for fitness swimmers.

Most aerobic activities exercise the large muscles in the legs and so, except for providing cardiovascular conditioning, are of little use for swimmers. And, strange though it may be, aerobic benefits gained primarily with leg muscles don't wholly transfer to an upper body sport like swimming—and vice versa. It's simply the nature of the beast that if you want to do supplementary training for any activity, you must work out using similar muscles in similar ways. That goes for strength as well as aerobic conditioning.

Supplement your swimming by strengthening the shoulders and chest, primarily.

Aerobic Exercise

WALKING, RUNNING, STAIR CLIMBING MACHINE, CYCLING

Advantages

These will usually allow a rest for the part of the body most often injured in swimming—the shoulders.

All are good aerobic conditioners.

Disadvantages

All emphasize lower body conditioning and do little for the arms and shoulders.

All require a gradual start-up. Even if you're fit from swimming, you should go slowly at first in these activities.

AEROBIC DANCE

Advantages

It offers some arm and shoulder conditioning.

Most programs stress shoulder flexibility.

Most programs provide good trunk strengthening.

Since there are a variety of exercises, there's relatively low risk of injury in any one of them.

Disadvantages

Aerobic dance requires a gradual start-up, especially for swimmers unaccustomed to weight bearing.

It takes a great deal of time to achieve the aerobic gains.

ROWING

Advantages

Rowing emphasizes at least some of the muscles used in swimming—the lats and back muscles.

It puts shoulders through a reasonably wide arc of motion.

Disadvantages

It does not exercise the muscles that rotate the shoulder.

It takes additional stretching to exercise the shoulders through a complete range of motion.

CROSS-COUNTRY SKI TRAINER

Advantages

The machine can be adjusted to provide a good workout for the arms and shoulders.

It is unlikely to cause impact-type injuries for swimmers not used to weight bearing.

It emphasizes the muscles that extend the hips, which are also used in swimming.

Disadvantages

It exercises the lower body more than is necessary for swimming.

It puts shoulders through a relatively limited range of motion. It can be a good idea to add stretching exercises.

Muscle Work—Strengthening and Stretching

Swimming is primarily an endurance activity. Follow the *endurance* prescriptions for the exercises to follow.

The most important exercises for swimming involve the shoulders and chest. We've marked them with an asterisk (*). These exercises are aimed primarily at free-style swimming.
- Wrist/forearm
    Flexors (page 320)
        Wrist and finger flexors must be strong to bring stability to your swimming paddle—that is, your hand.
- Arm/elbow
    Flexors (biceps) (page 306)
    Extensors (triceps) (page 295)
- Shoulder
Shoulder muscles are responsible for the major propelling force in swimming (primarily the pecs and lats), as well as the control necessary to fine-tune your stroke.
    Pushing muscles (pecs) (page 271)
  *Pulling muscles (lats) (page 277)
    Raising muscles (deltoid and traps) (page 284)
  *Rotation muscles (rotator cuff) (page 293)
        These are the muscles that stabilize the shoulder joint and control your hand/arm placement throughout the stroke. And these are the muscles that are most frequently injured.

- Trunk
    Stomach (page 247)
        Strong stomach muscles help you to avoid overarching your
        back.
- Hip
    Hip flexors (page 225)
    Hip extensors (buttocks) (page 229)
    Rotators (page 243)
        Primarily for the breast stroke.
    Leg
        Thigh, knee, lower leg, and ankle conditioning is not as
        important as upper body work in swimming. You simply
        might want to maintain a general strengthening program.

Swimming Tips

*Unskilled swimmers should take lessons from a qualified swim-
ming teacher.* Unlike running or walking (or even cycling), which
require only a fairly low level of ability to realize a good workout,
fitness swimming demands reasonably precise technique. If you
can't swim pretty well, it's awfully hard to get a good aerobic
workout from swimming. If nothing else, poor technique requires
a lot of effort, which can make the exercise too vigorous for aerobic benefits. Besides that, you can become breathless and tired
long before realizing a meaningful workout.

Take lessons. Not only will you reduce your likelihood of injury,
but you'll enhance the effectiveness of the exercise. And, perhaps
most important of all when it comes to exercising in the water,
you'll feel safer and enjoy yourself more.

*Using a snorkel can afford a workout for people unable to
breathe correctly in the water.* It's important, for safety reasons if
nothing else, that you're able to use proper breathing technique
when you swim. But if you simply can't, using a snorkle can still
allow you to get in your laps.

Use swim fins to build up strength and confidence. If it's hard
for you to swim more than a few laps, using fins can increase your
pleasure in swimming while you build up strength and confidence.
That's the way Rick did it.

*As in running and walking, time and not distance is the impor-
tant factor in an aerobic swimming program.* It's not how many
laps you swim but how many minutes you swim that counts. Remember, your goal should be to sustain an aerobic heart rate for at
least twenty minutes three times a week.

Try working around an injury by doing another stroke. All swimming strokes exercise the arms and shoulders. However, unless you're already used to doing the new stroke, you may have to approach it gradually so as to avoid being hurt.

Alpine Skiing

Jerry is twenty-seven. He has taken up skiing for the first time this season. A pretty good athlete and already in reasonable aerobic condition, he has found that although he has been able to ski through the beginning hills pretty quickly and now rides the chair lifts to the top with everyone else, by the end of the run his legs are aching. Moreover, he has a hard time edging—long traverses are murder for him. And by the next morning his legs feel as though they've been pounded with hammers.

"It comes down to strength," Garrick says. "Particularly in your quads." He rests his fingers on Jerry's leg, just above the knee. "Here, make a muscle. Tighter. Feel how soft that is? You want to work up your quads until they're rock hard when you tighten them. You may be able to get by with relatively weak legs in other sports, but skiing is one activity that absolutely demands leg strength if you're to be successful at it and enjoy it."

Not that skiing isn't a finesse sport as well—it is. But, unlike tennis, for example, finesse in skiing comes from the use of large, weight-bearing muscles, primarily in the legs and trunk. While it may require a reasonable level of aerobic fitness to ski long runs without stopping, skiing really isn't an aerobic activity like running or walking—it demands significant strength.

It also may involve significant injuries. The irony is that while ski injuries are relatively uncommon, they can be as serious as those of any sport, including football. For example, the knee injuries resulting from falling while skiing are among the most severe anywhere. So are ligament injuries of the knee and thumb, fractures of the leg, and dislocations of the shoulder. And there's little that you can do about it in the way of conditioning or strengthening. No matter how strong you are or what kind of aerobic shape you're in, if you fall just right (or just wrong, that is), you may be in for a serious injury.

Overuse injuries are another story. They may be less serious, but they're still bothersome. Ignored, they can turn into serious problems themselves. You can partially prevent these with appropriate strengthening programs. And because many of the common injuries caused by other activities are often brought to the surface while skiing, exercise can be an especially effective preventive measure.

So, although exercise may not prevent serious injury, it can help you out with the less significant varieties. And it can make your skiing easier, more fun, and more economical. At thirty dollars or so per daily lift ticket, the more you're able to ski, the less expensive each run becomes.

So how to go about it? First, it's important to realize that, like running (and unlike tennis), skiing is a symmetrical activity, using both left and right sides equally. It's impossible to cheat and get along by favoring one side or the other. A weakness on one side will affect your entire performance. So you have to bring both sides to comparable condition.

But it's difficult to simulate the actions of skiing with other fitness activities. Many programs have been touted as good off-the-slope conditioning—including jumping from side to side over benches, squat jumps, and hill running—but while these activities may indeed exercise muscles important in skiing, they also carry their own risk of injury. For most people, it's probably safer, and just as effective, to use readily available strengthening techniques.

The most effective aerobic programs are those that exercise the same muscles as those used in skiing. Such programs provide not only aerobic benefits but strengthening benefits as well. And they need not acclimate your body for impact, as should running exercises. The impact forces in skiing (other than skiing into a tree, that is) are usually not as much of a problem as those of running.

Good aerobic conditioning is especially helpful in skiing because the higher the altitude, the greater the cardiovascular demands on the body—there's less oxygen, and therefore you must work harder to get enough of it. In general, the better-conditioned you are at sea level, the better-conditioned you'll be at higher altitudes. You'll acclimate more quickly, too.

If you're not rehabilitating an injury, an effective supplementary workout program for skiing might combine a lower body aerobic conditioner such as cycling, and exercise to strengthen your thighs, primarily.

Aerobic Exercise

CYCLING

Cycling is the best of the readily available aerobic conditioning exercises for skiing. (A cross-country ski trainer is great too, but it's not always readily available.)

Advantages

It exercises muscles (primarily the quadriceps) essential for skiing.

You can adjust the resistance to keep up with your conditioning demands.

There's a low likelihood of injury.

It's often used to rehabilitate knee injuries suffered while skiing. (In this case, you should do at least some cycling with your injured leg only, using a toe clip to help you pull up. Otherwise, your good leg will do a disproportionate amount of the work.)

Disadvantages

You must take care to stretch your hip muscles, as sitting on the bike has a tendency to tighten up the muscles at the front of the hip. (See quadriceps stretch, page 220.)

It doesn't simulate the isometric component of skiing—that is, holding the bent-knee position for relatively long periods of time.

It may result in some of the overuse knee problems suffered by skiers.

It provides no upper body conditioning.

STAIR CLIMBING MACHINE

Advantages

It exercises the primary muscles used in skiing—the quadriceps in the thigh and hip extensor muscles in the buttocks.

The machine is adjustable to your current level of fitness.

It's nonimpact.

Some machines provide a workout for your arms and shoulders as well.

Disadvantages

It may cause problems for people with overuse knee injuries.

The machines are not readily available at fitness facilities and are expensive to buy.

It's difficult to emphasize one leg or the other, which may be necessary if you're rehabilitating a previous injury.

RUNNING

Advantages

It's among the most accessible aerobic exercises, one that many people already do.

You can gradually add running hills to your workout to enhance muscles necessary in skiing.

Disadvantages

Too much running has a high risk of producing injuries.

Knee injuries suffered while running can hinder skiing.

It doesn't condition the arms and shoulders, unless you use hand weights with exaggerated arm movements.

WALKING

Although some people may consider walking too easy to provide good conditioning for skiing, if you walk at a rapid pace over hills and valleys it can provide excellent thigh and aerobic conditioning.

Advantages

It exercises muscles necessary for skiing.

It's unlikely to cause injuries that hinder skiing.

Disadvantages

You need to walk hills to increase thigh strength for skiing purposes, but walking hills also increases the likelihood of knee problems.

Walking doesn't exercise the shoulders and arms, unless you use exaggerated arm swings or add hand weights.

In some parts of the country, the weather just before and during ski season is not conducive to walking.

CROSS-COUNTRY SKI TRAINER

Even though cross-country skiing and alpine skiing are quite different activities, these training machines are good for both types.

Advantages

This exercise emphasizes appropriate muscles for skiing.

It provides a workout for the arms and shoulders.

It's adjustable to meet your fitness needs.

Disadvantages

These machines are not widely available in fitness facilities and are expensive to buy.

AEROBIC DANCE

Advantages

Much of the lower body work in aerobic dance exercises muscles used in skiing, but not as specifically as other activities do.
It provides some conditioning for the arms and shoulders.
It conditions the leg muscles—the calf muscles in particular.
Most programs offer good back and stomach strengthening.

Disadvantages

There's probably not enough emphasis given to the muscles—primarily the quadriceps—used in skiing.
Considering the time required, aerobic dance does relatively little for the muscles used in skiing. (An hour of cycling would probably be of more value.)

ROWING MACHINE

Advantages

Rowing provides good exercise for the back, shoulders, and arms.
It provides good exercise for the quadriceps.
It's adjustable to your own fitness level.

Disadvantage

It gives more emphasis to shoulder and back conditioning than thigh conditioning.

Muscle Work—Strengthening and Stretching

For skiing purposes, you should follow the *endurance* prescriptions for the exercises to follow, as well as the prescriptions for *strength training*. You might alternate the exercises day to day.
The most important exercises for skiing involve the thighs. They're marked with an asterisk (*).
• Wrist/hand
  Wrist and finger flexor muscles (page 317)
    Enables you to strongly grip ski poles, especially if you're

relatively weak in the arms and shoulders.
- Shoulder
    Pecs and lats (pages 269, 277)
        For stability in poling.
    Deltoids (page 284)
        To help stabilize the shoulder for planting poles.
- Trunk
    Low back and stomach (pages 247, 257)
        Being able to rotate your body is essential for turning.
- Hips (page 229)
- Knee/thigh
    *Quadriceps (page 201)
        The most important muscle group. In addition to the usual quad strengthening exercises, be sure to emphasize the phantom-chair isometric exercise. It accustoms the quads to hold the bent-knee position necessary in skiing.
- Ankle/leg
    Calf (page 187)
        Calf strength and flexibility are important because the ski boot forces your legs to bend forward.
    Front of the lower leg (page 198)
        Recent evidence suggests that these muscles play a greater role in edge control and alleviating fatigue than previously imagined.

Skiing Tips

Begin your conditioning program at least six weeks before the beginning of the ski season. It takes this long to realize the benefits of the program, and you'll be over the aches and pains of the program before you actually begin skiing.

It's important to continue the program throughout the ski season. For most people, skiing is a weekend activity at most, a schedule that doesn't provide enough conditioning. An off-slope conditioning program is necessary.

Limit your first day or two of the season to half days (especially if they're the beginning of a week-long skiing vacation). Go at noon and buy a half-day ticket. You'll lessen the likelihood of being too stiff or uncomfortable to ski at all the second or third day.

Beginning skiers should always *start by taking lessons from a certified ski instructor.* The better skier you are, the less likely you are to suffer an injury—if for no other reason than the fact that better skiers are less likely to fall down. Over 80 percent of all ski injuries are the result of falling.

Cycling

Lynette is thirty-two years old and a recent recipient of an academic reentry scholarship. She lives in student housing. The complex is at the bottom of a hill, the university at the top. Lynette used to take the campus bus to classes. Now she rides her bike.

That is, she *tried* to ride her bike. On the very first morning she left herself too little time, pumped up the hill like a madwoman, arrived at class late and so winded and exhausted she thought she was going to throw up, spent the entire class sweating and trembling, shakily walked her bike back downhill, and went to bed for the rest of the day.

"That was the worst day I've ever had," Lynette says. "But I'm going to do it if it kills me."

"Well, maybe we can figure out a way that it won't," says Garrick. "You could ride a stationary bike, you know. No hills, good exercise, don't have to lock it up outside class."

"That's boring," Lynette says. "I want to ride to school."

"Okay. How long a ride is it?"

"It took me about twenty minutes. I'm not sure, though. I was probably in shock by the end."

Garrick laughs. "There really is something to starting things gradually."

"Amen," says Lynette.

"So to begin with why don't you walk your bike about fifteen minutes and ride the rest? Just make sure that at first the riding part is on the top of the hill, after it flattens out. You can just about coast all the way home, right?"

"Right."

"Then two or three days later, add a couple more minutes to the riding portion. A few days later, add another few minutes. Keep it up until you're on your bike the entire way."

"But that'll take *forever*," Lynette says. "I'll graduate first."

Garrick leans over and fixes her with his stern-doctor stare. "Remember how it felt when you tried to ride the whole way?"

"You're right," Lynette says. "I'll do it."

Cycling is simply one of the best aerobic conditioners there is. In fact, competitive cyclists are among the best-conditioned athletes of all, surpassed only by cross-country skiers. And they may have the best-developed quadriceps of any athletes—you can often identify a cyclist by nothing more than a bulging thigh.

Cycling is such a good exercise, it's hard to come up with an alternative program that delivers anywhere near its aerobic benefits. There's simply no better preparation for cycling than to cycle. And in this case, there may be no better way to achieve a good general aerobic workout. It's a fine, generally safe activity.

Safe, that is, if it's stationary cycling you're talking about. Once you get out on the road, all bets are off. In fact, the primary decision facing a would-be cyclist is which way to go—exercise bike or road bike? There's no answer to the question, of course. It's primarily a matter of taste and goals. And some people happily combine the two activities. For those who are wondering which way to go, however, here are some advantages and disadvantages of each.

Exercise Cycling

Advantages

It's safe—no risk of injury from outside sources.

You can adjust the workout for your range of motion in hips, knees, and ankles.

It allows you to vary your foot rotation on the pedal.

You can control the vigor of the workout by increasing the resistance or speed.

It's readily available. Virtually all fitness centers have exercise bikes, and you can buy a good exercise bike for less than the cost of four pairs of good running shoes.

Probably one of your neighbors will have one if you don't, and more than likely it's not being used.

You can work out regardless of the weather.

You can work out while doing something else—reading a newspaper, a book, watching the evening news.

Disadvantages

It's *boring*.

It may be difficult to do if you have knee problems.

It does little to condition the upper body.

Outdoor Cycling

Advantages

It's not boring. It can be one of the most interesting and invigorating of aerobic exercises.

There are many cyclists for company and many cycling clubs and events in which to participate.

Disadvantages

It's dangerous—primarily because of motor vehicles. Numerous cyclists are killed and injured, often through no fault of their own. Bike paths help, but they're comparatively few and far between. And there's the discomfort, and danger, of breathing auto exhaust in more urban areas.

Unless you live in a particularly flat area, your workout may be controlled by the terrain.

You're at the mercy of the weather—not only because it's cold riding in winter, but also because inclement weather may mean poor traction and therefore an increased risk of falling and being injured.

There's nothing better than cycling itself. And for high-level cyclists, there are few—if any—activities that will adequately maintain the leg strength and endurance necessary.

You can supplement your cycling by strengthening your hips, thighs, and lower legs, primarily.

But if for one reason or another—an injury, perhaps—you just can't cycle, or if you simply want to supplement your cycling for the sake of variety, if nothing else, be sure to choose an activity that emphasizes exercising the legs. Here are a few.

Aerobic Exercise

STAIR CLIMBING MACHINE

The action is remarkably similar to cycling. The height of the stair equals the diameter of the bike crank.

Advantages

The motion is similar to that of cycling.
It is adjustable to your own fitness level.
It exercises muscles similar to those used in cycling.
It is not dependent on the weather.

Disadvantages

It requires you to bear more weight than in cycling.
It may result in (or worsen) the same knee problems that afflict cyclists.

The machines are not readily available in fitness facilities and are expensive to buy.

CROSS-COUNTRY SKI TRAINER

Advantages

It does a good job of strengthening the quadriceps.

It requires less hip and knee motion than cycling (which can be important if you're recovering from an injury that restricts motion).

It provides some upper body conditioning—not so important for cycling but important for daily living.

It is not dependent on the weather.

Disadvantages

Ski trainers are not readily available at fitness facilities and are expensive to buy.

Using your arms and shoulders may be hard at first for cyclists not used to exercising the upper body.

It requires instruction and practice to use the machines properly.

RUNNING

Advantages

Running is already a common, easily learned activity.

It emphasizes the muscles of the legs.

It's weight-bearing and so enhances bone strength.

Disadvantages

If you don't approach it gradually, the impact can produce injuries—shin splints, stress fractures, etc.—that cyclists usually don't have to deal with.

It doesn't exercise the quadriceps as much as cycling does.

It may cause or worsen many of the same knee problems cyclists suffer.

WALKING

Advantages

It exercises the legs.

It's an easy, accessible activity.

It doesn't demand as much hip and knee motion as cycling—an advantage if you're nursing an injury.

Disadvantages

It must be enhanced by walking hills in order to strengthen the thigh muscles enough for cycling.

Some walking injuries, particularly those involving the knee, are similar to those seen in cycling.

AEROBIC DANCE

Advantages

The variety of movements and muscles used supplement the more specific muscle use in cycling, enhancing general fitness.

It's readily available through classes and tapes.

It's good for flexibility. (Cycling does little for flexibility.)

It usually provides good back and stomach strengthening—good for cycling as well as general fitness.

Disadvantages

It's not intensive enough for the specific muscles used in cycling.

You must approach it gradually, as it's a weight-bearing and, in some cases, impact exercise.

Some of the injuries, especially knee problems, are similar to those in cycling.

ROWING MACHINE

Advantages

The same leg muscles (the quadriceps) used in cycling are emphasized.

You can adjust the machines to your own fitness needs.

It does a good job of back strengthening.

Disadvantages

It exercises muscles, primarily the shoulders and arms, not used extensively in cycling.

It requires some instruction and practice to do well.

Rowing machines are not generally available in fitness facilities and are expensive to buy.

They may cause problems if you have back complaints.

Muscle Work—Strengthening and Stretching

Although cycling is primarily an activity of the legs, you have to maintain the rest of your body in good condition as well. If your upper body muscles are weak, they easily tire, making it hard to maintain good cycling posture and perhaps leading to injuries. Follow the *endurance* prescriptions for the exercises to follow.

The most important exercises for cycling involve the hips, thighs, and lower legs. We've marked them with an asterisk (*).

• Forearm/wrist
    Wrist flexors (page 317)
        Wrist flexors help maintain wrist position when gripping the handlebars.
• Arm/elbow
    Flexors and extensors (pages 295, 306)
        Help maintain stable elbow position.
• Shoulder
    General shoulder conditioning
        Shoulder muscles do little in cycling and so may be disproportionately weak.
• Trunk
    Back (page 257) (extension)
    Stomach (page 247)
        To combat back arching, which can lead to early fatigue while cycling.
• Hip
    Flexors (page 222)
    *Extensors (buttocks) (page 229)
        Assist the quads in pushing down on the pedals.
• Knee/thigh
    *Quadriceps (page 201)
        The single most important muscle in cycling. Emphasis should be toward modest strength with great endurance.
    Hamstrings (page 216)
        Important primarily to help extend the hips. Include leg presses, rowing, etc.
• Ankle/leg
    *Calf (page 187)
        May not be as important as we used to think it was.

Cycling Tips

For road cycling, have a good bicycle shop properly set up and size a bike for you. Improper equipment is a common cause of cycling injuries, especially for the recreational cyclist.

It can be a good idea for beginning cyclists to begin with an exercise bike. Many beginners have had past injury problems, so having a bike set up for maximum speed may not be appropriate. It can be important to be able to change the way your bike is set up, and stopping to change seat height and foot position on the pedals is hard to do when you're riding around the countryside. In contrast, exercise bikes are made to be easily adjustable. And when you're not worrying about traffic, hills, gravel, and pedestrians, it's possible to pay better attention to knee and hip comfort.

Place your feet on the pedals as they fall naturally. A common problem is placing your feet on the pedals with toes pointing straight forward. But people's feet don't necessarily fall that way. If your feet naturally point to the outside, for example, your knee must compensate by rotating in addition to functioning as a hinge, its proper role. The result can be knee problems.

Place the seat at a height that allows comfortable knee motion. The higher the seat, the less your knee has to bend—often a good strategy for people with knee problems.

Begin with no resistance and gradually work up to twenty minutes of cycling. If you're reasonably healthy, start at ten minutes and increase by five minutes every other day. Even with no resistance, a new exercise using muscles in a repetitive manner may produce some aches and pains. Expect them and don't worry. In most cases they'll go away soon.

When you're able to ride for twenty minutes, gradually introduce resistance. Begin by riding with resistance for the first three to five minutes, then remove it for the remainder of the twenty minutes. Gradually increase the time of resistance at a rate of no more than five minutes every other day, continuing to ride for twenty minutes total. Then increase the resistance for the first five minutes and continue the same pattern.

The initial resistance should not be more than 50 percent of the total resistance available in the machine. If this much is too much, use less. Then gradually build up.

Aerobic Dance

Marina is thirty and an aerobics instructor. She looks like an advertisement for the benefits of working out: tall, sturdy, not an ounce of fat, with an intensity that cuts through to the very back of the class. This is *it,* her expression says. There's nothing better than this. This is what I was born to do.

Well, that's not quite true. She was also born to be a medical lab technician, a student working toward a Ph.D. in biology, and a single mother. After class she slings her giggling three-year-old over her shoulder like a sack of flour and strides off to her bicycle, straps the child into the kiddy seat, and pedals through traffic to her apartment.

The only problem Marina has had with aerobic dance is doing it too intensely. She's been to the Center for Sports Medicine so often that Garrick calls her his "resident instructor." After suffering a stress fracture early on, she had to learn—under protest—to cut back to teaching four classes a week rather than six. But she still gives lecture-demonstrations to community groups and writes about aerobic dance for a local sports and fitness newspaper. And she's been approached about doing a videotape. It's the perfect complement to the rest of her life, a way for her to unleash some of the furious energy that stays bottled up in labs and classrooms.

In the evening, after the little one is asleep, she'll study her biology, hit the sack about ten-thirty, and wake up at five-thirty sharp to start the whole business over again: school, the lab, and then the best part of her day, donning leotards and again bouncing and stretching in front of the class with a look that says, this is *it*.

Garrick shakes his head in wonder. "Sometimes I think people like Marina aren't from our planet. They're supranormals, living things at a greater intensity than the rest of us. You'd think she'd burn out, but she thrives on it. Funny about aerobic dance—some people absolutely live for it."

Aerobic dance is the most popular organized physical fitness activity in the country. And for good reason. Aerobic dance provides an excellent workout. It combines strengthening, stretching, and aerobic conditioning.

In fact, it may be one of the best general conditioners you can find. Good aerobic dance programs encompass all the elements of an effective fitness program. They start with a warm-up and stretching section, progress through an aerobics portion (complete with pulse taking), and then finish with a cool-down, stretch, and specific strengthening program. You'd be hard pressed to find anything better than that. And the recent expansion of many aerobic programs into low-impact, nonimpact, and more dance-related classes offers a choice for those already involved as well as possibilities for others who for one reason or another haven't participated up to now.

Besides their thoroughness, good aerobic dance programs are distinguished by the availability of instruction and advice. In contrast to running, swimming, tennis, and most other exercise activities, in aerobic dance the instructor is right there throughout the session. And if you're not interested in formal classes, aerobic dance videotapes are available to an extent unchallenged by any other exercise.

And many aerobic dance programs are better than they used to be. Initially some programs were too vigorous, giving their participants the feeling that unless they were uncomfortable and breathless during the session and afterward, they hadn't gotten an adequate workout. Not so.

The idea in aerobic exercise is to breathe regularly, to train your body to more efficiently utilize life-giving oxygen. There are other kinds of exercise in which you hardly breathe at all—sprinting fifty yards in the pool or on the track, for example—thereby burning stored energy rather than breathed-in energy. This kind of exercise is called "anaerobic," and it's the way you build up specific muscles. But if it's aerobic exercise you're after, being substantially out of breath just doesn't do the trick.

Aerobic exercise does lots of good things for your body. It helps lower blood pressure and cholesterol levels. It tunes up your cardiovascular system. Over time it actually changes your metabolism so that you tend to use accumulated fat for energy more than before. It helps you do other athletic activities better. It simply makes you feel better. And all that is the result of maintaining an aerobic heart rate and *not* being out of breath. When it comes to aerobic exercise, pain is *not* gain.

Yet the old notion persists. A few years ago the Center for Sports Medicine was asked to evaluate an aerobics program to make sure it was proper and safe. The major flaw we found was that the program was too vigorous. As a result, the participants received an anaerobic workout rather than an aerobic workout. We slowed down the tempo and abbreviated some of the movements so that people maintained an aerobic heart rate and no more.

When the studio used the new program, a number of the participants complained. It was too easy. They didn't feel they had really worked out. One student actually quit because she didn't feel tired or sore the next day and assumed that she couldn't have gotten an adequate workout. She just didn't get the point. If you do aerobic exercise properly, you work out and survive to work out another day.

Another part of most aerobic programs is stretching. And here's an area in which some of these programs may go too far. Stretching before and after specific exercise is a good idea. Stretching to prepare yourself for an activity that demands a lot of flexibility is a must. But stretching for the sake of stretching may not be useful or advisable—it can cause injuries all by itself. The problem with some aerobic stretching programs is that they have no well-defined goal. While increased flexibility may be desirable for most people, many of these programs tend to push people too hard, aiming for a level of flexibility far beyond all but the most naturally flexible. And when you push yourself beyond your ability, you risk injury.

Good alternative training for aerobic dance is particularly hard to find because of the breadth and completeness of aerobic dance programs. So, more than with almost any other activity, you must choose bits and pieces from other activities in order to fill in the gaps left by aerobic dance. And you have to be careful. Because aerobic dance provides a little of everything but not a lot of anything, any alternative activity will almost certainly be more stressful on specific parts of the body. For example, twenty minutes of running will exercise the legs more and provide more impact than twenty minutes of aerobic dance. The result may be a higher risk of injury—doing the *same* thing for twenty minutes is harder on your body than doing a variety of things for the same amount of time.

So it may well be that the best alternative training for aerobic dance is aerobic dance itself—that is, bits and pieces of an aerobics program picked to complement your ongoing aerobic dance workouts.

You can supplement that by strengthening your shoulders, lower back, hips, thighs, and lower legs, primarily.

Aerobic Exercise

WALKING

Advantages

It exercises the lower body and provides impact, both of which are similar to aerobic dance.

It's readily available and easy to do.

There's no equipment necessary.

Disadvantages

You must gradually work up to an aerobic walking program.

You must pay close attention to heart rate, as a well-conditioned aerobic dancer may have to walk (and use an exaggerated arm swing) very vigorously to reach an aerobic heart rate.

You should supplement a walking program with stretching exercises, as walking does little or nothing for flexibility.

You should supplement a walking program with upper body work, as walking (even with hand weights and an exaggerated arm swing) will not equal the kind of upper body conditioning possible in aerobic dance.

Although walking injuries are relatively few, some of them are similar to those experienced by aerobic dancers.

You should be careful concerning how long you walk. An hour's walking is harder on the body than an hour's aerobic dancing. Better to duplicate the twenty to thirty minutes of the aerobic portion of the class.

RUNNING

Advantages

Availability—running can be done just about anywhere.

It requires minimal equipment. (Remember that aerobic dance shoes are *not* appropriate for running. Use running shoes.)

It exercises the lower body, providing (heavy) impact training.

Disadvantages

The impact and stress on the lower body is greater than in aerobic dance.

You should gradually work up to an aerobic running program. (See the Walk-to-Run Program on page 131.) *Don't* start by running hills.

It requires running shoes—aerobics shoes are *not* a good idea.

You should be careful concerning how long you run. An hour's running is harder on the body than an hour's aerobic dancing. Better to duplicate the twenty to thirty minutes of the aerobic portion of the class.

It affords minimal upper body conditioning.

It affords minimal flexibility conditioning.

Many of the injuries common to runners are similar to those of aerobic dancers.

CYCLING

Advantages

It's adjustable for your level of fitness.

It exercises many of the same leg muscles that are used in aerobic dance.

It's often available at aerobic dance studios or at home.

It's possible to do even if you're suffering from common aerobic dance injuries such as shin splints, stress fractures, and foot problems.

Disadvantages

You must begin gradually.

You should be careful concerning how long you cycle. An hour's cycling is harder on the body than an hour's aerobic dancing. Better to duplicate the twenty to thirty minutes of the aerobic portion of the class.

It does little for the arms and shoulders.

It offers no flexibility training—indeed, cycling has a tendency to tighten the muscles that flex the hip.

It doesn't offer impact training.

ROWING MACHINE

Advantages

It's adjustable to your level of fitness.
It exercises the arms, shoulders, and back.

Disadvantages

It may not be readily available.

You should be careful concerning how long you row. An hour's rowing is harder on the body than an hour's aerobic dancing. Better to duplicate the twenty to thirty minutes of the aerobic portion of the class.

It may require instruction and learning technique.

It may be difficult to do if you're suffering from common aerobic dance injuries such as back or knee problems.

It offers no impact training.

CROSS-COUNTRY SKI TRAINER

Advantages

It exercises the entire body.
It's adjustable for your level of fitness.
You can use the machines even if you're suffering from common aerobic dance injuries such as stress fractures.

Disadvantages

It requires instruction and a period of learning.
It may not be readily available.
It offers no impact training.
It offers little or no flexibility training.
You should be careful concerning how long you use these ma-

chines. An hour's skiing is harder on the body than an hour's aerobic dancing. Better to duplicate the twenty to thirty minutes of the aerobic portion of the class.

SWIMMING

Advantages

You can do it even though you're suffering from most aerobic dance injuries.

It offers a good workout for the upper body.

Disadvantages

It offers no impact training.

It offers minimal exercise for the legs (in contrast to aerobic dance).

It requires learning.

It's not readily available.

You should be careful concerning how long you swim. An hour's swimming is harder on the body than an hour's aerobic dancing. Better to duplicate the twenty to thirty minutes of the aerobic portion of the class.

AEROBIC DANCE

Advantages

You can remove the segment of an aerobic dance program that is causing problems and retain the rest. For example, if you have shin splints or a stress fracture in your lower leg, you can still do the initial warm-up and stretching exercises, then work out on an exercise bike while the rest of the class is doing the aerobic portion, then return to the class for the cool-down and floor exercises. Or if you have tennis elbow, say, you can do many of the exercises, simply excluding or modifying those focusing on the upper body and arms. In this way, aerobic dance can be the most flexible of exercise activities.

You can ask the instructor's advice as to how best to conduct your workout.

If you're not able to attend class at all, you can use a videotape that offers a comparable program.

Disadvantages

Aerobic dance requires access to a studio or videotape.

An aerobics studio may not offer other aerobic capabilities— such as an exercise bike or rowing machine.

Muscle Work—Strengthening and Stretching

Aerobic dance offers at least some use of more muscle groups than most of the other common fitness regimens. But it doesn't exercise the muscles in a precise, repetitive manner, as does golf or tennis. So, to supplement aerobic dance with muscle work, follow the *endurance* prescriptions for the exercises to follow.

Remember, however, if you're hurt you must bring the injured muscles up to the level of the healthy ones. You can't simply dance an injury into shape. You have to strengthen a weakened quadriceps or hamstring muscle, for example, or it will remain weaker than the opposite side. In this case, follow the prescriptions for *overcoming a specific weakness* on page 175.

The most important exercises for aerobic dance involve the shoulders, lower back, hips, thighs, and lower legs. We've marked them with an asterisk (*).

- Wrist/elbows and forearms/arms

   These aren't extensively exercised in aerobic dance. You may want to strengthen these areas of the body for other reasons, but it's not necessary for aerobic dance.

- Shoulder

   *Pulling muscles (rhomboids especially) (page 277)

      These muscles are important, as they pull your shoulder blades together, improving posture and getting rid of round shoulders. These muscles weaken with almost any shoulder problem, so they usually require some special effort.

   *Raising muscles (deltoids) (page 284)

      These muscles are important because in aerobic dance you elevate your arms for much of the aerobic portion of the program. If you're not strong enough to do so, you either may not be able to do the exercise properly, or you enlist other muscles to help out—that can cause shoulder problems. These exercises are particularly important for women, as usually women are relatively weak in the shoulders and arms. They can be a good conditioner for people planning to try aerobic dance sometime.

- Back/trunk

   Neck (page 263)

      Six-position isometrics will enhance your range of motion as well as strengthen your neck.

   Stomach (page 247)

   *Low back (page 257)

      Emphasize flexibility—most aerobic dance programs require some back flexibility.

- Hip

   Adductors (page 239)

   Abductors (page 235)

*External rotators (page 243)
> Strengthening these muscles is important because many of the movements in aerobic dance are performed in at least a slightly turned out position.

Internal rotators (page 243)
Flexors and extensors (pages 222, 229)
- Knee/thigh
  *Quadriceps (page 201)
  > Probably the most important muscle to strengthen. One of the most common problems in aerobic dance involves the kneecap and is usually the result of weak quadriceps.
  > Isometric exercises are particularly important here, as you must approach quad strengthening exercises with caution. Done too hard, they can cause the very problems you're trying to alleviate.

  Hamstrings (page 216)
  > Emphasize flexibility here.
- Leg/ankle
Strengthening the muscles in these areas is important because ankle sprains are the most common of all athletic injuries.
  Calf (page 187)
  > Most people, men and women, wear shoes with elevated heels of various heights, but aerobic dance is performed with a relatively low heel. The discrepancy can cause relatively weak and tight calf muscles and Achilles tendons and can lead to Achilles tendinitis.
  *Front of the leg (page 198)
  > Strengthening these muscles may help to reduce the risk of shin splints.
  *Ankle (page 197)
  > To combat ankle sprains. These muscles also help support the arch and discourage pronation.

Aerobic Dance Tips

The major problem with aerobic dance is that because it's so complete and exercises so much of the body, virtually all who do it—regardless of their level of fitness—will experience some unaccustomed aches and pains. That can discourage some people early on. But *don't* necessarily view aches and pains as an indication that you're not up to aerobic dance or that you're being taught improperly. Most likely neither is the case. It's just the nature of the beast.

The best way to do aerobic dance is consistently and frequently. If you work out only once a week, you'll have the same aches and pains every time, because you're simply not working out enough to achieve a training effect. As with any aerobic exercise, you should do aerobic dance at least three times a week (and not more than six, even if you're an expert). Three days is perfect for a beginner.

Most injuries occur during the aerobic portion of the program. If you're just beginning, a good strategy may be to do the warm-up and stretching portion, then stop the aerobic portion after five minutes. Walk in place or do the exercises with minimal movement to eat up the rest of the aerobic time, then do the cool-down and the floor portion—as long as they're comfortable. The next time, increase the aerobic portion by two to three minutes and the other sections by one minute. (Follow the same progression with low- or nonaerobic classes as well.)

You should be doing full classes for a minimum of six to eight weeks before advancing to the next higher level.

If you're using a videotape watch the tape all the way through before trying to do the exercises. This way, you'll be able to assimilate the instructions and information that you might ignore if you're trying to keep up with the exercises.

Follow the same progression as above.

When you can comfortably get through an entire program for a couple of weeks, you might try taking a class. Remember, the class may be different from the tape. Be cautious about working out too hard the first time.

Weight Training

Gino was forty-five before he weighed as much as five pounds more than he had at age eighteen. The trouble was, the entire five pounds seemed to gather around his stomach. For the first time, his pants became tight around the waist. He had to tug to button the lower buttons of his dress shirts. Worst of all, his wife and two children began looking at him strangely.

When he came home after a day's work they seemed to greet him by casting furtive glances at his stomach. His teenage son began giving him resounding whacks in the midsection to go along with his loud "Hi, Dad, what's up?" His ten-year-old seemed to snuggle in deeply when she hugged him around the midsection. And his wife started delighting in grabbing his love handles in bed.

Gino was aghast. This just wasn't in the cards. He would not tolerate gaining weight. So he began pushing away the ice cream, cut down on cheese, and stepped up the veggies. And he paid a visit to the Center for Sports Medicine.

"I just can't stand it," Gino says. "The hair might go, but a potbelly? Never."

Garrick laughs. "You don't mean to tell me that you don't like getting old?"

"Naw," Gino says. "I don't care if I get old. I just don't want to *look* old. I'm going to step up the weights."

"You already do weight training?" asks Garrick.

"Some. I take my kid to morning weights before his swim practice and lift with the team."

"So you've had instruction on how to use the machines?"

"Yeah. I've been through the routine."

"What about aerobic exercise?" Garrick asks. "That's what takes off the weight."

"That's what I need," Gino says. "Fix me up, Doc. I'm ready to go."

And how. Gino attacked the machines with a vengeance. He already knew how to use weight training machines (which was important, because you should never lift weights without instruction), and he'd begin by exercising the legs, then go to the abdominal machine, then do sit-ups on the incline board, then exercise the shoulders and chest with bench presses and pectoral curls, then the biceps and triceps, and top the whole thing off with twenty minutes of aerobic exercise on the electronic rowing machine, making very sure the little cartoon pacer on the video screen never came close to passing him by.

And, lo and behold, it worked. In two months he lost the five pounds, cinched up his belt, and went about his business—not, however, without a bit of chest puffing and strutting. Now if only there were something he could do about the receding hairline.

The reasons for embarking on a weight training program are as varied as the participants. Some lift to strengthen a part of their body so that they'll be better equipped to do a favorite sports activity. Others go to the weight room to undo the damage resulting from an injury. Still others get involved in weight training for the sake of lifting itself. Weight training has become a sport of its own.

As such, there's really no way to train for weight training—it's its own means and end. The best you can do is pick the style of weight training that most closely suits you and your goals. As a supplementary exercise to improve your performance in other activities, the same approach applies: pick the kind of weight training that does the job for you. There are a variety of styles and equipment available—isometrics, free weights, and weight training machines. Much of this book is devoted to suggesting which approach might be best for you. There's no one way—it all depends on your exercise goals. Knowing your reasons for working out is up to you —we can suggest a course of action from then on.

What we've tried to do in this chapter is deal with some of the problems you might encounter in weight training programs and present a variety of weight training prescriptions for you to follow when you get to work. We'll repeat some of them as appropriate in the next chapter.

Aerobic Exercise

Few if any popular weight training programs produce a true aerobic training effect. The closest to it is provided by "circuit training," in which you go from one machine to another in a predetermined sequence without pausing in between. At least that's the idea. In theory, this approach is supposed to give you an aerobic workout.

The reality is usually somewhat different. First, it's virtually impossible to go from machine to machine without pausing. Even when there's no one ahead of you, you have to physically move from one machine to the other, adjust each to your level of weight, and seat yourself properly. Even with free weights, you have to choose the proper barbells or dumbbells. These things take time, and here time is the enemy. And if you're in good shape to begin with, you can ill afford time in between exercise. The better condition you're in, the more difficult it is to raise your heart rate to an aerobic level and the quicker your heart rate drops after exercise. (The less well trained person retains a higher heart rate longer, as the heart is frantically trying to catch up.) Any pause at all may spell aerobic doom.

Another problem arises from the fact that many weight training exercises raise your heart rate higher than it should be for aerobic purposes. Weight training can easily become an anaerobic activity —good for muscle building but not the same as aerobic exercise. It's awfully hard to maintain a consistent aerobic heart rate by doing weight training. So if it's aerobic fitness you're after, a weight training facility is probably not the place to find it.

It's not, that is, if you do weight training only. But many weight training facilities offer other types of equipment. Many have exercise bikes, rowing machines, and perhaps even treadmills, cross-country ski trainers, or stair climbing machines. And increasingly weight training facilities offer aerobic dance classes. So you may be able to solve most of your workout demands at one place.

Weight Training Tips

For many people, a general weight training program is a new experience. Many men have been involved in weight training in the past to supplement sports, such as football, wrestling, or swimming. Assuming that such programs were appropriate for the sport —a questionable assumption at best—it's important to remember that the exercises you did were devised to allow you to block better, or pull yourself through the water more quickly, or any of a number of specific tasks. But being a good blocker means little when you're playing tennis. Developing a good freestyle stroke doesn't help your golf much. So going to the weight training facility and doing the same exercises you did when you were nineteen and a swimmer may do you little good when you're a thirty-five-year-old tennis player. You have to start all over.

A good general weight training program will exercise all of the major muscles in your body—many of which you don't often use in daily living. So beginning a program may result in all sorts of new aches and pains. And the older or less well conditioned you are, the more you'll hurt. Be prepared.

Assessing your condition before beginning is very important. It's a good idea to turn to Chapter 2 to make sure you're at least relatively balanced one side to the other, as virtually all weight training exercises work both sides equally. As in the other activities we've talked about, you simply won't be able to work yourself into shape unless your program is first directed specifically toward correcting your deficiencies.

Obtain instruction. An instructor should go through every machine with you, showing you how to use it and helping you lift in order to find out how much weight you should start with. And periodically your instructor should check you out to ensure that you're continuing to lift properly. Everyone, especially beginners, picks up bad habits. They should be caught early. (And always use a spotter for free weights and other potentially dangerous lifts.)

Be honest with yourself. Left to their own devices, people (especially men) often cheat so as to start with as much weight as possible—you feel tougher and less out of shape that way. But at the very least this approach will lead to rapid fatigue and frustration once you actually begin. You won't be able to progress to heavier weights because you started out too heavy, and you may become injured along the way.

Lift regularly. The ideal frequency is three times a week. Any less may afford you some gains, but the going will be slow, and you may never rid yourself of aches and pains. Any more may actually impede your progress. Your body needs time to recover from tough workouts. Working out too often can be harmful at the worst and inefficient at the least.

In general, lean toward more reps and less weight. It's safer that way. For example, if a program calls for twelve reps before going on to a heavier weight, you might do twenty or twenty-four before advancing. Likewise, if the schedule suggests increasing the weight by one plate or 10 percent, it might be a good idea to increase by a half plate or 5 percent. If you're going to err, err on the side of caution.

Absences in weight training have the same effect as in aerobic training—you lose it faster than you gain it. After a couple of weeks off (especially if you've been sick), *don't* pick up where you left off. Decrease all weights by a half to three-quarters, depending on how long you've been away. You'll find that you'll be able to increase faster than you did when you first began, and you won't hurt yourself in the meanwhile.

Injuries don't necessarily have to stop your entire program. As with aerobic dance, one of the advantages of a good weight training program is its diversity. You can continue doing any lift or using any machine that doesn't involve the injured part.

In Chapter 5 we'll give specific weight training prescriptions as they apply to the exercises in your own workout program.

Stretching

These days, stretching is *in*. There are books and videotapes dealing with stretching, as well as stretching classes, and stretching is a major component of aerobic dance classes as well. But why? What good does it do to stretch? Is there any particular value in being flexible?

Well, it *is* impressive to be able to touch your head to your knees or your ankle to your ear. It's guaranteed to draw oohs and ahs from onlookers. But beyond that, much of the zeal for stretching seems to be based on the assumption that increased flexibility prevents injuries. The more supple you are, the more fit you are—or something like that.

Not so. The truth is that inflexible people are no more likely to be injured than flexible people—assuming, that is, that you're flexible enough to perform the task at hand. For example, you must be extremely flexible to be a gymnast or ballet dancer. The tasks involved in these activities require excessive ranges of motion. So an inflexible ballet dancer might indeed be hurt when attempting a grand jeté, just as an inflexible gymnast is going to be pretty uncomfortable going into the splits.

In these cases, flexibility is necessary for a particular activity.

But most of us don't need to go into the splits from day to day. Most of us couldn't do a grand jeté if Makarova herself were there urging us on. We simply don't need to be that flexible.

Tennis players and swimmers provide a less extreme example of the same point. Both activities require more than average shoulder flexibility. Rearing back to serve or pumping through a freestyle lap puts unusual demands on your shoulder's ability to extend, flex, and rotate. Here's where stretching can help make doing these sports more comfortable, enjoyable, and safer.

But if you've ever been to a swim meet you've probably noticed swimmers putting their arms and shoulders through all sorts of contortions in an effort to limber up. One swimmer grabs another and pulls an arm back, and up, and back, and up, until the first swimmer hollers uncle. No swimming stroke requires that much flexibility. The upshot is that at the Center for Sports Medicine we see swimmers who have hurt themselves, not by swimming but by stretching.

The point is that stretching inappropriately and without a specific goal in mind may lead to frustration (some people are born—and will die—inflexible) and injuries. If you do stretch, stretch for some practical purpose—not to see if you can assume a pretzel shape just for the sake of doing it.

And don't stretch to be as flexible as the instructor—it's an exercise in futility. Instructors are hired because they're flexible enough to demonstrate all kinds of exercises. They've had training that you haven't and have devoted an amount of time to these pursuits that you most likely will never match. The instructor is there to provide an example of how to go about things, not a mirror image to be copied.

When it comes to strengthening programs, stretching is particularly important. But, depending on the program, you may not even be aware that you're stretching. For example, programs that stress lifting heavy weights through a limited—but powerful—range of motion will produce muscles that are abnormally tight. If you then subject these "muscle-bound" muscles to tasks that require a greater range of motion than was necessary in your training, you may be risking injury. In these cases, it can be important to stretch the muscles involved.

Other strengthening programs incorporate stretching into the muscle work itself. One of the advantages of many weight training machines is that they force you to lift through an entire range of motion, in effect making you stretch as you strengthen. Next time you climb into one of these machines, notice how you have to stretch just to begin the exercise and stretch again when you return the weight to rest.

Whichever way you do it, however, it's important to combine

stretching and strengthening. Muscles work best when they're strong *and* flexible. But have a reason for your stretching. Remember that stretching for its own sake can cause more problems than it solves.

Stretching Tips

Always stretch slowly and progress gradually. Never bounce into stretches. It's easy to lose control of the stretch that way—instead of stretching a muscle you might tear it.

Be careful of gravity-assisted stretches. Gravity helps you stretch, yes, but it also makes the stretch harder to control. For example, it's easier to touch your toes when bending down from a standing position than it is by reaching forward while sitting on the floor. Gravity doesn't give you a hand when you're on the floor—you're on your own there. But it's also easier to tear a hamstring muscle with gravity on your side than it is by relying on your muscles alone. If you must do gravity-assisted stretches, take it slow and easy.

Rather than trying to do much in any given day, your goal should be to become more flexible over a period of weeks or months. This is especially good advice for older adults. As we age, our bodies become used to moving in particular ways. Stretching may be a totally new experience for muscles used to long-established patterns. Take it easy.

You should feel the stretch in the appropriate place. If you're stretching for a particular sport or activity, it's important that you stretch in the same position as that demanded by the activity. For fitness stretching, in which the goal is stretching muscles for their own sake rather than to be able to do a particular task (not necessarily a good idea in any case), you should know which muscle the stretch is directed toward and where that muscle is in the body. If you feel the stretch in that muscle, you'll know you're doing it right.

You should never *feel the stretch in your joints.* It's virtually impossible to stretch joints. Stretching joints means stretching ligaments, and ligaments aren't particularly elastic. They have a tendency to tear rather than stretch.

Strength and flexibility go together—a weak muscle is a tight muscle. All of the stretching in the world will do little to increase the flexibility of a weak muscle. You must stretch and strengthen at the same time. Following an injury, the need to strengthen is even more important. Not only will an injured muscle reject attempts to stretch it, but it may be even more prone to injury in the meanwhile. Strengthening is as important as stretching in regaining normal flexibility after an injury.

You should stretch about as frequently as you do other fitness activities—about three times a week if the effects are going to be lasting.

Stretch just to the point of discomfort and hold for about fifteen to twenty seconds. Then repeat the stretch, this time trying to go just a bit farther. If the stretch hurts, back down.

Don't bounce into stretches. Stretch slowly and gently, and progress gradually.

In the next chapter we'll show you which stretches to do as they pertain to the strengthening exercises we recommend. And these will be stretches you can count on, stretches that, if done correctly, are unlikely to result in injuries. In addition, in some cases we'll point out the potential dangers of commonly done stretches —which ones *not* to do.

Stretching and strengthening—two sides of the same coin.

5 Working Out for Strength, Endurance, and Flexibility

I t's time to put *Personal Trainer* to work for you. The following sections present exercises for strength, endurance, and flexibility. At first we'll talk about them in general terms—what isometric exercise is, for example, and the difference between working for endurance and power. Then we'll present specific exercises that you can do to enhance your condition.

One final word before we begin: when it comes right down to it, the best way to do any activity better is simply to *do* it. The best way to improve skiing is to ski a lot. The more tennis you play, the better you'll play. The following exercises will help, no doubt about it. But they won't take the place of actually getting out and doing the activity. Doing the activity and exercising too—now that's a different story. There's nothing better than that.

Training for Strength and Endurance

Now things get very interesting. We come to muscles, and there are lots of them. You must treat muscles individually, and in groups, and as they relate to one another. Muscles work in subtle, wondrous ways. No one muscle works alone—they band together, help one another out, assume and relinquish responsibility in the execution of the wide variety of motions our bodies perform.

For example, when you swing at a golf ball your body doesn't rely on any one muscle group, but rather the cooperation of a host of them. Hands, forearm, upper arm, shoulder, back and stomach, hip and groin, thigh and lower leg—muscles in all these areas must work together. The club head, not unlike a tennis racket or your hand holding a baseball, is like the end of a whip. Your muscles must work together in two ways: first, to get the end of that whip moving as fast as possible so the greatest amount of energy can be imparted to your fingertips or the racket or club head; second, to steer or direct that energy in the proper direction. (The longest drive in the world doesn't mean much if it's lost in the rough; the fastest serve in the world is worthless if it's out.)

For the first of these functions, getting the end of the club moving fast, your body must transmit force from the big muscles in your thighs, back, and shoulders out to the end of your arm. They must contract rapidly in order to get the upper body moving. Once it is moving, the rest of the body must remain more or less rigid so the energy can travel through it. The proper backhand in tennis, for example, achieves its power from the trunk and shoulder muscles, but if the elbow and wrist aren't strong and rigid the energy will be lost before it ever gets to the racket. Thus, the job of many muscles is merely to hold joints stable and rigid so that energy can be transmitted through them.

The "steering" function is more subtle. It doesn't require a lot of strength, just precision. It's this function that requires endless hours of practice, grooving your swing or stroke. No matter how well conceived, strengthening exercises are no substitute for actually doing the activity, for actually whipping the club head through the ball and watching it soar 250 yards down the fairway.

Let's say you're having trouble with your swing. You're not strong enough or not flexible enough, and instead of 250 yards your balls are only getting out there about 150, and rather than soaring they're bouncing and rolling and dribbling off, and into the rough at that. It's clear that you have to do something. But just how do you go about strengthening all the muscles involved in swinging a golf club?

To start with, you have to know at least a little bit about how muscles work and which ones are responsible for which actions. Then the idea is to move them in ways similar to the motion of your favorite activity, but this time against resistance, weight or otherwise, so that they have to work harder than usual to accomplish their accustomed tasks. A muscle that has to work hard builds up so it can handle the increased demands. Then, the next time you step up to the tee and swing, your muscles will contract and relax with increased vigor. The result is a lowered handicap and more fun on the course.

At least, that's the idea. Done intelligently, this kind of strength training can pay impressive dividends. The problem is that often it's not done intelligently, and often it's not done with specific goals in mind. The results can be little if any benefit at least and injury at worst. So, once again, knowing *why* you want to become stronger is crucial—it dictates what muscles you exercise and how you go about it.

It may not be obvious, but endurance is a function of strength just as much as sheer power is. Strong muscles don't tire out as readily as weak muscles. Strong muscles can work for a longer time. But you don't exercise for power in the same way as you do for endurance. The difference involves the amount of weight you lift and how often you lift it. For endurance training, you lift less weight more times.

A familiar example for many people may involve weight training machines. Take the leg extension machine. Let's say that you can lift 150 pounds on the machine. You may have to sweat and strain, work so hard that you feel as though your thigh muscles are about to pop through the skin, and afterward end up panting, with jelly legs, after just five reps. That's power training—lifting as heavy a weight as possible as many times as you can stand it.

On the other hand, you might cut the weight in half, down to 75 pounds, and do many more reps—three sets of twenty or thirty, let's say—as quickly as possible. That's endurance training. Neither approach is better than the other. They simply have different ends. Again, determining your goals is crucial.

Another example of endurance training as opposed to power training involves that old chestnut of an exercise, the one that any person who ever played high-school sports or toiled in the armed services knows only too well—push-ups. For power, do the push-ups in the classic manner: on your toes, body extended, up and down as many times as possible. And then, if you can muster it, just one more time. You may even try doing them with extra weight—a child sitting on your back, say. For endurance, try doing push-ups from your knees. They're much easier that way, as there isn't as much body to raise and lower. You thereby reduce resistance, putting less of a burden on your poor overworked muscles, enabling you to do the exercise many more times than before.

Again, for power, heavy weights and few reps. For endurance, lighter weights and many reps. We'll point out which is which as we go.

ISOMETRIC EXERCISE

This is one of those familiar terms that not too many people fully understand. For some it may smack of earlier days of weight training, in which Charles Atlas and others advertised the benefits of such techniques as "Dynamic Tension"—simply a term for isometric exercises. Did a bully kick sand in your face at the beach? A short source in isometric weight training will turn things around in a jiffy. Sooner than you think, you'll be the one kicking sand, and you'll walk off hand in hand with the pretty girl.

There must have been something to it, as those ads, and the world of weight training that they represented, have prevailed. And just as Charles Atlas promised, isometric exercise really is easy to do and uncommonly accessible. In fact, there's no other strength training technique that is so adaptable to any circumstance.

That's because isometric exercise requires no equipment at all. It simply involves contracting muscles without moving any weight or resistance. So you don't need a weight training machine, you don't need barbells or dumbbells, you don't need spring-loaded devices to stretch and squeeze. All you need is something—your other arm will do—that prevents you from moving the muscles you're exercising.

Let's take an example. Say you want to strengthen the triceps, the muscles in the back of your upper arm. They're the muscles that allow you to straighten your arm—as when you're whipping the club head through the golf ball. You can do so isometrically by pushing your arm against an immovable object—again, your other arm will work just fine. Place your hands one against the other and push, one arm trying to push the other away, the other resisting with all its might. The result should be a standstill—no movement at all. That's isometric exercise.

Isometrics may seem simple—and compared to other activities they are—but isometric exercises still must be done with some precision. It's important to concentrate on contracting the muscle and to do so as hard as you can. You should hold the contraction for at least six seconds and repeat it five to seven times, with two or three seconds of rest in between. Ideally, you should try to do a set of five to seven contractions three or more times a day. Attempting to do thirty or forty of the contractions at one time is not as effective as you might think, because after about the third contraction—if you're doing them properly—your muscles will start to fatigue, making the exercises less effective.

You can do the same kind of thing with any muscle group in your body. The unmoving resistance can take the form of a friend, a wall, a doorway, a heavy table or sofa, a tree, or even the family car—anything that's strong enough, or unyielding enough, to prevent any movement on your part.

Advantages

You can do it anywhere. No equipment, no partner, no gym or studio—all you need is yourself.

It's difficult to hurt yourself. Because you're controlling the resistance, it's hard to have too much or too little. It may be the safest of all weight training techniques.

It's a good starting point or complement to other weight training techniques. Before running out and buying a set of dumbbells or joining the local fitness facility, you can begin weight training on your own by doing isometrics. And even after you've branched out to other kinds of exercise, isometrics can provide a good complement.

It's good for rehabilitation of irritated or inflamed joints. Since you don't move during isometric exercises, a joint that may hurt at various spots along its range of motion needn't be forced into painful positions. You can avoid the spot that hurts.

Disadvantages

It strengthens mainly at the position in which the exercise is done. If you exercise with your arm bent at a 90-degree angle, your arm will be strengthened mainly in that position. So, for thorough strength training, you should do isometrics in many positions along the range of motion. That's both time-consuming and boring.

It's hard to measure progress. You're probably getting stronger, but there's no way to measure that increase in strength. Without some sort of feedback, it's easy to lose interest.

ISOTONIC EXERCISE

No, it's not the name of a cold drink. It's the term that describes the kind of weight training most of us are familiar with: moving weight through space. Lifting free weights, using weight machines, working against the resistance of springs or elastic material—all of these are types of isotonic exercise.

The least familiar of these, at least for people who are used to fitness facilities, are the exercises involving elastic materials like Thera-Band, surgical tubing, and inner tubes. We'll suggest specific exercises using these materials in a moment, but first some general advantages and disadvantages of the technique.

Advantages

The materials are portable. It might be tough to pack a set of barbells in your overnight bag, but it's mighty simple to slip in a couple of lengths of surgical tubing. You can take the elastic to work with you, on vacation, even set it up in the car. You can take it and use it just about anywhere.

They're cheap. Just a few bucks is all you need to set yourself up with a variety of strengths of Thera-Band or the other kinds of elastic materials. With the exception of isometric exercise, it's the most economical of all weight training techniques.

Disadvantages

They're inexact. You can do a pretty good workout with elastics, but you can't measure how much weight you're lifting. That may or may not be a problem, depending on the reasons why you're exercising.

They may break. It may not happen often, but these materials sometimes do break. More likely is the possibility that they may work loose from their tether. In either case, they can snap out at the person using them. A good caution is *never* to face the elastic material when you're working out.

They provide increasing resistance past the midpoint in the range of motion, when you're becoming weaker. As you stretch the elastic, it becomes more resistant. For that reason, it can be surprisingly easy to overdo working out with elastics and pay for it the next morning with memorable soreness—but rarely real injuries.

They're difficult to use with large muscles. It's awfully hard to get a good workout for muscles in your thigh, hip, and back, for example, because the elastics simply can't provide enough resistance to do much good. For strengthening large muscle groups, it's best to go on to other techniques.

Training for Flexibility

Flexibility and strength go hand in hand. That is, they should. By any practical measurement, in terms of what you use your strength for, strength without flexibility isn't worth all that much. But it's functional flexibility that counts, not necessarily being able to touch your head to your knees or do splits.

For example, in your quest for a more powerful tennis serve you may have put on all kinds of muscle, but that increased strength isn't going to help you much if you're not flexible enough to rear back and hit the ball. You're also going to have trouble with an overhead, and your ground strokes may suffer as well. Likewise, you may be able to bench press more weight than you ever dreamed, but if you can't twist and bend enough to complete a backswing on the golf tee, you may not be able to drive one yard longer than before. Flexibility is fully as important as strength.

But flexibility for its own sake does not have any practical value at all. In fact, flexibility for its own sake may cause more problems than it solves.

There's no ideal amount of flexibility. Unless your activity demands it, what does it matter if you can touch your head to your knees? For a dancer that kind of extreme flexibility is important. For a gymnast it's important. For a tennis player, golfer, runner, swimmer, or walker—that is, for most of us—it most likely isn't. In fact, what does it matter if you can hardly touch your hands to your knees, even—unless your activity demands it? There's simply no relationship in the uninjured person between flexibility, or the lack of it, and the risk of injury. You may be the stiffest person in the world, but if your activity doesn't demand more flexibility, and you're not suffering in other ways, why increase flexibility for the sake of bending like a pretzel?

In fact, striving for flexibility for its own sake can cause injury. Extreme bending and stretching can be hard on joints, tendons, and ligaments. If you do decide to become extremely flexible, take great care that you do the stretching exercises slowly and gently. Progress gradually, more slowly than may seem necessary, so as to guard against overstressing your joints.

When you do weight training, be sure to work on flexibility as well. That means stretching gently before and after working out. And be sure that you lift through an entire range of motion. Certain devices, like Nautilus machines, encourage you to use your entire range of motion and to stretch when beginning and ending a lift. Others may not, and free weights certainly don't. In such cases, be sure to do more than simply lift through that limited range where you're strongest. You may be able to lift more weight that way, but you'll do your body a disservice. It's the kind of workout that causes people to become muscle-bound. Your muscles may look great but not have much practical usefulness. Exercise your muscles from full extension to full retraction and back again. Remember, flexibility is like strength: if you don't use it, you lose it.

The Exercises—Which to Do, When, and How

The following exercises are organized in two ways. First, they're arranged according to parts of the body: a section of exercises for the muscles of the ankle and calf, another for the knee and thigh, another for the hip and groin area, and so on. And each of these sections begins by suggesting what sports and exercise activities these muscles make possible. For example, beginning on page 200, in the Knee and Thigh section you'll find out that the quadriceps muscles in the thigh allow you to run, jump, and walk —pretty basic stuff. You'll also find out that the quads are the most important muscles for cycling and for even more specialized functions such as pushing off while serving a tennis ball or absorbing shock while skiing. So if your fitness goals involve running, jumping, or walking—a pretty safe bet—there's simply no more important muscles in the body to keep strong and flexible than the quads.

But if you've read Chapter 4, How to Train for Your Favorite Sports Activity, you already know that. Chapter 4 took a different tack, presenting popular athletic activities and suggesting specific exercises to enhance them. The sections on running, walking, and cycling, among others, have already directed you to specific quadriceps strengthening and flexibility exercises. You can arrive at the same place using either approach.

So, number one, the sections are arranged according to parts of the body. Number two, the exercises themselves begin with the most accessible, simplest exercises, those requiring no equipment, and continue on through more sophisticated exercises requiring limited equipment, all the way to exercises requiring the most equipment and the most instruction. So let's say you're a runner (or a walker, cyclist, tennis player, or skier—when it comes to quads the list is almost endless) and you're interested in strengthening your quads. Beginning on page 201 you'll find quadriceps strengthening exercises you can do anytime, at home or at work, on the highway or in an airplane, in a meeting or in bed, with no equipment, no preparation, and no bother. You'll also find exercises requiring careful instruction, precise technique, and equipment you'll find only at a fitness facility. And with all these exercises you'll find stretches to do before and after, so that you're working on flexibility and strengthening at the same time. You'll also find a listing of possible problems to look out for as well as suggestions on how to solve those problems so as to achieve the best possible workout.

So the progression goes from simple and accessible to sophisticated and involved—but *not* from least to most beneficial. That's the beauty of it all. It's *not* necessary to start with the first exercises and progress to the later ones. In most cases, if you're not injured to begin with, *any of these exercises can be as good for you as any other*. It all depends on what your fitness goals are and how much time and energy you have to devote to working out. Simply do those exercises that are most convenient and congenial *for you*—this is a book of *personal* fitness training, after all. If you like the exercises and they give results, stay there. If you want to try others, that's fine too. There may be no reason to move from exercise to exercise—*unless you want to*.

The point is that everyone is different, with different fitness goals and different ability to achieve those goals. And different people have different access to equipment and are able to devote different amounts of time to working out. All we can do is suggest exercises—you're the only one who knows how they feel and what they're doing for you. This is a partnership, one that requires trust and good judgment on both sides. Don't feel obligated to follow these prescriptions to the letter. Listen to your body. If the weights we suggest are too heavy for you, by all means go lighter. If they're not heavy enough, increase your load carefully. If you want to do more or fewer repetitions than we suggest, you're the boss. Just be smart about your body and, if in doubt, don't overdo. It's much wiser to go too slowly rather than too quickly.

Read the recommendations that follow carefully, weigh them in the light of your own means and goals, and go ahead from there. And rest assured that every suggestion is made with your best interests in mind. The point of this book, after all, is to provide you with your own personalized fitness workout. Good luck—and enjoy.

General Exercise Prescriptions

What follow are prescriptions of how many exercises to do and how often to do them. As you get more and more involved in your training, you'll gradually become your own personal trainer, your own best expert. At the least you can use these prescriptions as a starting point; at the most, if you follow them to the letter, they won't steer you wrong.

ISOMETRIC EXERCISES

• Hold all isometric exercises for at least six seconds. Do five to seven exercises at a time, at least three times a day.

ISOTONIC EXERCISES

• *Without weight or resistance*—gradually work up to three sets of twelve exercises daily.
• *With weight or resistance*—before using weights, be sure to read carefully any safety and operating directions and ask for instruction and supervision. Do not do the same heavy lifts more than three days a week.

For Strength

• First, find a weight or resistance that you can lift eight times but not as many as twelve times.
• Gradually work up to three daily sets of eight to twelve reps at that weight.
• When you can handle twelve reps at that weight, do two or

three daily sets of eight to twelve reps of a weight increased by no more than ten percent of your original weight.

• Do not progress to a heavier weight more quickly than every third workout day.

For Endurance

• First find out how much weight or resistance you can lift by starting with a weight you *know* you can handle, then adding to it. Hold for two to three seconds. That's your single lift maximum weight.

• Do two to four daily sets of thirty-plus reps at 50 percent maximum weight.

• When you can handle that weight, do two to four daily sets of thirty-plus reps of a weight increased by no more than 10 percent of the original weight.

• Do not progress to a heavier weight more quickly than every third workout day.

For Weight Training Combined with Other Exercises

• First find out how much weight or resistance you can lift by starting with a weight you *know* you can handle, then adding to it. Hold for two to three seconds. That's your single lift maximum weight.

For an average person

• Do one set daily of fifteen to twenty reps on each machine at 50 percent of your maximum weight.

• When you can handle that weight, do one set daily of fifteen to twenty reps at an increased weight of no more than 10 percent of the original weight.

For an athlete

• Do one set daily of fifteen to twenty reps on each machine at 70 percent of your maximum weight.

• When you can handle that weight, do one set daily of fifteen to twenty reps at an increased weight of no more than 10 percent of the original weight.

• Do not progress to a heavier weight more quickly than every third workout day.

After an Injury

• First, find out how much weight or resistance you can lift and hold for two to three seconds. That's your single lift maximum weight.

• Do two or three daily sets of ten reps at 50 percent of maximum weight.

• When you can handle that weight, do two or three daily sets of ten reps at 75 percent of maximum weight.

• When you can handle that weight, do two or three daily sets of up to ten reps at 100 percent of maximum weight.

• When you can handle that weight, do two or three daily sets of up to ten reps of an increased weight of no more than 10 percent over your original maximum weight.

• Do not progress to a heavier weight more quickly than every third workout day.

The prescriptions should be self-explanatory. For an example, let's follow one of them through from beginning to end.

A Blueprint

In Chapter 4 (page 130), we recommended that runners do the endurance training workout to strengthen their quadriceps muscles. Here's how to start. First, determine your single lift maximum weight as the endurance prescription suggests. You do that by finding a weight you can hold for two to three seconds. A runner using the leg extension machine, say, might be able to hold *100 pounds* for that long. That's the weight to base the rest of your workout on.

To begin with, do two to four daily sets of thirty or more repetitions at 50 percent of your maximum weight. In this case, that's *50 pounds*, right?—that is, half of the original 100 pounds. So the first level of training will involve doing thirty or more leg extensions lifting 50 pounds, two to four times a day—a pretty good workout.

Once you're able to handle that amount of weight—and that means no excessive straining, no hurting while you do the exercise or afterward, no excessive soreness the next day—you can begin to increase the amount you're lifting. *Don't move on until you're ready,* never more quickly than every third workout day. There's no special virtue in progressing quickly, when you're not ready to progress. All of us move at our own pace. If you're not lifting as much as the person who preceded you on the machine, it means nothing. Stick to your own pace and your own goals. You'll avoid injury that way and be happier in the process.

When you're ready to move on, increase your weight by no more than 10 percent of the original weight. In this case, that means 10 percent of the original 100 pounds—or 10 pounds. So your next sets will involve lifting 50 pounds plus 10 pounds—in other words, 60 pounds.

When you're again ready to lift a heavier weight—and that means no sooner than three workout days later, remember—add another 10 pounds. Now you're lifting 70 pounds. And so it goes until you arrive at your original 100-pound standard. When that happens, you'll find that you're strong enough to establish a heavier single lift maximum weight. And go on from there.

The other workout prescriptions are similarly straightforward and easy to follow. Refer to them as you work out.

A final suggestion: don't be overwhelmed by the possibilities here. There are lots of exercises, lots of combinations to help you improve your level of fitness and performance in your favorite sport. You could spend all day, every day, working out. You could devote all your time to it—or so it may seem.

Take it easy. The idea is to integrate your personal fitness workout into the rest of your life. Most of us have only so much time to devote to exercise, so use that time wisely. Don't go overboard. Stay afloat and on course. Begin gradually, proceed intelligently, remember your goals. In general, don't work out more often than every other day, and don't go faster than the prescriptions suggest. That's the way to approach it. That's the way to get results.

Good luck and good exercising.

The Calf and Ankle

The motion of the ankle is mostly controlled by muscles next door, in the calf and lower leg. The calf muscles are called the gastrocnemius and the soleus. Below them and to the outside of the leg are the peroneal muscles. These are the most prominent of the muscles that allow you to move your ankle—to twist, turn up and down, roll in and out. They also hold your ankle steady.

Calf and lower leg muscles provide propulsion for running, jumping and walking. Without strong calf and lower leg muscles, it's difficult to do any activities based on these movements successfully.

These muscles help pull your body forward when you plant your foot, as in cross-country skiing or high-speed walking. They stabilize the ankle for cutting and turning. They allow you to point and rise up on your toes, as in dance and many other activities—for example, when kicking in freestyle swimming.

Before beginning the exercises, review the General Exercise Prescriptions in the introduction to this chapter (page 183).

Strengthening the Calf

ISOMETRIC EXERCISES

Toe Raises

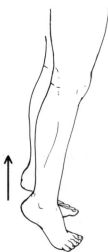

Stand with knees straight and raise your heels slightly (about ½ inch) off the floor. Hold for as long as possible. When you become stronger, try doing one leg at a time.

This exercise strengthens the gastrocnemius, the larger of the two calf muscles.

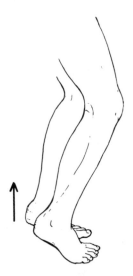

Stand with knees slightly bent and raise your heels slightly (about ½ inch) off the floor. Hold for as long as possible. When you become stronger, try doing one leg at a time.

This exercise strengthens the soleus, the smaller of the two calf muscles.

ISOTONIC EXERCISES

Straight-Knee Toe Raises

Stand flatfooted and, keeping your legs straight and your feet pointed straight ahead, rise up and down onto your toes. This exercise uses your own body weight for resistance. You can do the exercise one leg at a time, and if necessary use the off leg to help out if the exercise is too difficult for one leg alone.

This exercise strengthens the larger muscle in the calf, the gastrocnemius.

To enhance the motion, do the exercise on a slant board or step onto a higher board. You can gradually increase the angle of the slant board or height of the step board.

You can do this exercise with both legs at once or, if one side is weak, with one leg at a time.

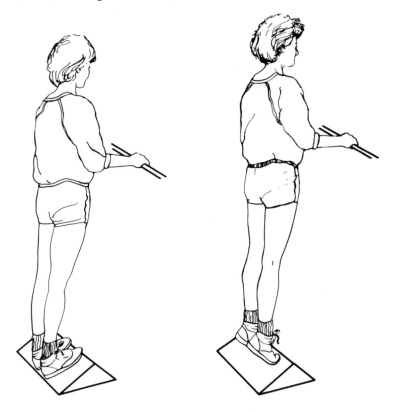

This exercise combines stretching with strengthening, as every time you sink down you do a gravity-assisted stretch. For that reason, be sure to do the exercise carefully and gently. Don't bounce into toe raises.

Problem: Pain in the back of the ankle at the top of the lift.
Solution: Don't rise up so high.
Stand with your toes on the block so you can start the lift in a slightly stretched position.
Problem: Difficulty in balancing.
Solution: Rest your fingertips on the back of a chair or other support.
Problem: Pain in the back of the ankle or calf at the beginning of the lift.
Solution: Decrease the height of the block or angle of the slant board—your toes are too high, stretching your Achilles tendon and calf muscle too far.

Bent-Knee Toe Raises

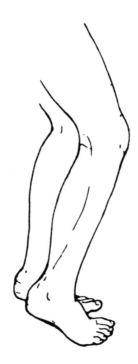

Stand flatfooted as before, and, with knees slightly bent and your feet pointed straight ahead, rise up and down onto your toes. This exercise strengthens the smaller muscle in the calf, the soleus.

It may be hard to do the exercise on a slant board or step board, as bending your knees already flexes the ankles. They may not be able to flex that much more in order to step onto the exercise boards.

You can enhance either exercise by carrying dumbbells or placing a barbell on your shoulder.

Problem: Knee pain.
Solution: Increase or lessen how much you bend your knee until the pain is gone.
Strengthen the quadriceps (see page 201).
Problem: Pain in the front of your ankle at the beginning of the exercise.
Solution: Don't bend your knees so far—thereby straightening the ankle.

Squats

This exercise strengthens quads primarily, and hip muscles and calves as well. Squats are a combination exercise—an exercise that works out more than one muscle group at the same time.

Start by slightly bending your legs and gradually go lower as you become stronger. You don't have to squat all the way to benefit from the exercise.

Keep your feet pointed straight ahead, about shoulder width apart. Don't flex your knee beyond 90 degrees. (Note that with your thigh parallel to the floor, your knee is flexed beyond 90 degrees.) Don't arch your back. Arching your back invites injury —keep it flat.

You can enhance the exercise by carrying dumbbells or placing a barbell on your shoulders. The barbell may be in front of or behind your neck—either position is effective.

Lunges

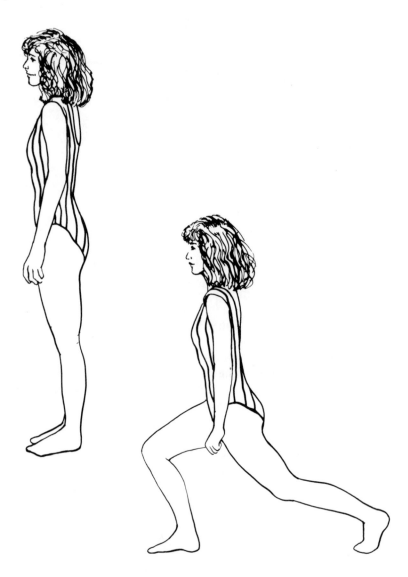

Lunges strengthen quads primarily, and hip muscles and calves as well.

Keep your feet pointed straight ahead, about shoulder width apart. Don't arch your back. Arching your back invites injury—keep it flat.

You can enhance the exercise by carrying dumbbells or placing a barbell on your shoulders. The barbell may be in front of or behind your neck—either position is effective.

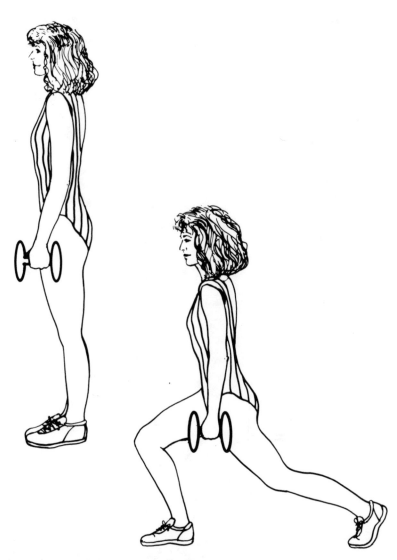

Problem: Pain around and behind kneecap.
Solution: Stop motion before reaching painful spot.
Change foot position. Usually, turning in slightly will help. Occasionally, turning out will help.
Problem: Back pain or back arching.
Solution: Lessen weight.
Strengthen abdominal muscles (see page 247).
Do pelvic tilts (see page 51).
Wear an abdominal belt.

USING WEIGHT TRAINING MACHINES

Toe Raises

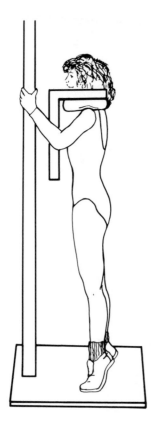

Place pads on shoulders or on knees and rise up and down onto your toes. These machines provide an easy way to add weight or increase motion. They can stretch as well as strengthen.

With the standing machines you can do the exercise with your knees straight or bent.

There are a number of variations of toe raise machines. Any one of them will provide a good strengthening workout for your calf muscles. The only difference among these machines is really the position of the knees. Bent knees emphasize the smaller muscle in the calf, the soleus. Straight knees emphasize the upper calf, or gastrocnemius muscle.

Whether you're sitting, lying down, or standing does not influence the effectiveness of the exercise. Doing the exercise sitting or lying on your back places the "weight" at your feet. Doing the exercise standing means the weight must be borne by your shoulder—that might hurt.

Problem: Pain over the ball of your foot.
Solution: Wear shoes.
Wear shoes with a slightly stiffer sole.
Problem: (On sitting machine) Pain above the knee where the weight rests.
Solution: Move the pad slightly higher on your thigh.
Place a folded towel between the pad and your thigh. (The folded towel should be slightly larger than the pad so as to distribute the weight over a larger area on your leg.)
Problem: Pain in the back of your ankle at the top of the lift.
Solution: Don't rise up so high.

OTHER STRENGTHENING EXERCISES

Leg presses, squats, and lunges strengthen a number of muscles at the same time. They don't strengthen calf muscles in particular, but they can be better than nothing. Because you use your calves in combination with other muscles in these exercises, you more closely duplicate real-life situations.

Problem: Back pain.
Solution: Decrease weight.
Decrease the speed at which you do the exercise—there's a greater tendency to overarch your back when you work out quickly.
Strengthen your stomach muscles (see page 247).
Problem: Pain in your ankle or calf at the beginning of the exercise.
Solution: Move weights away from your body so that your ankle isn't as flexed at the beginning of the exercise.
Problem: You can't feel the workout in your calves.
Solution: Try a machine that exercises the calf muscles in particular—do toe raises, for example (page 194).

Strengthening the Lower Leg

USING EXERCISE AIDS

The following exercises strengthen the peroneal muscles and other small muscles that help provide motion for the ankle, using such aids as Thera-Band, surgical tubing, and inner tubes.

Pull foot to the outside and up against resistance.

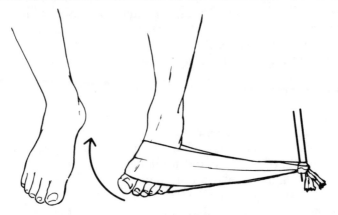

Pull foot to the inside and up against resistance, keeping your toes pointed.

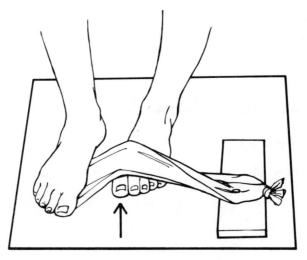

Pull foot up and toward you against resistance.

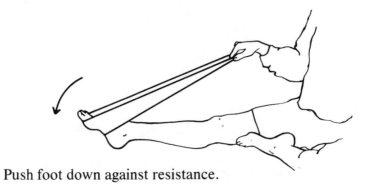

Push foot down against resistance.

Problem: Pain at the beginning or end of the exercise.
Solution: Shorten your range of motion.
Problem: Pain in the knee.
Solution: Stop twisting your leg below the knee.
Problem: Pain in your ankle.
Solution: Point your toe more or less according to how your ankle feels.

CYCLING

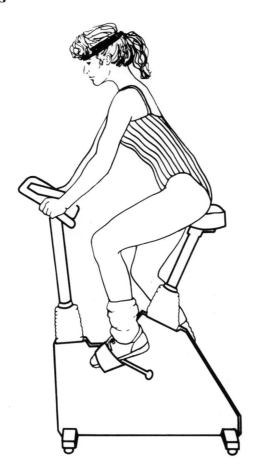

Cycling doesn't strengthen the calf and lower leg muscles solely, but it's a good general exercise for all the muscles in the body from the hips down. During the downstroke, the calf muscles are particularly involved, if only to hold your ankle steady so as to transmit the force from your quadriceps to the pedal, and during the upstroke the muscles closer to the ankle are involved.

STRETCHING

The Knee and Thigh

The knee itself contains no muscles—few joints do. Its motion
is controlled by the muscles next door, in the thigh. These muscles
are called the quadriceps and hamstrings, and they're two of the

body's largest. They work together to straighten and flex your knee as well as to hold it steady. They're also involved when you flex and extend your hip.

Pretty basic stuff. When it comes to athletics, these functions translate into movements that are at the heart of just about any sporting activity.

The thigh muscles are the base muscles for running, jumping, and walking. It's tough to think of more than a few activities that don't require at least one of these skills. In other words, if you're to be successful doing any of the great majority of sport and fitness activities, you must have strong thigh muscles.

They're the base muscles for cycling—particularly the quadriceps. The well-developed quads of accomplished cyclists are the tip-off.

These muscles enable you to push off while serving in tennis—particularly the quadriceps. They serve as shock absorbers while skiing—particularly the quadriceps. They are used in running backward—particularly the hamstrings—a quite useful skill in tennis, soccer, basketball, football (especially for defensive backs), etc.

Before beginning the exercises, review the General Exercise Prescriptions in the introduction to this chapter (page 183).

Strengthening the Quadriceps

ISOMETRIC EXERCISES

Quad Sets

For running, walking, jumping, cycling, kicking, and skiing.

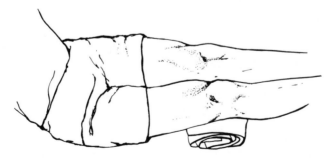

Extend your leg and tighten your quadriceps as much as possible. Hold for at least six seconds.

Bent-Knee Quad Sets

While sitting, push your foot into the floor as though trying to get up. Hold for at least six seconds.

Wall Sitting

With your back against a wall, support yourself in a semicrouch, as though sitting in a chair. Hold for as long as possible. You can do these exercises in a variety of positions and angles.

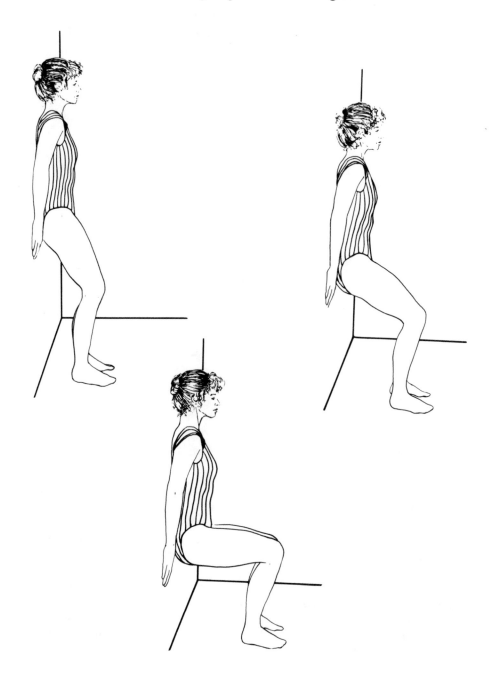

ISOTONIC EXERCISES

Squats

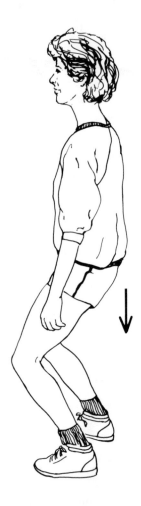

This exercise strengthens quads primarily, and hip muscles and calves as well. Squats are a combination exercise—an exercise that works out more than one muscle group at the same time.

Start by slightly bending the legs and gradually go lower as you become stronger. You don't have to squat all the way to benefit from the exercise.

Keep your feet pointed straight ahead, about shoulder width apart. Don't flex your knee beyond 90 degrees. (Note that with your thigh parallel to the floor, your knee is flexed beyond 90 degrees.) Don't arch your back. Arching your back invites injury —keep it flat.

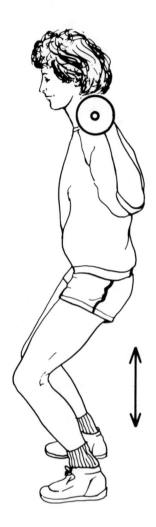

You can enhance the exercise by carrying dumbbells or placing a barbell on your shoulders. The barbell may be in front of or behind your neck—either position is effective.

Lunges

Lunges strengthen quads primarily, and hip muscles and calves as well.

The forward leg is the one being strengthened.

Keep your feet pointed straight ahead, about shoulder width apart. Don't flex your knee beyond 90 degrees. Don't arch your back. Arching your back invites injury—keep it flat.

You can enhance the exercise by carrying dumbbells or placing a barbell on your shoulders. The barbell may be in front of or behind your neck—either position is effective.

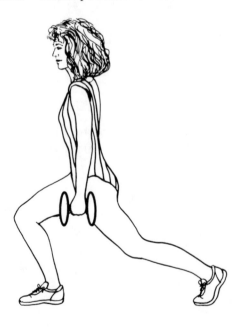

Problem: Pain around and behind kneecap.
Solution: Stop motion before reaching painful spot.
Change foot position. Usually, turning in slightly will help. Occasionally, turning out will help.
Problem: Back pain or back arching.
Solution: Lessen weight.
Strengthen abdominal muscles (see page 247).
Do pelvic tilts (see page 51).
Wear abdominal belt.

USING EXERCISE AIDS

Weight Boot

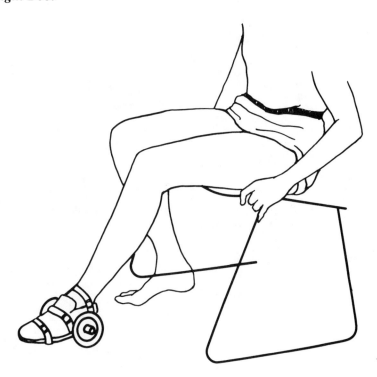

Heavy weights may be more than your ankle can handle. Be careful. You can use a weight boot for knee extensions, but be sure to let your foot down to the floor between lifts. If you don't, the weight boot will tend to pull your knee apart—the heavier the boot, the more stress on your knee.

Elastic Material or Wall Pulleys

As you extend your knee the angle of pull changes, often lessening the resistance.

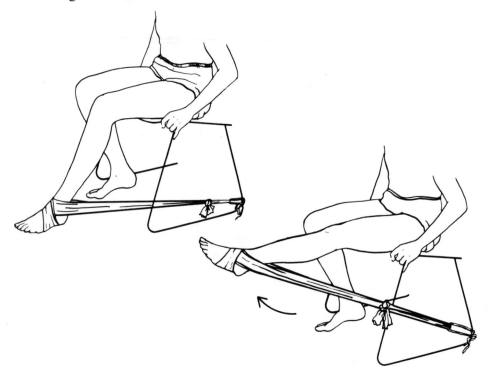

It may be difficult to attach the device to your leg or foot. (See illustration below for how to do it.)

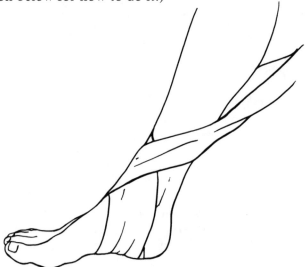

USING WEIGHT TRAINING MACHINES

Knee Extensions

Place the pad or weight just above your ankle on the front of the leg. Short people may wind up with the pad across their foot or ankle. This position may produce too much weight for the area. If possible, adjust the machine accordingly. If not possible, look for another machine.

If your leg strength is approximately equal side by side, and you're not injured, you may lift with both legs at the same time. If not, lift with one leg at a time. If your legs are not similarly strong, any inequalities will remain unless you exercise each side separately.

Problem: Tendency to arch your back.
Solution: Lessen weight.
             Press the small of your back into the backrest of the machine.
Problem: Tendency to thrust hips forward.
Solution: Lessen weight.
             Hold on to handles on machine.
             Use waist strap (provided on some machines).

Problem: Tendency to bounce into lift.
Solution: Lessen weight.
Begin lift slowly.
Adjust the machine so you start the lift with legs partially extended, where you're stronger.
Problem: Inability to bend knee far enough to get into machine.
Solution: Adjust the seat back so you sit more upright.
Work on quadriceps flexibility (see page 219).
Adjust the machine so that you begin the lift with legs partially extended.
Problem: Inability to carry weight to fully extended position.
Solution: Lessen weight.
Problem: Pain all the way through lift.
Solution: Lessen weight.
You may be injured—rehab injured part.
Problem: Pain at specific point in lift.
Solution: Lessen weight.
Strengthen vastus medialis muscle (see page 201).
Do one set up to the position that causes pain. Then readjust the machine and do a second set from the position of pain to full extension.
Use the good leg to support weight to beyond the painful spot and then go back to lifting with the bad leg.

Sitting Leg Presses

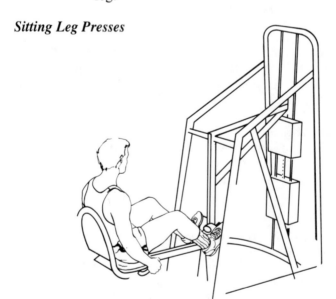

This exercise primarily strengthens the quadriceps. You can adjust the seat back and forth for more or less knee bend.

Standing/Lying Leg Presses

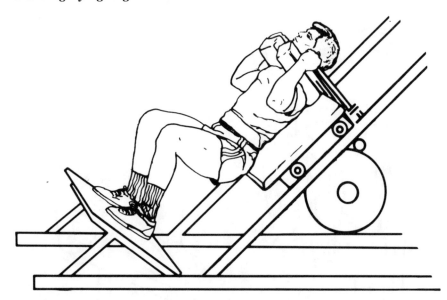

These strengthen the quadriceps and hip extensor muscles (gluteals) as well.

Inverted Leg Presses

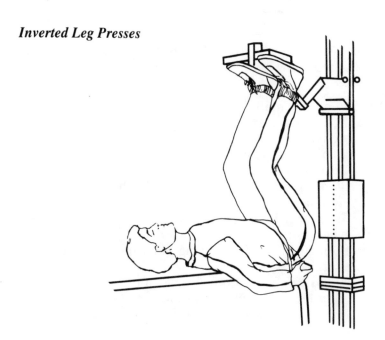

Usually not equipped with cams to even out resistance through the range of motion.

Single-Leg Presses

Better for assuring equal strength in both legs. The other varieties may allow cheating without the exerciser being aware of it.

Problem: Can't begin lift.
Solution: Lessen weight.
Adjust seat away from weights so your knees and hips aren't bent so far.
Problem: Back pain or back arching.
Solution: Stabilize upper body by using handholds or waist restraining belt.
Strengthen abdominal muscles.
Problem: Knee pain.
Solution: Strengthen quads by doing other quad strengthening exercises.
Avoid painful portion of range of motion.
Alter foot position. Try turning feet in or out.
Move seat back from weights so that your knee doesn't have to bend so much. The farther the bend, the more pressure on the back of the kneecap. (Just the amount of bending necessary to climb stairs places two and a half times your body weight across

the back of the kneecap—an area roughly the size of a quarter.)

Problem: Pain in the front of your ankle (probably from squatting too deeply).

Solution: Move seat away from weights.
Wear shoes with raised heel. (Prevents ankle from bending so severely.)

The purpose of stair climbing machines, cross-country ski trainers, exercise bicycles, and rowing machines is to aerobically exercise and increase endurance of thigh muscles, among others.

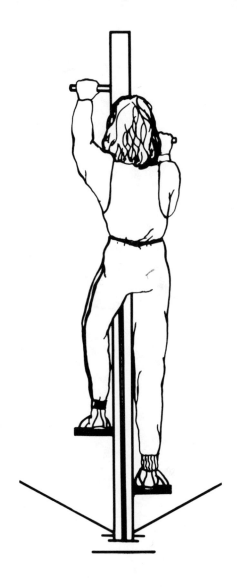

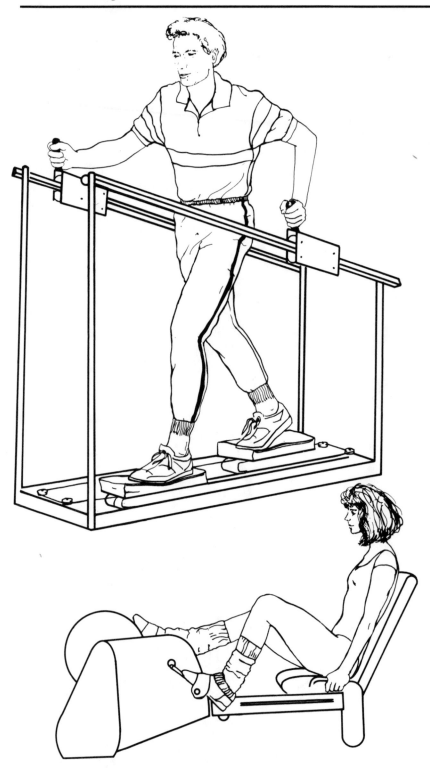

All strengthen quadriceps and gluteal muscles simultaneously. How much these muscles are strengthened depends on the position of your hips. For example, sitting down to exercise on a bike primarily strengthens the quads, while exercising standing up brings the gluteals into play more readily.

Some of these machines relieve strain on the quads by working in a reciprocal fashion. For example, exercise bikes with toe clips allow you to push down on one side while you pull up on the other.

Strengthening the Hamstrings

For running, walking, jumping, cycling, kicking, and skiing.

ISOMETRIC EXERCISES

Hamstring Sets

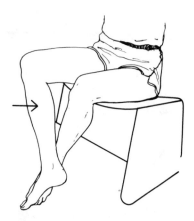

While standing or sitting, push the calf of one leg against the other leg. You can also do the exercise by pushing your heel into the floor or against a chair leg.

ISOTONIC EXERCISES

Hamstring Curls

You can do hamstring curls lying on your stomach, but the most effective way is standing.

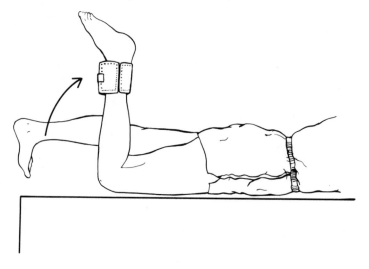

USING EXERCISE AIDS

You can use a weight boot or ankle weights, but be careful. The heavier the weight, the more stress on your knee and ankle.

Doing many reps with light ankle weights can increase endurance.

> **Problem:** You may have a tendency to flex your hip rather than bend only your knee, thereby diluting the strengthening effect on the hamstrings.
>
> **Solution:** Stand facing the wall with your thighs and the front of your pelvis pushed into the wall. In that way, you're forced to use your hamstrings only.

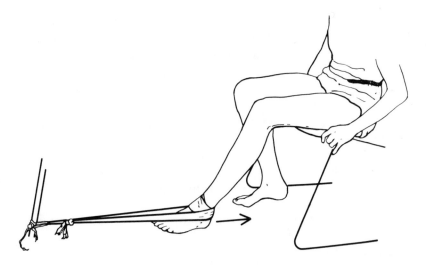

It can be difficult to work through more than the midrange of motion, as resistance becomes greater toward the end of the exercise.

USING WEIGHT TRAINING MACHINES

Machines differ primarily with regard to the position of the hip —sitting, lying, or in between. While you're sitting, your hamstrings are stretched. When you're lying down or standing, your hamstrings are in a relaxed position. Standing may be the most functional position of all. We use our hams for such activities as running and walking, all in the upright position, and it makes sense to exercise the muscles in as near their functional position as possible.

Be careful that the weight or pad isn't too high on the back of your leg. It should rest just above your ankle. This placement can be a problem for short people, as sometimes the machines aren't adjustable.

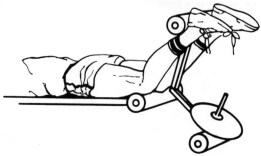

If both legs are equally strong, you can do the lifts with both at the same time. If not, exercise one leg at a time. It's too easy to let your stronger side compensate for your weaker side when lifting with both legs.

Problem: Difficulty in getting into machine because hamstrings are too tight.
Solution: Stretch hamstrings.
Adjust backrest so you're leaning back, thereby relaxing hamstrings.
Problem: Back pain or back arching at the beginning of the lift. (Especially on machines requiring you to lie flat on your stomach, when hams are not strong enough to initiate the lift.)
Solution: Lessen weight.
Place pillow beneath hips.
Use machine with bench bent to allow 10 to 20 degrees of hip flexion.

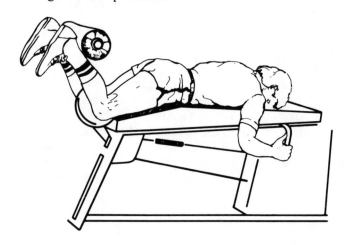

Problem: Back pain or back arching at the end of the lift—with or without pain in the quadriceps. (Probably because your quads are too tight to allow enough knee bending, or your hams are too weak to handle the weight at the end of the lift.)

Solution: Stretch quads (strengthen if weak).
Place pillow beneath hips.
Work on bent bench. Remember to keep your back flat.

Problem: Pain in the back of the knee when your leg is straight (on sitting machines). (Probably from tight hamstrings.)

Solution: Stretch hamstrings.
Adjust backrest to allow you to lean back.

Problem: Pain in the back of the knee when it's bent at the end of the lift.

Solution: Turn your feet in or out to relieve pain.

Backtracking

Pedaling an exercise bike backward (if your bike allows you to do so) or running or walking backward is a good hamstring exercise. It can also be a hazardous activity on rough or uneven ground. Be sure to glance behind you from time to time.

STRETCHING

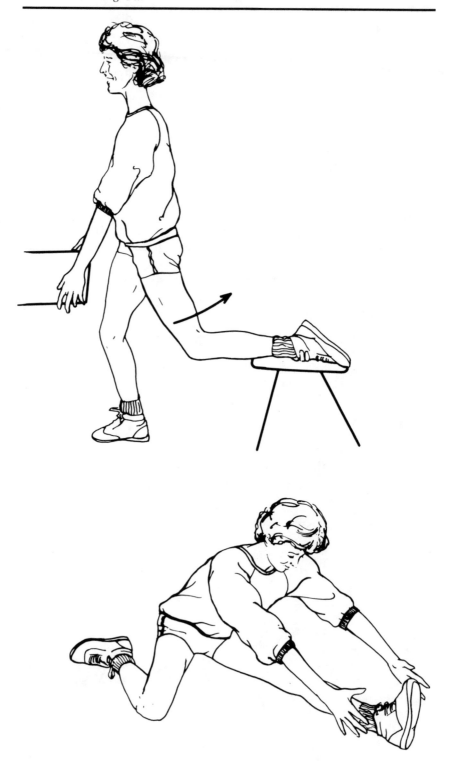

The Hip and Groin

Any number of muscles crisscross the hips and adjoining areas of the body. In fact, the pelvis, the ring of bone containing the hip joint, anchors all manner of muscles and bones, providing a transition from your body's torso to your legs. Chief among these muscles are the gluteals, in the buttocks, the groin or adductor muscles in the inner thigh, and the iliopsoas (ilio-so-as) muscle, which runs across the hips from the lower abdomen to deep in the groin.

These muscles work together to extend and flex the hips, to rotate the legs in and out, and to allow you to pull your legs apart and push them together. And they stabilize the hips and pelvis, playing a significant role in posture and gait.

The hip and groin muscles are the stabilizers and movers in all running, jumping, and kicking activities.

These muscles initiate the turning jumps in dance and figure skating, and the cutting maneuvers in soccer, tennis, and basketball. They are used in virtually every aerobic activity—walking, running, aerobic dance, rowing, skiing, and, to a lesser extent, cycling and swimming. The iliopsoas flexes the hip so you can kick a soccer ball straight ahead. By its strength and endurance, the iliopsoas determines the speed at which you can sprint. (You can't run any faster than you can bring your leg forward.)

Before beginning the exercises, review the General Exercise Prescriptions in the introduction to this chapter (page 183).

Strengthening the Iliopsoas

ISOMETRIC EXERCISES

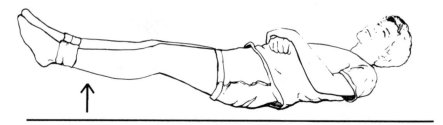

Lie on your back and raise your heels off the ground. Be careful to keep your lower back flat against the surface. This exercise may tend to increase swayback.

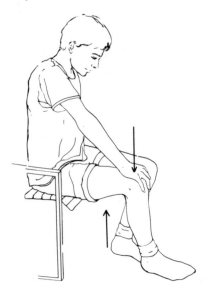

Sit with your hand on your knee. Press down with your hand and attempt to raise your thigh against your hand. You can do this exercise with both legs at once or one leg at a time.

Stand with your thighs and knees pressed into a wall. Attempt to push your thighs forward. You can do this exercise with both legs at once or one leg at a time. Both the front of the pelvis *and* the front of the thigh should be pushed into the wall. Be careful to keep your back flat. The tendency is to press the thigh forward and arch the back, pulling the front of the pelvis away from the wall.

> **Problem:** Back pain.
> **Solution:** Decrease the force of the exercise.
> Do stomach strengthening exercises and pelvic tilts (page 247).
> Concentrate on holding your back flat—don't over-arch.
> Concentrate on pressing the front of your pelvis into the wall.

ISOTONIC EXERCISES

Note: All the exercises to follow have the potential to produce or worsen low back problems by causing you to overarch your back while working out. It's important that your stomach muscles be strong to counteract this tendency. As a rule of thumb, if you can't do ten slow curl-ups (see page 247), you probably shouldn't do hip flexor strengthening exercises.

In any case, be sure to guard against overarching your back.

While standing, raise your knee in front of your body.

Sit-Ups

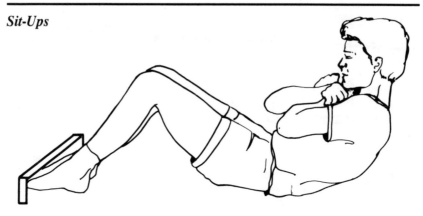

Do sit-ups with your feet hooked and knees straight or bent.

Problem: Back pain.
Solution: Strengthen your stomach muscles (see page 247).
Be sure the small of your back is pressed into the floor
—don't overarch.
Try bending your knees more or less.
Don't do the exercise.

Do sit-ups with your feet hooked and knees straight. This version is the more difficult to do. Both exercises strengthen the iliopsoas muscle primarily. Be sure to hold your back flat. Do not
overarch while doing the exercise. You should attempt this exercise only when you are able to do a full sequence of three sets of
twelve repetitions of the bent-knee, feet-hooked sit-ups.

Problem: Back pain.
Solution: Strengthen your stomach muscles (see page 247).
Be sure the small of your back is pressed into the floor
—don't overarch.
Don't do the exercise.

While lying on your back with your knees straight, lift your legs into the air. Be sure to keep your back flat.

Problem: Back pain.
Solution: Be sure the small of your back is pressed into the floor
—don't overarch.
Stop doing the exercise.

Sit-Ups Using an Abdominal Board

Sit-ups on an abdominal board exercise the hip flexor muscles as much as if not more than the abdominal muscles. They should always be done with the knees bent, so as not to encourage over-arching the back. In any case, it may be a good idea to wait until you've built up good strong stomach muscles before working with an abdominal board. (See page 254.)

The idea of abdominal boards is to effectively increase the weight of the upper body by forcing you to work more against gravity.

Be sure to guard against overarching the lower back. Bend your knees when doing the exercise and press your lower back into the abdominal board.

To engage a wider array of hip flexor muscles, gently twist your torso as you rise—do a set to one side and then the other.

Remember that if you're doing sit-ups the main workout for your hip flexor muscles occurs in the last two-thirds of the exercise.

Problem: Back pain.
Solution: Don't overarch your back. Press your lower back into the board, especially at the beginning of the exercise. Strengthen your stomach muscles (see page 247). Stop doing the exercise.

USING WEIGHT TRAINING MACHINES

Thigh Lifts

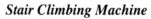

Take care not to overarch your back.

Stair Climbing Machine

Be sure to pull up with your lower foot—that exercises the hip flexors. Rather than strengthening the hip flexor muscles specifically, the VersaClimber® machine offers a combination exercise for a number of muscle groups in the body.

Problem: Knee pain
Solution: Lessen resistance.
Strengthen quadriceps (page 201).

Cross-Country Ski Trainer

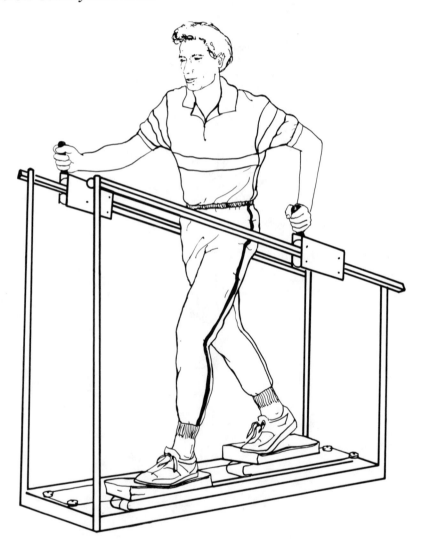

Actively push your back foot forward—that exercises the hip flexor muscles. Like the stair climbing machines, cross-country ski trainers are designed to provide an overall body workout.

Strengthening the Gluteals

ISOMETRIC EXERCISES

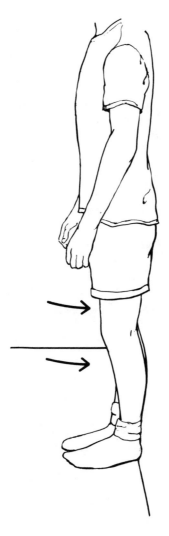

Stand with your back to a wall and attempt to push your heel and calf into the wall.

Lie on your stomach, bend your knee 90 degrees, and lift your leg up. Hold at least six seconds. You can do this exercise with both legs at once or one leg at a time.

Problem: Pain in the small of your back.
Solution: Place a pillow beneath your stomach (not under your hips, as that encourages overarching).

ISOTONIC EXERCISES

Squats

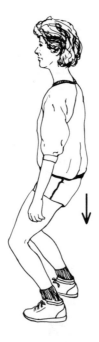

Strengthens quads primarily, and hip muscles and calves as well. Squats are a combination exercise—an exercise that works out more than one muscle group at the same time.

Start by slightly bending legs and gradually go lower as you become stronger. You don't have to squat all the way to benefit from the exercise.

Keep your feet pointed straight ahead, about shoulder width apart. Don't flex your knee beyond 90 degrees. (Note that with your thigh parallel to the floor, your knee is flexed beyond 90 degrees.) Don't arch your back. Arching your back invites injury —keep it flat.

You can enhance the exercise by carrying dumbbells or placing a barbell on your shoulders. The barbell may be in front of or behind your neck—either position is effective.

Lunges

Strengthens quads primarily, and hip muscles and calves as well.

Keep your feet pointed straight ahead, about shoulder width apart. Don't arch your back. Arching your back invites injury—keep it flat.

You can enhance the exercise by carrying dumbbells or placing a barbell on your shoulders. The barbell may be in front of or behind your neck—either position is effective.

Problem: Pain around and behind kneecap.
Solution: Stop motion before reaching painful spot.
Change foot position. Usually, turning in slightly will help. Occasionally, turning out will help.
Problem: Back pain or back arching.
Solution: Lessen weight.
Strengthen abdominal muscles.
Do pelvic tilts.
Wear abdominal belt.

Bent-Leg Lifts

While lying on your stomach with your knees bent, alternately raise your legs into the air. Be careful not to overarch your back.

Problem: Cramping in the back of your thigh.
Solution: Slightly bend or straighten your knee according to how your thigh feels.
Concentration on using the muscles in your buttocks, not your thighs.

USING WEIGHT TRAINING MACHINES

Single-leg machines are probably less likely to result in back problems. They are also more precise in strengthening, especially when one leg is injured—it's impossible to let your good side bear the brunt of the lifting.

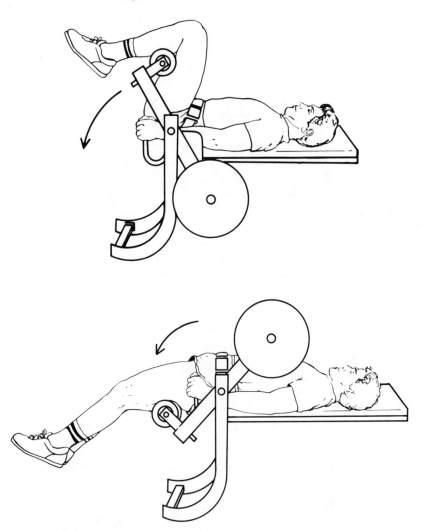

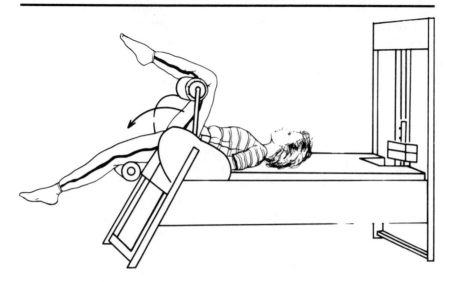

Be sure to place the pad behind the knee. Do not place the pad below the level of the knee—the knee must bear too much strain that way.

Problem: Back pain.
Solution: Lessen weight.
Don't overarch back.
Problem: Knee pain.
Solution: Be sure pads are directly behind knee, not below.

Virtually all squatting, running, rowing, and cycling machines utilize some degree of hip extension—and so strengthen hip extension muscles such as the gluteals. (See illustrations on page 229.) These machines exercise the muscles functionally, as they're used during sports activities, and so may provide an advantage for that reason.

The disadvantage is that it's difficult to know just how much of a workout your hip extensor muscles are receiving—there's no way to measure it.

Strengthening the Abductors

ISOMETRIC EXERCISES

Sit or lie on your back with your knees together. Wrap a belt around your thighs to secure them together and push against the resistance as though trying to pull your thighs apart. This exercise is best done lying down, because then your hips are in the position in which they usually function.

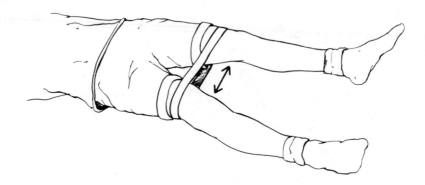

ISOTONIC EXERCISES

Leg Lifts

Lie on your side with your upper leg straight and your lower leg bent at the hip and knee. Lift your leg up toward the ceiling.

Lie on your side with both hips flexed. Lift your leg up from the side. Doing the exercise this way recruits different accessory muscles to help out.

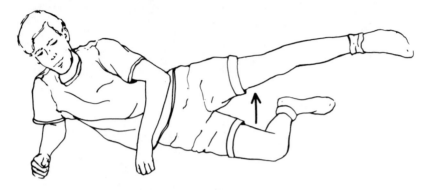

If you find the exercise difficult, try leaning your body upward on your elbow. That way, the exercise is easier to do. It allows you to use your muscles in the midrange of motion, where they're stronger.

If the exercise is still difficult, bend your knee as you lift your leg. That makes things easier.

Be sure to point your toe, and don't overarch your back.

Problem: Pain in your hip from pressure of the floor.
Solution: Use a half-inch-thick mat or folded towel beneath your hip bone.

USING WEIGHT TRAINING MACHINES

Abduction Machines

Be sure to place pads at knee level or above. When pads are lower than the knee, they direct too much force to the knee, especially if it's bent at all, which decreases its stability.

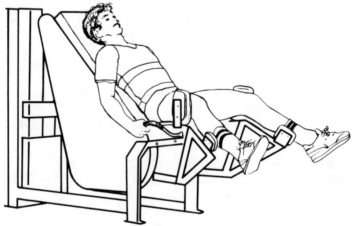

Problem: Knee pain (usually on the outside).
Solution: Pads too low—place pads higher on leg.
Lessen weight.
Strengthen your quadriceps muscles (see page 201).
Problem: Back pain (with standing machines).
Solution: Don't overarch back.

Strengthening the Adductors

ISOMETRIC EXERCISES

Lie flat on your back with a pillow between your knees. Try to crush the pillow by pushing your thighs together.

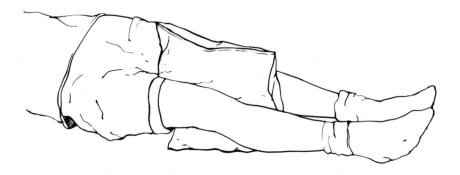

Problem: Painful cramping in your groin and inside of the thigh.
Solution: Use a larger pillow.

ISOTONIC EXERCISES

Side Leg Lifts

Lie on your side with your upper hip and leg bent (to get them out of the way). Lift your lower leg into the air.

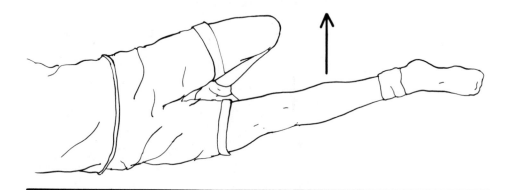

If the exercise is difficult, try it with your lower leg bent.

You may find the exercise uncomfortable for your lower hip-bone. If so, use a mat or stiff mattress.

Problem: Pain in your hip from pressure of the floor.
Solution: Use half-inch-thick mat or folded towel beneath your hipbone.

USING EXERCISE AIDS

Any of the previous exercises can be done using Thera-Band or low wall pulleys. The extra resistance works the muscles harder.

You can use ankle weights as well, but only for those exercises involving a straight knee while lying down. If your knee is bent, the added resistance puts strain on the knee, which increases injury risk.

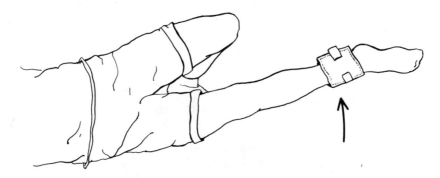

With any exercise aids, the farther down on your leg you put the weights or attach the pulley or elastic, the more they "weigh," thereby increasing resistance and increasing the force exerted on the knee.

Problem: Knee pain.
Solution: Lessen weight.
Place weight or strap higher on leg, even above the knee.
Problem: Low back pain.
Solution: Lessen weight.
Don't overarch your back.

USING WEIGHT TRAINING MACHINES

Adduction Machines

Be sure to place pads at or above the level of your knee. Lower than that, the pads direct too much force to the knee, risking injury.

The sitting machines may be hard to get into, especially if you're injured, as they demand a certain level of flexibility at the beginning. The exercise itself is more difficult to begin from a stretched position.

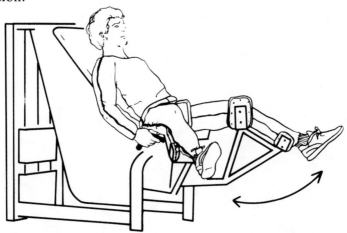

Problem: Knee pain.
Solution: Pads may be too low—place them higher on the leg.
Lessen weight.
Problem: Difficulty in beginning exercise.
Solution: Adjust the machine so you can start with your knees
closer together.
Do unaided exercises before tackling the machine.
Lessen weight and work up to appropriate weight.
Problem: Back pain (on standing machine).
Solution: Lessen weight.
Don't overarch back.

Strengthening the Turnout Muscles

ISOMETRIC EXERCISES

Lie on your stomach with your knees bent at a 90-degree angle.
Place a pillow between your ankles and attempt to crush it by
pressing your ankles together. Be sure to keep your knees and
thighs together.

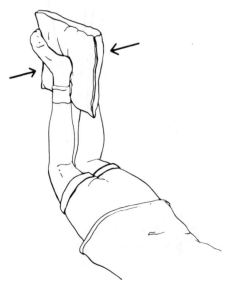

Problem: Cramping in the back of your thigh.
Solution: Concentrate on doing the exercise with the muscles
in your buttocks, not in the back of your thigh. Your
buttocks should be tight and firm during the exercise.

Full Body Lifts

This exercise provides a workout for both sides simultaneously. It also provides an isometric workout for the arms and shoulders.

Problem: Low back pain.
Solution: Don't overarch back.
Strengthen stomach muscles.
Try standing alternate-leg lifts.
Stop doing the exercise.

Although this exercise is primarily for the back, it requires hip extension to pull up straight enough so that the back muscles become engaged. So it strengthens the gluteal and other hip extensor muscles as well.

Problem: Low back pain.
Solution: Don't overarch—it's easy to do.
Strengthen stomach muscles.
Stop doing the exercise.

STRETCHING

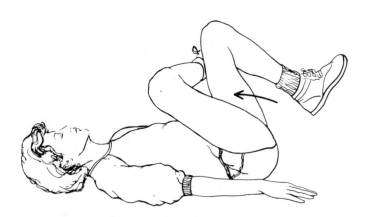

The Stomach, Back, and Neck

The stomach and back make up the trunk of the body, its foundation and stabilizer. Some of the body's largest and most powerful muscles are involved in this area. Prominent among those are the paraspinous muscles, the large, ropy muscles that straddle the backbone, and the abdominal muscles, which connect the pelvis to the rib cage. They work together to stabilize the entire body and to provide twisting, flexing, and extension movements.

The neck muscles work to support and stabilize your head and allow head movement.

The most important function of the stomach and back muscles is to stabilize the trunk, allowing your arms and legs a stable platform from which to operate. Virtually every sporting activity, from serving a tennis ball to hitting a golf ball to running and jumping, requires this stable body platform. In fact, there is virtually no sporting activity in which the stomach and back muscles are not involved.

Stomach and back muscles allow your body to rotate, so that you can throw, swing, row a boat, dance.

Stomach and back muscles allow you to bend backward and forward—especially important motions in such sports as diving, gymnastics, and dance.

The neck muscles primarily position and support the head. True neck strength is used in some sports—wrestling and football, for example. And neck strength and endurance are important for activities such as breathing in swimming.

Before beginning the exercises, review the General Exercise Prescriptions in the introduction to this chapter (page 183).

Strengthening the Stomach

ISOMETRIC EXERCISES

Generally, isometric exercises for the back, stomach, and neck involve holding positions rather than working against resistance or opposing muscles. They're not particularly effective strengthening exercises—for example, simply tightening your stomach muscles is not a very good way to strengthen the muscles, because it's difficult to get feedback as to just how good a contraction you are actually getting. For the most part, isotonic exercises work better.

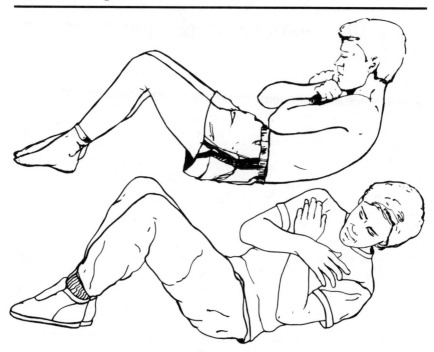

Lie on your back and begin curl-up exercises. Stop partway and hold the position. If you twist slightly to the side, you engage a wider range of stomach muscles.

Problem: Unable to get your shoulders off the floor without overarching your back.
Solution: Just barely lift shoulders off the floor.
Try the exercise even though your shoulders are on the floor.
Try bending your hips and knees slightly more.

ISOTONIC EXERCISES

Curl-Ups

Lying on your back, with arms relaxed over your chest, your feet on the floor with knees bent, slowly curl up until your shoulder blades clear the floor. Be sure to press the small of your back into the floor. Count to six going up, hold for a count of six, then count to six going back down.

Curl-ups are among the best exercises to strengthen abdominal muscles solely. Sit-ups are more well known, but they engage other muscles, primarily hip flexors, to help out in the exercise. And sit-ups encourage arching of the back, which should be avoided. (If you do regular sit-ups—especially if you hook or stabilize your feet—the very muscles you're using to pull yourself up are the muscles that cause your back to arch.) If you do sit-ups, be careful to press your lower back into the floor as long as possible.

To engage a wider array of abdominal muscles, do curl-ups with your body twisted slightly to the right and then another set with your body twisted slightly to the left. A good formula is to do one curl-up straight, one to the left, and one to the right. Count the entire sequence as one rep.

Take care with the position of your arms and hands.

Start the exercise with your hands at your sides—that's easiest.

When you're stronger, touch the sides of your head with your fingertips—that's harder.

When you're even stronger, stretch your arms and hands above your head—that's hardest.

Do as many slow curl-ups as possible while still keeping your lower back pressed into the floor.

Problem: Back pain.
Solution: Don't overarch—flatten back into floor.
Do fewer repetitions.
Don't rise up so high.
Problem: Neck pain.
Solution: Don't pull your neck forward with your hands.
Just touch your fingertips to the sides of your head, no more.

V-Ups

Lying on your back, with arms outstretched, bend at the waist and raise torso and legs to a V position. Then lower torso and legs to the floor.

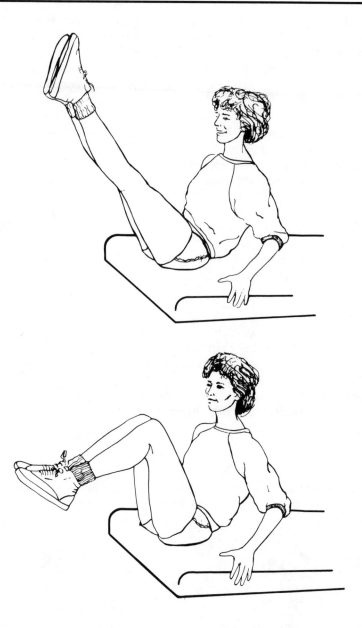

An easier variation of V-ups involves sitting on the edge of a chair or table and raising your legs. Try this version if the exercise is too difficult at first. If even this version is too difficult, try doing it with your knees bent.

A more difficult variation of V-ups involves placing your fingertips near your ears. Try this version once you've become stronger from doing regular V-ups.

Most difficult of all is to extend your hands above your head and raise arms and legs to meet in a jackknife position. Try this version once you've become stronger from doing modified V-ups.

Problem: Neck pain.
Solution: Don't thrust neck forward when pulling up.
Don't pull neck forward with hands behind head.
Keep torso straight.
Problem: Back pain.
Solution: Don't overarch back, especially when in V position.

USING EXERCISE AIDS

Bending Exercises

These exercises can be done safely if you concentrate on not overarching your back and keeping your knees slightly bent.

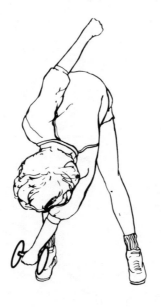

Use light weights or resistance. There's some question as to how effective the weights really are—you can do the exercises unaided as well. Use as much resistance as you can handle without excessive straining.

Problem: Back pain.
Solution: Don't overarch your back.
Try an easier position—with your arms at your sides.
Be sure your knees are slightly bent.

Curl-Ups and Sit-Ups Using an Abdominal Board

Curl-ups and sit-ups on an abdominal board exercise the hip flexor muscles as much as if not more than the abdominal muscles. They should always be done with the knees bent, so as not to encourage overarching the back. In any case, it may be a good idea to wait until you've built up good, strong stomach muscles before working with an abdominal board.

The idea of abdominal boards is to effectively increase the weight of the upper body by forcing you to work more against gravity.

Be sure to guard against overarching the lower back. Bend your knees when doing the exercise and press your lower back into the abdominal board.

To engage a wider array of abdominal muscles, gently twist your torso as you rise—do a set to one side and then the other.

Remember that if you're doing sit-ups the main workout for your stomach muscles occurs in the first third of the exercise. That's why curl-ups are the best exercise for stomach muscles alone—sit-ups engage other muscle groups.

Problem: Back pain.
Solution: Don't overarch your back. Press your lower back into the board, especially at the beginning of the exercise. Strengthen your stomach muscles (see page 247). Stop doing the exercise.

USING WEIGHT TRAINING MACHINES

Be careful to avoid overarching your back—press the small of your back into the backrest. Many of the machines utilize a pull-over motion, which encourages you to keep your back either flat or gently curved in a safe direction.

Machines that use pads rather than straps are more effective in exercising your abdominal muscles. They discourage your hip flexor muscles from doing the exercise instead of the abdominal muscles.

Placing your hands across your body rather than holding on to the machine can further discourage overarching the back.

When using abdominal strengthening machines at a fitness facility or elsewhere, be sure to carefully read the instructions and, until you're sure of your technique, ask for supervision.

> **Problem:** Back pain.
> **Solution:** Don't overarch the back. Make a conscious attempt to keep the back flat or bent forward.

Strengthening the Back

ISOMETRIC EXERCISES

Lie on your stomach and begin a back curl-up exercise. Stop partway and hold the position.

> **Problem:** Low back pain.
> **Solution:** Lessen the back arch. Just barely lift your collarbones from the floor. The arch should start gradually from the base of your skull to your legs—not just at your lower back.

ISOTONIC EXERCISES

Back Arches

Lying on your stomach, pull your torso and legs into the air. Be careful to make a gentle arch along the entire back instead of jerking upright and bending primarily at the lower back.

At first you can do the exercise most easily by keeping your arms at your sides and raising your torso only.

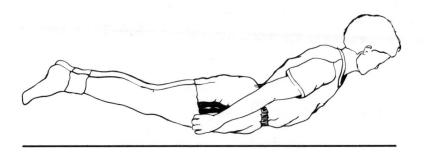

The next step, when you're strong enough, is to raise both torso and legs, still keeping your arms at your sides.

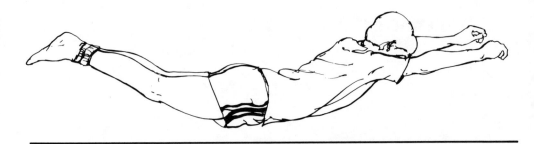

The exercise is most difficult when you extend your arms above your head and raise both torso and legs.

Problem: Back pain.
Solution: Ease up on exercise. Do fewer back arches in an easier form. Then work back up to harder and longer sets.

Don't bounce into exercise. Try to make the back arches smooth and gentle.

USING EXERCISE AIDS

Back Arches

Note: Do not consider doing these exercises until you've already developed substantial abdominal and back strength through the exercises we've suggested earlier.

After hooking your feet into the bench and dropping your torso down toward the floor, raise yourself straight up until your torso is slightly past parallel to the floor.

Be careful not to bounce into the exercise, thereby putting unnecessary pressure on the lower back. Gently arch your back throughout the entire spine.

The exercise can be made even more challenging by extending your arms above your head.

Problem: Back pain.
Solution: Ease up on the exercise. Do fewer reps, or simply go back to doing back arches on the floor, and gradually build up once again.
Rise up slowly and gently, bending through the length of the spine, not just in the lower back.

USING WEIGHT TRAINING MACHINES

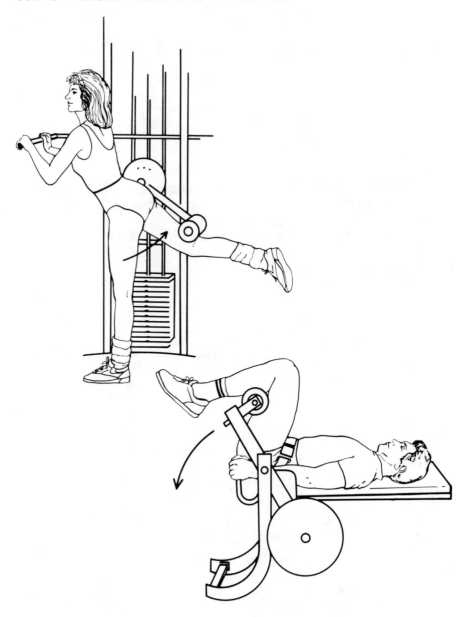

Back machines are of two sorts. One kind is a hip extension machine that goes beyond simply extending the hips by using a weight across the back of the legs or thighs. (We discuss this type above. See page 234.)

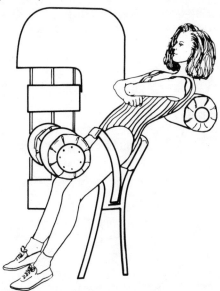

Another kind places the resistance pad across the upper or middle back.

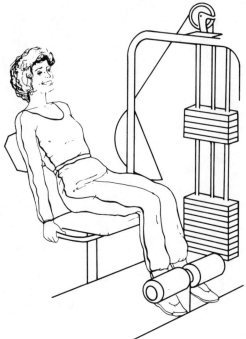

Machines that support the feet or thighs do a good job of isolating the back muscles.

Back rotation machines do a good job of exercising the back muscles, not simply the shoulders.

With all back machines, be sure not to overarch. Whenever possible, press your lower back into the backrest. When using machines at a fitness facility or elsewhere, be sure to carefully read the instructions and, until you're sure of your technique, ask for supervision.

Problem: Back pain.
Solution: Don't overarch the back. Make a conscious attempt to keep the back flat or bent forward.

STRETCHING

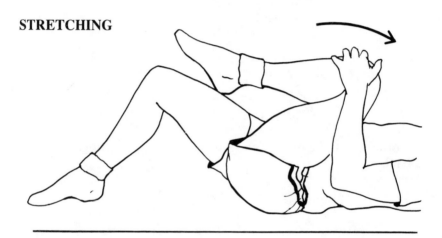

Strengthening the Neck

ISOMETRIC EXERCISES

Generally, isometric exercises for the back, stomach, and neck involve holding positions rather than working against resistance or opposing muscles. They're not particularly effective strengthening exercises—for example, simply tightening your stomach muscles is not a very good way to strengthen the muscles, because it's difficult to get feedback as to just how good a contraction you are actually getting. For the most part, isotonic exercises work better.

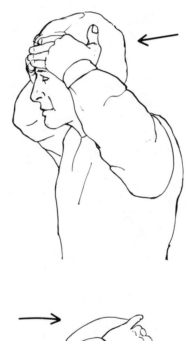

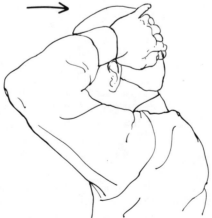

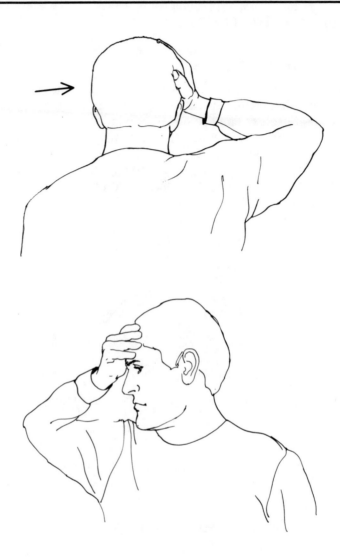

Push your head against the resistance of your hand. There are six possible directions: bending your head to the front, back, and each side and turning your head to each side.

ISOTONIC EXERCISES

When using free weights, the only practical exercise is to bend your neck backward against the weight. Be careful that the weight is not too heavy, especially when you begin to tire.

USING EXERCISE AIDS

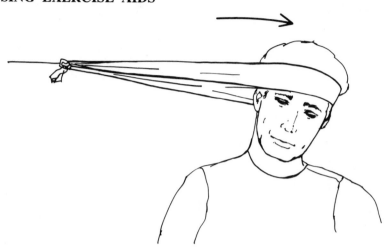

When using wall pulleys, it's possible to strengthen the neck by moving in four directions—back, forward, and to both sides. Again, be careful that the resistance is not too strong.

USING WEIGHT TRAINING MACHINES

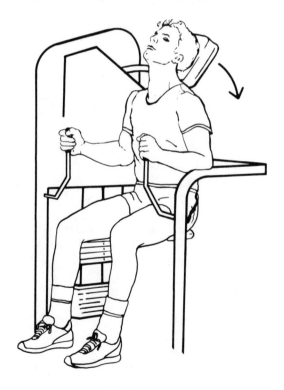

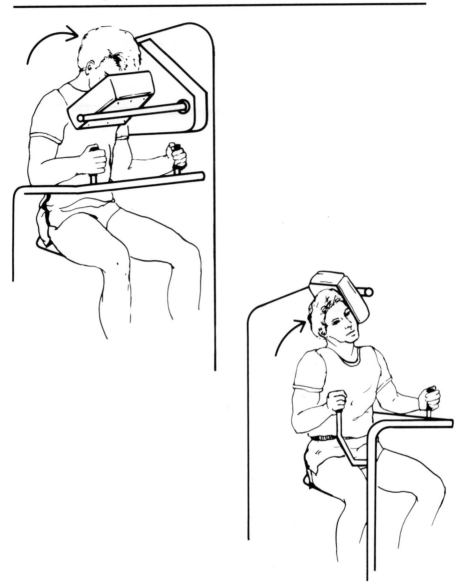

Be sure to breathe while doing the exercise—exhale when working against resistance, inhale when releasing resistance. With all these exercises there's a greater than usual tendency to hold your breath—fight it.

> **Problem:** Neck pain or pain in your shoulders, arms, or hands.
> **Solution:** Reduce the resistance.
> Reduce your range of motion.
> Stop doing the exercise.

STRETCHING

The Shoulder and Chest

There is no joint quite like the shoulder. It is at once the most flexible and the least stable joint in the body. Because it's held together primarily by muscles and tendons rather than ligaments (like the knee and ankle) or its own bone-to-bone stability (like the hip), it allows a wide degree of motion. But that motion depends on the health of all the muscles and tendons involved. Just one injured or weakened muscle can wreak havoc with virtually every movement of the entire shoulder.

These muscles are primarily the pectoral, or chest, muscles, which provide the shoulder's pushing motion; the latissimus dorsi and trapezius muscles in the back, which allow the shoulder to pull; the deltoids, those muscles on top of the shoulder at the very top of the arm that allow you to raise your shoulder; and the rotator cuff muscles, which form a hood or cuff covering the top of the joint and, with the help of the other muscles, allow shoulder rotation.

The shoulder has two main functions in sports: doing specific tasks like hitting or throwing a ball, pulling an oar, pulling the body through water; and providing balance, as in skiing or the arm swing in walking or running. We tend to ignore this latter shoulder function, but although it may be less obvious, it's no less important. Try to run with an arm in a sling or ski one-armed and you'll see why.

In some activities the shoulder has an additional function—that of support. Push-ups are an example of an exercise activity that demands strong, stable shoulders to support the body while your arms work.

Strong shoulder muscles are needed for all sporting activities using the arms.

Strengthening the Shoulder

Virtually all of the muscles around the shoulder can be strengthened by just three exercises: pull-ups, push-ups, and dips. They require little specialized equipment and can be modified to decrease and increase resistance. To a large extent they've been supplanted by the use of elaborate machines that allow the isolation of various muscle groups and more precise feedback regarding progress, but still these three simple exercises better simulate the activities for which we use our shoulders, chest, and upper back than do many of the machines. It's hard to go wrong with them.

The advantages of using weight training machines are that there is less worry about precise technique (because the machine forces you to do the particular lift correctly) and less likelihood of hurting yourself, because a weight stack is used and it is thus impossible for the weight to fall on you.

There are disadvantages. The machines isolate muscles so well that the surrounding muscles are not used, so the way the body works in real-life situations is not so nearly simulated. Also, many of the machines initiate the lift from a stretch position. That can be good, because it decreases the tendency to become muscle-bound from lifting only through the strongest portion of the arc of motion, or bad, because the muscle is very weak at this point, even though eccentric cam machines effectively lessen the weight.

The shoulder is a complicated joint. For ease of understanding, we've divided its motions into five: pushing, pulling, raising, rotating in, and rotating out. The exercises to follow strengthen the shoulder by utilizing these movements.

Before beginning the exercises, review the General Exercise Prescriptions in the introduction to this chapter (page 183).

ISOMETRIC PUSHING EXERCISES

Stand facing a wall with your arms extended and hands against the wall. Lean into the wall and push against your body weight. The idea is not to move but to hold yourself in equilibrium for at least six seconds.

ISOTONIC PUSHING EXERCISES

Push-Ups

Place your hands slightly more than shoulder width apart about at the level of the shoulders. The farther ahead of your body you place your hands, the more you strengthen the shoulder muscles.

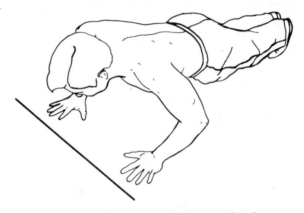

Hold your body rigid without arching your back.

The top of the exercise is when your elbows are straight—the bottom is when your chest, not your stomach, just touches the floor.

Problem: The exercise is too hard.
Solution: Do push-ups from your knees.
Do push-ups leaning against a wall or high table.

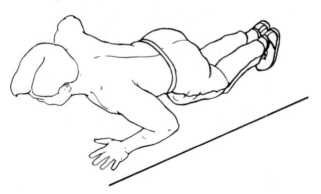

Do bench presses to strengthen your pectoral (chest) muscles (see page 273).

Problem: Your back hurts.
Solution: Strengthen your stomach muscles (see page 247).
Do fewer push-ups. (Your back tends to arch as you grow tired.)
Problem: The backs of your wrists hurt.
Solution: Strengthen wrist flexor muscles (see page 317).
Problem: The push-ups are too easy.
Solution: Raise your feet up on a bench.
Add weight to your back.

Dips

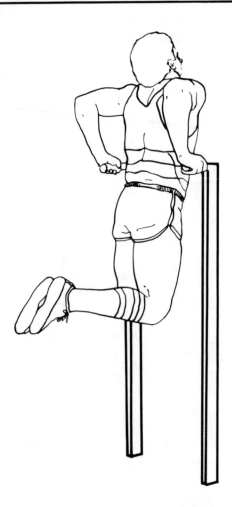

Dips are more difficult than push-ups, because they employ your entire body weight for resistance, rather than the approximately 75 percent used in standard push-ups.

Your hands should be slightly more than shoulder width apart.

The top of the exercise is when your elbows are straight; the bottom is when your elbows are bent, with arms behind your body. You should feel the stretch across your chest.

Try to work up to three sets of twelve daily. Dips are a very difficult exercise. Don't be discouraged if you can't do more than a few at the beginning.

Problem: You're unable to do even one dip.
Solution: Stand on a stool to begin the exercise and just lower into the down position.

Problem: Pain across your chest during the bottom of the exercise. (The cause is too much stretching of the pectoral muscles in the chest.)

Solution: Put your feet on the floor or on a bench so as not to drop so low.

USING EXERCISE AIDS

Bench Press

Lie on bench, feet flat on floor.

Hold the barbell about 6 inches wider than shoulder width. Holding your hands wide apart emphasizes outer pectoral muscles —hands closer together emphasizes inner pecs.

Keeping your elbows out, lower the bar to your chest.

Keep your head on the bench. Be careful not to overarch your back. Do not raise your hips off the bench.

Inhale going down—exhale pushing up.

You should always use a spotter so the weight can't fall on you by mistake.

Problem: Pain on top of your shoulder.
Solution: Place your hands farther apart on the bar.
Problem: You can't hold the bar level (probably because one shoulder is stronger than the other).
Solution: Strengthen the weak side by using dumbbells (see below).

Bench Press Using Dumbbells

Lie on the bench, feet flat on the floor.

Hold dumbbells at arm's length, palms facing.

Lower dumbbells straight down to the sides of your chest, keeping your arms close to your sides. Then push back to starting position.

Inhale going down, exhale going up.

Flys

Flys involve a hugging motion against resistance, which primarily strengthens the pectoral muscles in the chest.

Lie on bench, feet flat on the floor.

Hold dumbbells together at arm's length above shoulders, palms facing each other.

Lower dumbbells out to each side of your chest. Your elbows should be bent at the lowest point in the lift and straightened as you push back up across the front of your body.

Inhale going down, exhale going up.

Don't overarch your back. Keep your head on the bench.

USING WEIGHT TRAINING MACHINES

Bench Press Machines

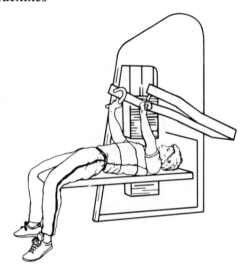

Virtually all of these machines and others like them are variants of bench presses. They primarily strengthen the pectoral muscles in the chest.

Machines requiring you to lie down might encourage overarching of the back. Be careful.

Press the small of your back into the bench or backrest.

Problem: You can't lift adequate weight because one side is weak.

Solution: Use a machine allowing differing weights for each side.

Strengthen the weak side with dumbbell presses or flys (see page 274).

Problem: Back pain.
Solution: Decrease weight.
Strengthen your stomach muscles (see page 247).
Try a sitting machine and press the small of your back into the backrest.
Use a machine allowing independent arm movement. (Helps you not to overarch your back.)

Fly or Chest Machines

These machines isolate the pectoral muscles even further.

Machines that force you to sit on a slant combine a hugging motion with some lowering of the arms. They strengthen all the pectoral muscles.

Machines in which you bring the weight straight across the chest emphasize the upper pectorals more.

Machines that require you to hug the weights across and up by raising your arms emphasize the upper pecs even more strongly.

Be sure to press the small of your back into the backrest.

Problem: Pain in the elbow (most often in machines where the pads rest against your forearm).
Solution: Try a machine that rests the pads against the front of your elbow.
Strengthen your wrist flexor and extensor muscles (see pages 317, 315).
Reduce weight.

Problem: Pain in the back of the shoulder (sometimes accompanied by a feeling of anxiety when you begin the exercise—especially in people who have previously suffered a shoulder dislocation).

Solution: Adjust the position of the bench or seat so that you don't begin the exercise with your arms stretched so far back.

Strengthen the front of your shoulder, primarily the deltoid muscle (see page 285).

Avoid this machine.

ISOMETRIC PULLING EXERCISES

Sit in an armchair with your arms resting on the arms of the chair. Grasp the arms and pull backward.

ISOTONIC PULLING EXERCISES

Pull-ups

Place your hands about shoulder width apart. As far as strengthening the shoulder is concerned, it doesn't matter whether your palms are toward you or away from you.

Gradually work up to three sets of twelve daily. Pull-ups are difficult. Don't be discouraged if you can do only a few to start with.

Problem: You're unable to do even one pull-up.
Solution: Start in the elevated position by standing on a box or chair. Then raise your feet and gradually lower yourself down. Repeat the exercise by standing on the chair again.
Use a low bar that allows you to keep your feet on the floor. Then angle your body to do the exercise.

Strengthen your lattissimus dorsi muscles by using a lat bar (see page 279).

USING EXERCISE AIDS

One of the major symptoms of shoulder injuries is a loss of motion. Many shoulder exercises, however, especially those done on machines, require a wide range of motion. Doing shoulder exercises with free weights and elastics can be especially valuable when you're recovering from an injury, because you can usually limit the exercises to a comfortable range of motion.

Lat Pull-Down

Lat pull-downs primarily strengthen the lattissimus dorsi muscles in the back. Pulling down with a wide grip emphasizes the upper portion of the muscles. The narrow grip emphasizes the lower portion.

Pull the bar straight down to the upper chest.

Exhale going down; inhale going up.

Problem: Pain in the back of the shoulder (when using the wide grip).

Solution: Use a narrower grip so as to put less strain on the back of the shoulder.

Problem: Low back pain.
Solution: Don't overarch your back.
Strengthen your stomach muscles (see page 247).
Lessen the weight.
Problem: You can't hold the bar level.
Solution: One side is stronger than the other, so strengthen the weak side by doing one-arm rows (see below).

One-Arm Rows Using Dumbbells

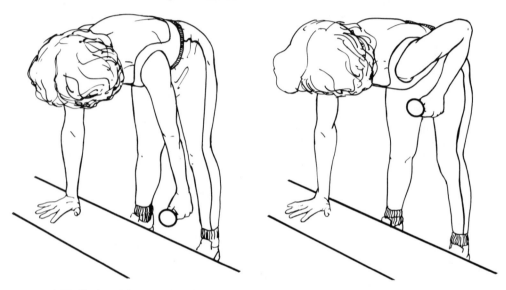

Pull dumbbell straight to your chest, keeping your arm close to your body.
Inhale going down; exhale going up.

USING WEIGHT TRAINING MACHINES

Rowing

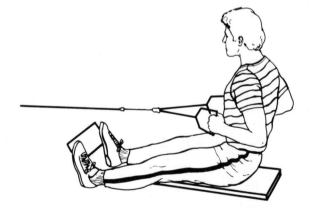

Rowing exercises primarily strengthen lattissimus dorsi and upper back muscles.

Bend slightly forward during the exercise. Do not rock back and forth at the waist. Be careful not to overarch your back.

Pull directly to your chest.

Exhale while pulling; inhale when letting back.

Problem: Back pain.
Solution: Decrease weight.
Strengthen your stomach muscles (see page 247).
Don't overarch your back.

Pulling Machines

Pulling machines differ in a number of ways. In some the weights are applied through the hands, so that although they primarily strengthen the shoulder muscles, they depend somewhat on strength in the arms and forearms to control the weights.

Other machines place the pads at the elbow, thus involving shoulder muscles almost exclusively.

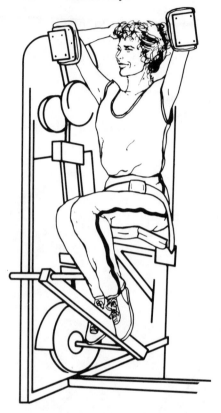

Some machines start the weights well behind the level of the head. Others begin with the arms in front of the body. The farther the weights are up or behind your head, the more your pectoral muscles are utilized in the first part of the exercise.

Some machines simply bring the arms down to the sides, rather than pulling down in front of the body. These machines exercise the pectoral muscles as well as the lats.

Problem: Shoulder pain at the beginning of the exercise (as well as apprehension of pain—a common problem in people who have suffered shoulder injuries).

Solution: Use a machine that allows you to start the exercise with your arms toward the front of your body. Avoid these machines.

Problem: Pain in the elbow.

Solution: Try a machine with pads on the upper arms rather than one requiring you to use your hands, wrists, or elbows.

Pull-Over Machine

Pull-over machines combine pushing, in the first half of the exercise, and pulling, in the last part of the motion. They strengthen the pectoral muscles as well as the lats.

Press your lower back into the backrest.

ISOMETRIC RAISING EXERCISES

Sit in front of a heavy table or counter. Extend your arms to the front and a bit out to the sides, with hands under the surface. Raise your arms against the table.

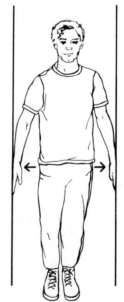

You can do a similar exercise by standing in a doorway and extending your arms from your sides so that your hands are pushing against the doorjamb. Push your arms against the sides of the doorway.

ISOTONIC RAISING EXERCISES

USING EXERCISE AIDS

Military Press

Primarily strengthens the deltoid muscle at the top of the arm.

Sit with feet firmly on the floor.

Hold bar at shoulders, then with a slow, steady motion press upward to arm's length.

Exhale going up; inhale going down.

Problem: Pain at the top of the shoulder.
Solution: Widen your grip on the bar.
Problem: Pain in the lower back.
Solution: Use a bench with a backrest and press your back into it.
Strengthen your stomach muscles (see page 247).
Don't overarch your back.
Reduce the weight.
Problem: You can't hold the bar level.
Solution: One side is stronger than the other, so strengthen the weak side by doing presses using dumbbells (see page 286).

Presses Using Dumbbells

Raise dumbbells alternately—one up and then down, then the other up and down. Exhale going up; inhale coming down.

Keep your palms facing in and elbows close to your body.

Keep your back straight—don't overarch.

Various Raises and Presses

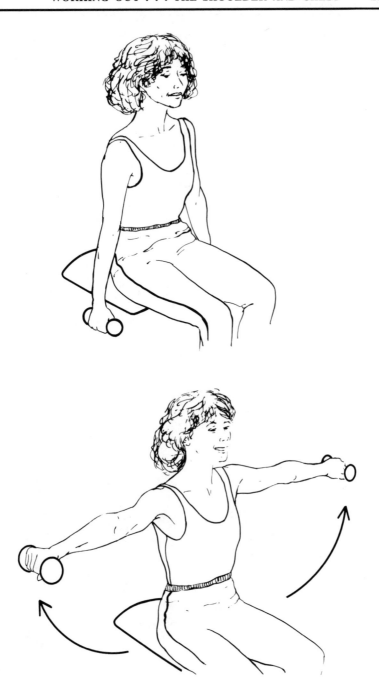

Keeping arms straight, raise dumbbells a little above shoulder height.

Exhale going up; inhale coming down.

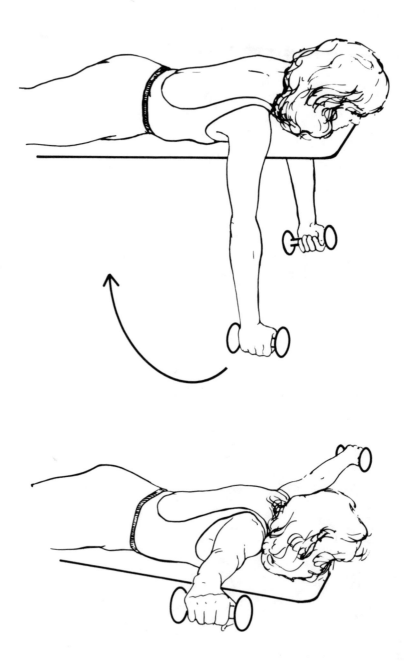

Lying on your stomach, with elbows locked and arms straight, raise dumbbells to shoulder height.

Exhale going up; inhale coming down.

Shrugs

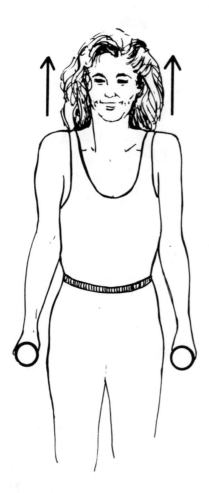

Shrugs primarily strengthen the trapezius muscle in the back and neck.

Holding dumbbells or a barbell, shrug the shoulders—raise them and rotate them in a circular motion from front to rear.

Inhale when doing exercise; exhale when at rest.

USING WEIGHT TRAINING MACHINES

By positioning the pads differently, raising machines emphasize different portions of the deltoid muscle at the top of the arm. All strengthen the upper trapezius in the back and neck as well.

This machine primarily strengthens the middle part of the deltoid muscle.

This machine primarily strengthens the front part of the deltoid muscle.

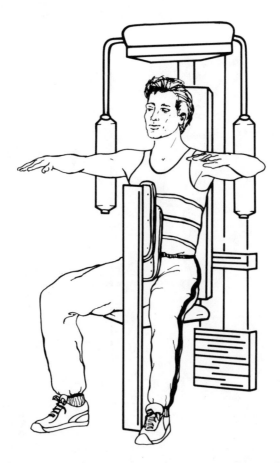

This machine primarily strengthens the back part of the deltoid muscle.

     Problem: Shoulder pain at the beginning of the exercise (as well as apprehension of pain—common in people with previous shoulder injuries).

     Solution: Lower the seat so your arms start out more to the front of your body.
Strengthen the deltoid muscle with dumbbell presses (see page 274).
Avoid these machines and this position.

STRETCHING

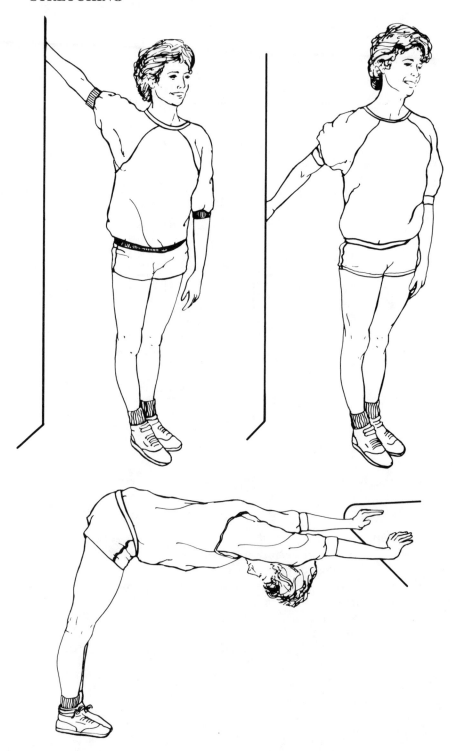

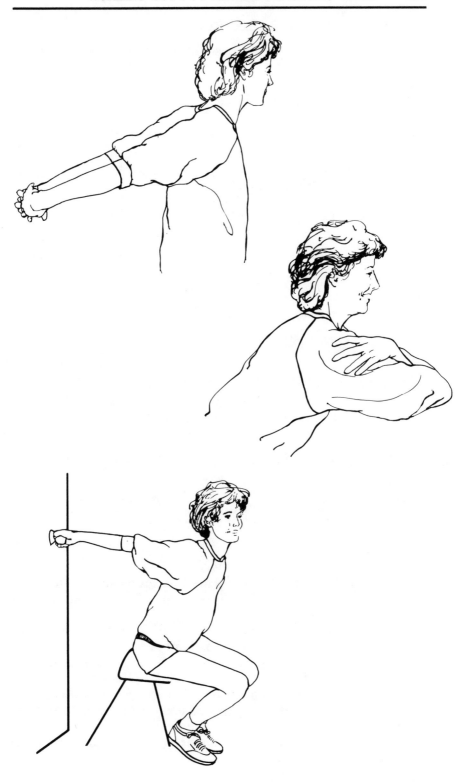

ISOMETRIC ROTATION EXERCISES

Sit in an armchair with your hands on the outsides of the chair arms. Pull your hands together—that is, hug the chair.

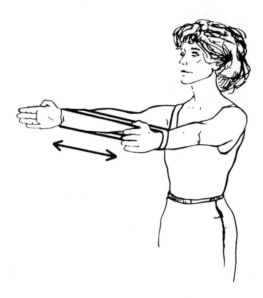

Stand with your arms raised, shoulder width apart in front of you. Loop a belt around your wrists and pull your hands away from each other against the resistance of the belt.

The Arm

Like the knee and ankle, the wrist and elbow contain no muscles. Their motion is controlled by the muscles nearby—in the case of the wrist, the muscles in the forearm; for the elbow, the muscles in the upper arm. The primary muscles in the upper arm are two of the best-known in the body: the biceps and triceps. Those in the forearm are more numerous and may not be as familiar by name, but their function is no less important. These muscles allow your elbow and wrist to bend—to flex and extend and to rotate.

The upper arm muscles make possible all forms of throwing or striking. In other words, common and not-so-common sports such as baseball, football, basketball, tennis, racketball, handball, squash, golf, lacrosse, jai alai, and ping-pong are a function of the upper arm muscles. So are gymnastics, boxing, and weight lifting.

The upper arm muscles allow you to swim.

The forearm muscles help make possible all of the above sporting activities and more: they stabilize the wrist and allow your hand to grasp and let go. It may be their most important function of all.

Because the muscles in the arm and forearm are relatively small, it's difficult to find specific exercises for them that don't either require some form of equipment or involve the larger muscles of the chest, shoulder, and back—pull-ups and sit-ups are examples of those. There are simply no unaided muscles for the arm.

Before beginning the exercises, review the General Exercise Prescriptions in the introduction to this chapter (page 183).

Strengthening the Triceps

ISOMETRIC EXERCISES

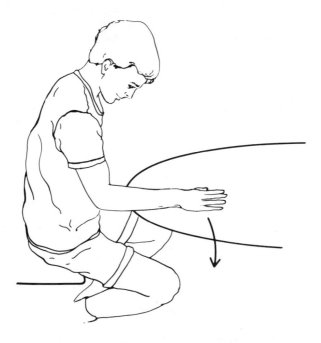

Sit at a table with your elbow bent to 90 degrees and palm down. Push down against the table as though attempting to straighten your elbow. This exercise strengthens the muscle that extends the elbow, the triceps. (It also strengthens the pectoral muscles in the chest.)

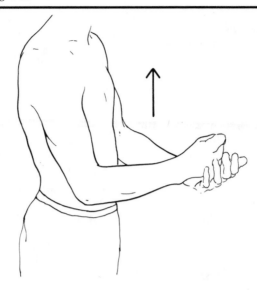

With your elbow bent at 90 degrees, place your hand in the hand of your other arm. Try to straighten your arm while resisting the motion with your other arm. The result should be a standoff—no movement. This exercise strengthens the extensor muscles—triceps—of one arm while strengthening the flexors—biceps, primarily—of the other. It also strengthens the pectoral muscles in the chest.

ISOTONIC EXERCISES

Push-Ups

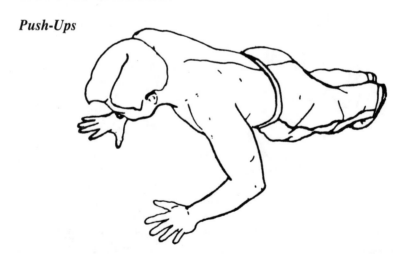

The nearer your hands are to being beneath your shoulders, the more you strengthen your elbow extensor muscles, the triceps.

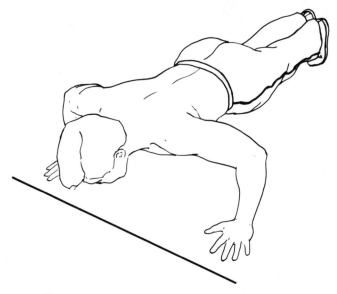

If you place your hands well to the sides, you strengthen the pectoral muscles in the chest as well.

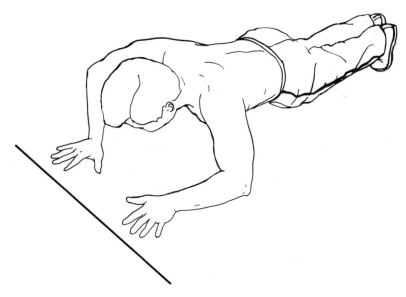

If you place your arms well ahead of your body, you strengthen your shoulder muscles to a greater degree than in the other versions.

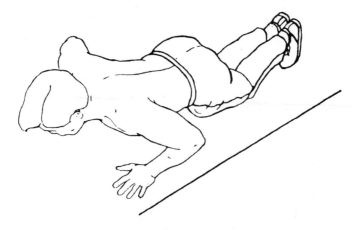

Unlike chin-ups, if you're unable to do push-ups you can de-crease your effective body weight by doing the exercise from your knees rather than your toes.

Problem: You can't push off the floor.
Solution: Do the push-ups from your knees rather than your toes.
Problem: You still can't push off.
Solution: Do push-ups off a wall, and as you become stronger, gradually incline forward.

Problem: Pain in the back of your wrists during the exercise.
Solution: Your wrists lack adequate motion or are too weak. Strengthen wrist flexor muscles (see page 317). Tape or wrap wrists in the meanwhile.
Do knuckle push-ups.

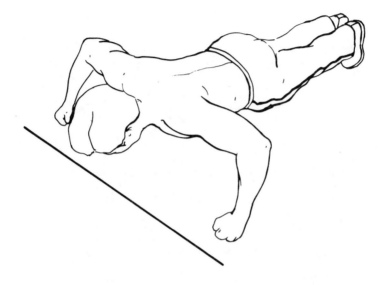

Move your hands forward of your body.
Turn hands outward and move them farther out to the sides.

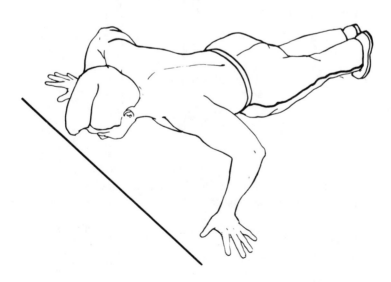

Problem: Back pain.
Solution: It's probably from arching your back in an attempt to keep your chest off the floor.
Strengthen stomach muscles (see page 247).
Do knee push-ups until you're strong enough to do the exercise properly.

Dips

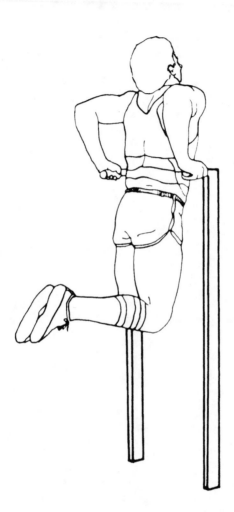

Dips strengthen the triceps as well as the pectoral muscles in the chest. They are actually super push-ups, because you have to lift your entire body weight instead of having some weight on your toes.

Dips are very difficult. Don't be discouraged if you can't do many.

Problem: Unable to do the exercise.
Solution: You're not yet strong enough. Strengthen triceps first (see page 295), then try the exercise.
Do push-ups until you're strong enough to try dips.
Do dips with your feet partially resting on the floor.

Problem: Wrist and forearm pain.
Solution: Do wrist curls (see page 318) to strengthen forearm muscles.
Problem: You can do the exercise only through a limited range of motion—can't dip all the way down and push back up.
Solution: Gradually extend your motion as you become stronger.
Do triceps curls (see page 302), concentrating on the extremes of motion—arm straight and bent.
Strengthen shoulder muscles (see page 268).

USING EXERCISE AIDS

Triceps Curls

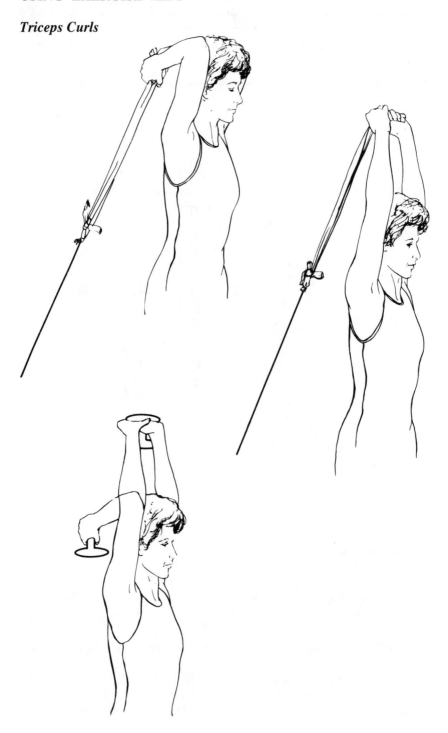

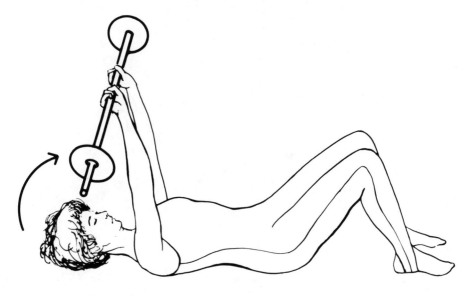

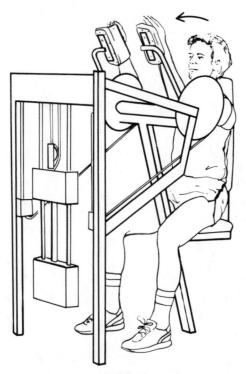

Triceps curls strengthen the triceps, which work to extend your elbow.

USING WEIGHT TRAINING MACHINES

Triceps curl machines stabilize the arm to prevent the shoulder muscles from being involved in the exercise. They allow you to strengthen the triceps solely.

It doesn't matter whether you do the exercise with palms up or down—although it's easier to control the weight with palms down.

Problem: Wrist pain.
Solution: Decrease weight.
Tape or wrap wrists.
Strengthen muscles that stabilize the wrist (see pages 315, 317).

All pushing-type machines usually exercise the triceps and other elbow-extending muscles—in conjunction with the chest and shoulder muscles.

STRETCHING

Strengthening the Biceps

ISOMETRIC EXERCISES

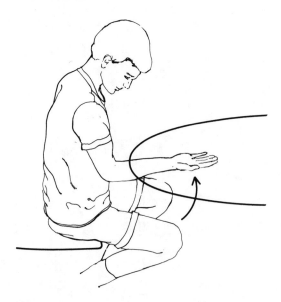

With your elbow bent at 90 degrees and palm up, place your hand beneath a counter or fixed table. Then attempt to lift by bending your elbow. This exercise strengthens the flexor muscles, primarily the biceps. It also strengthens the pectoral muscles in the chest.

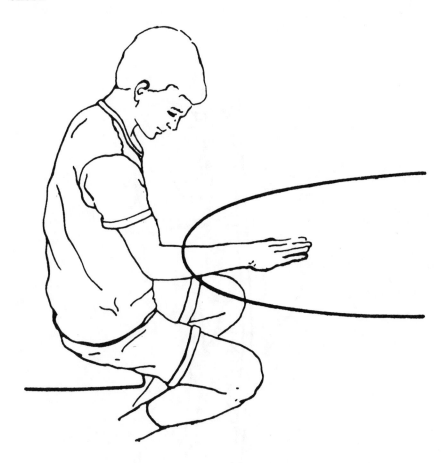

With your elbow bent at 90 degrees and palm down, place your hand beneath a counter or fixed table. Then attempt to lift by bending your elbow and pressing up with the back of your wrist and hand. This exercise isolates and strengthens one of the smaller flexor muscles, the brachialis.

ISOTONIC EXERCISES

Pull-Ups or Chin-Ups

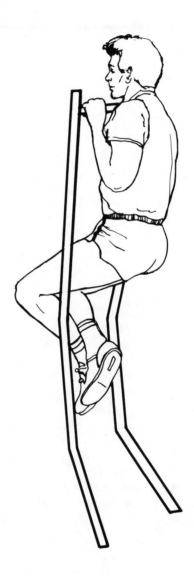

Pull-ups, which are done with your palms facing away from the body, primarily exercise the smaller elbow flexor muscles, such as the brachioradialis. For most people, this is a more difficult exercise than push-ups. And, like push-ups, pull-ups also strengthen the shoulder muscles—in this case the lats.

Pull-ups, done with your palms facing your body, primarily exercise the biceps.

If either exercise is too difficult, you might want to do a variant —hang as long as possible without fully extending your elbows. In effect, the exercise provides a kind of isometric exercise for the elbow flexor muscles.

The greater your range of motion, the more thorough the effect of the exercise. People often do these exercises through a restricted range of motion, rarely dropping all the way to full elbow extension, because the exercises are much easier to do if you don't fully straighten your arms. But the greater your range of motion during the exercise, the greater your strength throughout that range of motion. If your range of motion is limited, you build strength—and flexibility—only through that partial range.

Pull-ups and chin-ups are difficult. Don't be discouraged if you can do only a few at the start.

Problem: The exercise is too hard to do.
Solution: Try biceps curls (see page 310) until you're strong enough to do pull-ups and push-ups.

Do pull-ups with a low bar, leaning back with your heels resting on the ground (see illustration, page 277).

Problem: You can't hold on to the bar long enough.
Solution: Strengthen your grip with finger strengthening exercises (see page 320).
Problem: Wrist and forearm pain.
Solution: Your wrist flexor muscles are too weak. Do wrist curls (see page 318) until you're strong enough.
Problem: You can do the exercise only through a limited range of motion. You can't start with your arms fully extended or can't pull your chin above the bar.
Solution: Gradually extend your range of motion as you become stronger.
Do biceps curls, concentrating on the extremes of motion.
Problem: The exercise is too easy.
Solution: Use a weight belt.

USING EXERCISE AIDS

Biceps Curls

Biceps curls strengthen the biceps muscle primarily, and the smaller flexor muscles as well.

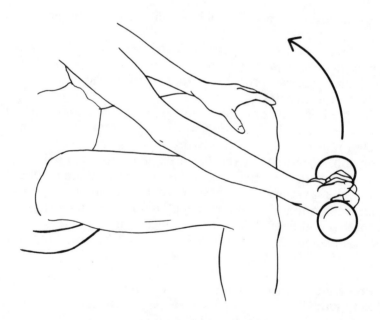

Using dumbbells, you can do the exercise one arm at a time. It allows you to equalize the workout for both arms. With double arm curls, your stronger side usually does most of the work.

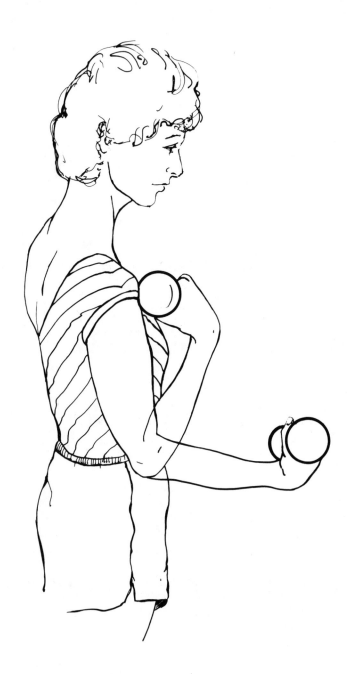

To exercise your forearm muscles as well, roll in your wrists at the top of the curl.

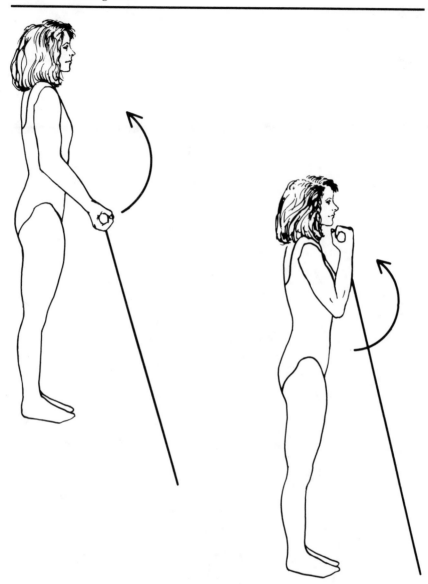

Using barbells, or a weight/pulley system, you can do the exercise with both arms at the same time.

You can do these exercises as well with your palms facing away from the body. That strengthens the smaller upper arm flexors as well as the biceps.

Problem: Front of shoulder hurts.
Solution: The pain is from using your shoulder muscles to help bring your arm forward. Do a "preacher curl," with

the back of your arm resting against a pad. That dis-
engages the shoulder muscles.

Problem: Wrist and forearm pain.
Solution: Your wrist flexor muscles in the forearm are too
weak. Decrease the weight.
Tape or wrap wrists.
Strengthen flexor muscles (see page 317).
Problem: When using Thera-Band, the curl becomes more dif-
ficult as you bend your arm—the resistance becomes
stronger past the midpoint of your range of motion.
Solution: Work only to the midpoint of your range of motion.
Lessen resistance during the end of the curl by start-
ing with more slack in the Thera-Band.
Remember: Always face away from any elastic materials.

USING WEIGHT TRAINING MACHINES

Most of the machines require that you do the exercise with
palms up. This position primarily strengthens the biceps. If you're
able to do the exercise with palms down, it primarily strengthens a
smaller flexor muscle, the brachioradialis.

These machines have a tendency to make you start the lift with
your elbow partially bent. It encourages less than a full range of
motion.

Problem: Wrist and forearm pain.
Solution: Your wrist flexor muscles in the forearm are too weak. Decrease the weight.
Tape or wrap wrists.
Strengthen flexor muscles (see page 317).

All pulling-type machines usually exercise your biceps and other elbow-flexing muscles (in conjunction with other muscles, such as those of the back and shoulder).

STRETCHING

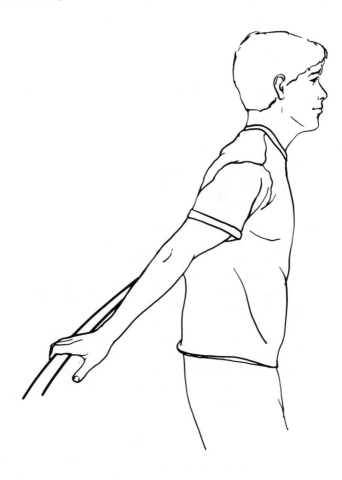

Strengthening the Wrist Extenders

ISOMETRIC EXERCISES

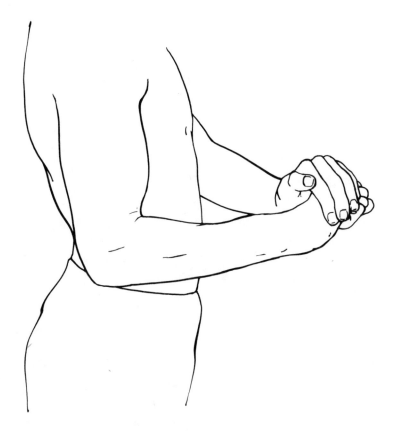

   With your elbow bent at 90 degrees and palm down, try to cock your wrist against the resistance of your other hand. The result should be no motion. This exercise strengthens the muscles in the forearm (the muscles involved in tennis elbow) that extend the wrist (as well as muscles in the other arm).

ISOTONIC EXERCISES

Reverse Wrist Curls

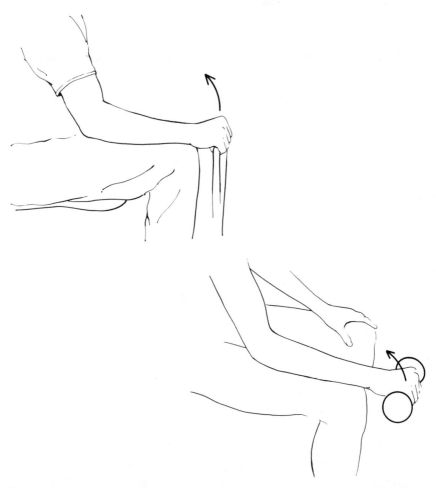

Rest your arm on your knee with your wrist and hand, palm down, hanging free. Curl your wrist toward you, using as much weight as is comfortable.

Reverse wrist curls strengthen the muscles in the forearm that extend the wrist.

You can begin doing reverse wrist curls with elbows bent. Then, as you become stronger, straighten your elbow. A straight elbow enhances the workout, as you stretch your muscles, making them more flexible—and making the exercise more difficult.

Reverse wrist curls will usually require less weight than normal wrist curls, as the extensor muscles are normally weaker than the flexors.

Problem: Pain over the back of your wrist at the beginning of the lift.
Solution: Decrease weight.
Shorten the curl so that you don't fully flex your wrist at the beginning.
Problem: Pain in the palm side of the wrist.
Numbness or tingling in the hand or fingers.
Solution: It's probably from tendinitis of the tendons on the front of the wrist. Stop doing the exercise. Apply ice for 15 minutes. Do gentle stretching for a few days until the pain or numbness has completely disappeared. Begin curls again with lighter weight. If the pain doesn't disappear, see a doctor.
Problem: Pain on the outside of the elbow.
Solution: Stop doing the exercise. Ice the area and do gentle stretching for a few days until the pain is gone. Then begin curls again with lighter weight.

Strengthening the Wrist Flexors

ISOMETRIC EXERCISES

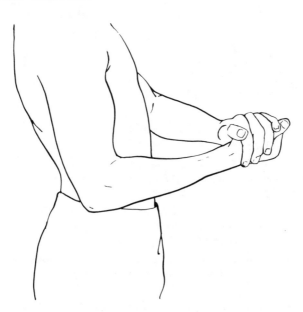

With your hands clasped together, try to bend your wrist against the resistance of the other arm. There should be no motion. This exercise strengthens the muscles that flex the wrist in both arms.

ISOTONIC EXERCISES

Wrist Curls

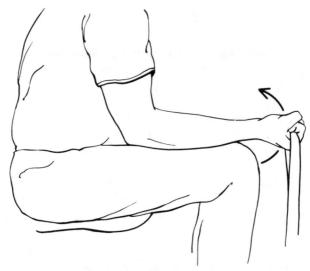

Rest your arm on a table with your wrist and hand, palm up, hanging free. Curl your wrist toward you, using as much weight as is comfortable.

Wrist curls strengthen the muscles in the forearm that flex the wrist.

You can begin doing wrist curls with elbows bent. Then, as you become stronger, straighten your elbow. A straight elbow enhances the workout as you stretch your muscles, making them more flexible, and making the exercise more difficult.

Problem: Pain over the back of your wrist at the end of the lift.
Solution: Decrease weight.
Shorten the curl so that you don't fully cock your wrist.
Problem: Pain in the palm side of the wrist.
Numbness or tingling in the hand or fingers.
Solution: It's probably from tendinitis on the front of the wrist. Stop doing the exercise. Ice the area. Do gentle stretching for a few days until the pain or numbness has completely disappeared. Begin curls again with lighter weight.
Problem: Pain on the inside of the elbow.
Solution: Stop doing the exercise. Ice the area and do gentle stretching for a few days until the pain is gone. Then begin curls again with lighter weight.

Wrist Rolls

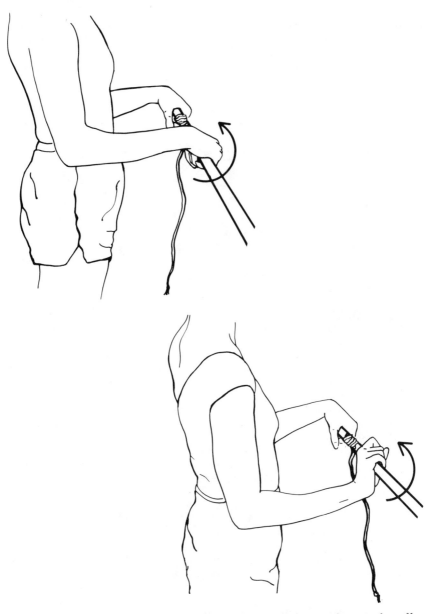

Attach a rope with a weight on the end to a bar or broom handle. Slowly wind the rope up around the bar with your wrists. Then let down in a controlled, slow manner.

You can do the exercise with your palms up (strengthens the muscles that extend the wrist) or down (strengthens the muscles that flex the wrist).

Strengthening the Fist-Making Muscles

ISOMETRIC EXERCISES

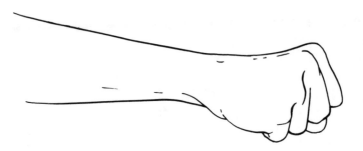

Clench your hand tightly in a fist. The exercise strengthens the muscles that flex your fingers, thereby improving your grip.

ISOTONIC EXERCISES

Grip Strengthening

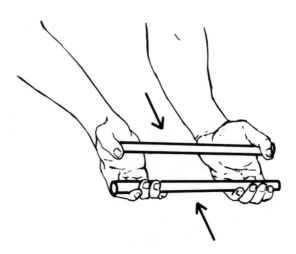

These exercises may be important in racket sports and other sports, such as fencing, gymnastics, and some field events, that require a strong grip.

Problem: Your hand is too small or weak to begin the exercise. (Many of these devices aren't suitable for women.)

Solution: Use a smaller device.
Squeeze a rubber ball or some other resilient material, such as Silly Putty®.
Problem: Painful snapping of knuckles during the exercise.
Solution: Lessen resistance.
Use a smaller device. (Avoid snapping, as it can lead to pain and swelling.)

Stretching

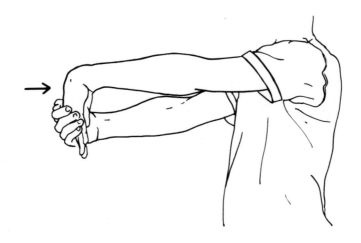

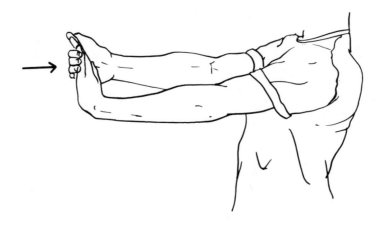

Postscript

Well, yes, there's a lot of information here. That's the idea —to provide a thorough, detailed, and safe guide to personal fitness training. But remember, not every exercise and every approach is right for you. The idea is to pick and choose what makes sense in terms of your exercise goals and needs. This is *your* book, to personalize in terms of who *you* are.

To do so, treat *Be Your Own Personal Trainer* as an extended consultation with Jim Garrick. Let the two of you devise your own personalized fitness program. Use Chapters 1 and 2 to assess your own personal condition and bring your body into a balanced state, ready to go ahead and work yourself into shape. It's the time when you get to know yourself better and discover what your needs and goals really are. Read Chapter 3 to look at the fitness possibilities that may exist for you, offered with a breadth and awareness gained from Garrick's daily immersion in the field. Chapters 4 and 5 offer exercises and approaches to help you realize your own personal fitness goals. Again, these are suggestions made to increase your fitness level *and* to keep you from getting hurt— through the unique perspective of Garrick's twenty-five years of experience as a sports medicine physician. By applying this information to your own situation, you will find an approach that's right for you alone.

A word to the wise: be steadfast and be patient. When it comes to the body, nothing good happens immediately. You can hurt yourself suddenly; lasting gains take time. Once you've found your fitness course stay with it, and little by little, perhaps even sooner than you might expect, you'll start to reap the benefits.

Life is more enjoyable when you're fit and active. Life is healthier when you're fit and active. And getting there is fun in itself. So, good luck to you. Here's all you need to know. Use it wisely and well.

Index